Giovanni Pietro Giussano, Henry Edward Manning

The Life of St. Charles Borromeo

Volume I.

Giovanni Pietro Giussano, Henry Edward Manning

The Life of St. Charles Borromeo
Volume I.

ISBN/EAN: 9783742814753

Manufactured in Europe, USA, Canada, Australia, Japa

Cover: Foto ©Thomas Meinert / pixelio.de

Manufactured and distributed by brebook publishing software
(www.brebook.com)

Giovanni Pietro Giussano, Henry Edward Manning

The Life of St. Charles Borromeo

ST. CHARLES BORROMEO.

*From the Portrait in the Ambrosian Library in the care of the
Oblates of St. Charles.*

THE LIFE

OF

ST. CHARLES BORROMEO

CARDINAL ARCHBISHOP OF MILAN

From the Italian of

JOHN PETER GIUSSANO

PRIEST AND OBLATE OF ST. AMBROSE

WITH PREFACE

BY

HENRY EDWARD CARDINAL MANNING

ARCHBISHOP OF WESTMINSTER

VOL. I.

BURNS AND OATES

LONDON	NEW YORK
GRANVILLE MANSIONS	CATHOLIC PUBLICATIO
	SOCIETY CO.
ORCHARD STREET, W.	BARCLAY STREET

1884

PREFACE.

THE Oblates of St. Charles in the Diocese of Westminster have long had the intention of publishing an English version of Giussano's Life of their Founder. Now at last this purpose, so many years delayed, is happily accomplished. The time of its fulfilment is opportune, for on the 4th of next November will fall the third centenary of St. Charles's death, at the early age of forty-six years.

He was born in 1538 when the Lutheran heresy was in its full sway. The schism of England was then complete; and the first meeting of the Council of Trent had been held at Vicenza. He died in 1584, when the north of Germany, Sweden, Norway, and Denmark were lost to the faith. The blood of many martyrs had been shed in England, and the decrees of the Council of Trent had already aroused the profound reaction which has raised the Catholic Church to its present spiritual purity and power. In the brief space of forty-six,. or rather of four and twenty years, St. Charles accomplished a work which has made him the patron of the Pastoral Office of the Church, as St. Thomas of Canterbury is the patron of its liberties.

No one can form an adequate conception either of the work accomplished by the Council of Trent, or of the wise and effective execution of its decrees by St. Charles, unless he shall have already acquired a knowledge of the state of the Church in Europe, and above all in Italy, at that date.

The great Western Schism, as it is called, when the kingdoms of Europe for many years subtracted their obedience from the Popes of doubtful election, had greatly weakened both the instinct of unity, and the recognition of authority. National churches began to assert their self-sufficiency, and Metropolitans openly claimed the power to confirm the election of Bishops. Both France and England learned this evil lesson of independence. In France it issued only in Gallicanism, but in England in a permanent schism. The Preamble of the 24th of Henry VIII. affirms this self-sufficiency in explicit terms. The whole of the north of Europe was thus prepared for separation. The Teutonic and Scandinavian races, of whom many had received the faith so late as the eleventh, twelfth, or even, as the Wends, the thirteenth century, were less intimately assimilated to the unity of the Christian world. They readily fell away, and their influence penetrated into Catholic lands, even into France and Italy. For three hundred years an intellectual movement not only anti-Catholic, but essentially anti-Christian, had been rising and spreading in Central Italy. It was the conscious and deliberate exhumation of Paganism. The languages and the literature the intellectual ideas and the moral aberrations, the scepticism and the sensuality of the Greek and the Roman world were revived, elaborately defended, and deliberately taught in books, in colleges, in theatres, in society. The intellectual taste and tone and fashions of the courts in Italy, and of the men who reigned over the public opinion of the time were explicitly Pagan. Not only the infidel philosophers, who kept lamps burning before the busts of Plato and Aristotle, wrote and spoke as Pagans, but grave theologians and pious authors invoked DII SUPERI, and warned sinners to repentance lest they should be *ad inferni triremes damnatos.* Under such an obscuration of the light of heaven, it is no wonder that the faith and morals of men became profoundly corrupt. The Church in the fourteenth, fifteenth, and sixteenth centuries was passing through an atmosphere infected and poisoned by a manifold pestilence. Only the Church of the Living God, like its Head, immortal, could have lived through such a miasma of spiritual death.

It was precisely to expel this plague that the Council of Trent laboured for eighteen years, and it was in a special manner that St. Charles was called to direct the Council of Trent. He was to be the first to carry its decrees into the life and action of the Church.

In the year 1560, and at the age of twenty-two, he was raised to the Sacred College, and became Secretary of State to his uncle, Pius IV. From that time the whole guidance of the Holy See over the Council in Trent passed through his hands. He ordered a special archivium to be prepared in his residence in which all the correspondence and documents of the Council were

laid up.   It had an outer chamber called the *Sanctum* for
its ordinary correspondence, and an inner chamber called
the *Sanctum Sanctorum*, in which the decrees and defi-
nitions of the Council were deposited.   The couriers
who brought letters from Trent were admitted at any
moment of day or night, and it was his express order
that he should be wakened up from sleep on their
arriving in the night.   The proposition of all matters
to be discussed in an Œcumenical Council resides in
the Head of the Church.   No new matter could be
introduced, and none withdrawn without the authority
of the Holy See.   How close an oversight of the proceedings of the Council this implies is obvious.   One
signal instance of it is on record.   A decree was proposed renewing the definition of the Council of Florence, in which the Roman Pontiff is declared to be the
Supreme Teacher of all Christians.   This caused much
debate.

Many of the Spanish and Italian Bishops desired to
make the implicit meaning of this decree to be explicit :
defining thereby what it was reserved for the Council
of the Vatican to complete.   But the French Bishops,
led by the Cardinal of Lorraine, offered so strong a
resistance that the matter was referred to Rome, and
the Cardinal Legates were directed to withdraw the
subject.   It is useless now to speculate what might
have been the history of the last three hundred years,
if the Council of Trent had declared the Doctor and
Pastor of all Christians, when he defines any matter
of faith and morals as Head of the Church, in teaching
the universal Church, to be by divine assistance pre-

served from error. The Four Gallican Articles
might never have existed, and the uncertainties and
contentions resulting from them would never have
arisen. But the Divine Head of the Church permitted it to be otherwise, and laid upon the Council
of the Vatican the duty of taking up again and
making perfect what the Council of Florence had
begun. All these grave questions of discretion must
have passed through the hands of St. Charles, and the
decision is in complete harmony with the prudent and
deliberate character which appears in the twenty years
of his episcopate in Milan.

The Council had lingered with many interruptions
from its first convocation in 1536 to 1563. The sit-
tings were suspended four or five times, sometimes for
months, once for four years, again for two, finally for
ten. At last it met in January 1562, and it was
closed in December 1563. The firm and vigilant
will of St. Charles then pressed the Council to its conclusion. It was confirmed by Pius IV. in January
1564, by the Constitution, *Benedictus Deus.* The
same Pontiff reserved to the Holy See the interpretation of the decrees of the Council, and constituted a
perpetual tribunal, called the Congregation of the
Council, for that purpose. In 1566 was also published the Catechism of the Council of Trent for the
guidance of the Pastors of the Church. These two
acts of supreme wisdom were known to be the result
of the counsels of St. Charles, and with these events his
career in Rome came to a close. On the Feast of St.
Ambrose in 1563, he was consecrated Archbishop of

Milan, and in spite of all efforts to retain him in the
service of the Holy See he hastened to reside in the
midst of his flock, for which in twenty years he wore
out his life.

The record of his episcopate is to be found in the
two volumes of the *Acta Ecclesiæ Mediolanensis.* They
consist of the decrees of six Provincial Councils, and
of eleven Diocesan Synods held by him; of the rules
and constitutions of various Confraternities of Devotion; and especially of the Congregation of the Oblates
of St. Ambrose, Patron of the Church at Milan.[1] There
is no part of a Bishop's diocesan administration which
is not to be found in these acts reduced to the most pre-
cise order and system. The whole legislation of the
province, and of the diocese of Milan is there deli-
neated like the work of a master builder in all its
structure, symmetry, and unity. *Sapientia ædificavit
sibi domum.* Wisdom has there built an imperishable
house. It is a whole of great proportions, complete
in outline and finished in the minutest details. Next

---

[1] The Acts of the Church of Milan are also printed in one volume of
1273 pages. No adequate idea of their extent and minuteness can be
given by a mere description. They are divided into eight parts :—

1. The Acts of the six Provincial Councils of Milan.

2. The Acts of the eleven Diocesan Synods.

3. The Edicts on various parts of Discipline, for Clergy and Laity.

4. Instructions as to preaching, administration of Sacraments, Fabric
of Churches, Festivals, and the like.

5. Institutions or Rules for the Archbishop's Household, for the Congregation of the Oblates, for the Confraternities of the Christian Doctrine,
of the Blessed Sacrament, of Charity, of St. Ursula, of the Oratory, of
Nuns, of the Seminary, &c.

6. Tabula or directions for Feasts, Vigils, Synods, Censures, and the
like.

7. Pastoral Letters, nineteen in number, and Sermons in Synods.

8. Forms and Instruments of Diocesan Administration.

to the Collection of the Œcumenical Councils there is no work of ecclesiastical and spiritual legislation so perfect as the acts of the Church of Milan. In them the Council of Trent is to be seen translated into provincial and diocesan administration for the reform of all orders of the Church.

And in these events appears a manifest work of Divine Providence.

The fifteenth century was marked by the fall of the Christian empire of the East. The Mahomedan Antichrist had already laid waste three of the four Oriental Patriarchates. Constantinople was the last to fall. The desolation of the Eastern Church was then complete. The following century was also marked by a visitation which has made desolate the sanctuaries of many kingdoms and realms of northern Europe; then Catholic Rome itself was sacked and outraged by every kind of sacrilege. While this work of deformation and of ruin was wrecking and rending dioceses and provinces from Catholic unity, a reformation was wrought within the Church itself. No evil was so strong as to escape its power, or so small as to escape its discernment. The five and twenty sessions of the Council of Trent have each a twofold effect; the one to define or to defend the irreformable faith; the other to reform the moral disorders and corruptions of external discipline, and of human traditions.

In the work of the sixteenth century, three men, three friends of one will but of various gifts and of manifold inspirations, worked to one end with great diversity of operation, but with perfect unity of aim.

To St. Ignatius was assigned the work of combating and reducing the intellectual aberrations and the manifold heresies of the Protestant revolt, and of conforming the way of life of the regular Orders to the needs of the modern world. To St. Philip was given the work of recalling Rome from the fascinations of the *renascimento* to the life of Christian perfection in the world, without cloister and without vows.[1] To St. Charles was committed the office of raising once more the priesthood to the state of perfection in which its Divine Founder created and left it.

The Divine Exemplar of sacerdotal and pastoral perfection was in the beginning manifested to the world in the Person of the only High Priest and Shepherd of souls.

When He ordained His Apostles to be priests He laid upon them His own priesthood, with the law of following in His footsteps and being like to Himself. His Priests were to be the images and likeness of His own perfection. They were to manifest that perfection among men; and not only to manifest it but to communicate it to others. They were to be *perfectores aliorum*, the perfectors of other men; and by impressing His perfection on others to perpetuate it to the end of the world. This law and office attaches to the priest-

---

[1] On the day after St. Philip died, May 27, 1595, Baronius wrote to the Oratory in Naples as follows: "I send you the *Capitolo*, that is to say, the Decree never to change the Congregation into a religious order with vows. The said *Capitolo* our Father left us in these his last days of convalescence, as his final testament, and the foundation-stone of the Congregation. It was deeply pondered by us all, and by all solemnly ratified and accepted; nor do I doubt that you, as his sons and heirs, will accept the last codicil of the holy and blessed testator."—*Life of St. Philip Neri*, by Capecelatro, Archbishop of Capua, vol. ii. p. 457.

hood as such, not only as it exists in the Bishop, but as it exists also in the Priest; called of the second order, not because there are two priesthoods, but because the episcopate contains the priesthood, but is an order distinct from the priesthood itself by divine institution. For this reason, St. John Chrysostom and Theodoret apply to Bishops and Priests alike the exhortations and injunctions of St. Paul to St. Timothy and St. Titus. When St. Paul says " that the man of God be perfect," he is not speaking exclusively to Bishops but inclusively to Priests: when the schoolmen taught that there can be no office higher than the priesthood, because of the consecration of the Body and Blood of Jesus Christ, they were right in their reasoning, because in the episcopate there is no power higher than the power of consecration and of sacrifice. Some of the schoolmen had taught that the episcopate is higher than the priesthood by jurisdiction alone. St. Charles perceived that, by the divine institution of the priesthood, perfection is required as a condition to receiving it; and as the law also of the Priest's life when invested with it; both for his own sake and for the effect of his life and priesthood upon others; or in other words, that the priesthood was instituted to reflect, to perpetuate, and to communicate His perfection to mankind. And this perfection is what in theology is called the essential perfection of the person, as distinguished from the instrumental state, into which the imperfect may enter to acquire perfection: but no man may enter the priesthood except to exercise perfection already acquired, in order to make others perfect. Perceiving this, and perceiving with the intensity of his saintly discernment how many both Bishops and Priests had declined from the high level and standard of their state, and that the decline of the priesthood is the ruin of the world, for the priesthood is the light of the world and the salt of the earth, the conclusion became inevitable and imperative :—Restore the light and savour of the priesthood, and the world will walk in its light and be seasoned with its purity. It was upon this point, therefore, that his zeal concentrated its whole intensity. No man more honoured and loved the sons of St. Dominic among whom he lived in Rome, and of St. Francis, who were his companions in Milan ; and all Regular Orders as such. But he saw that they were not the priesthood of the Universal Church divinely ordained for the care of the flock. He honoured them as instrumental states in which individuals may acquire perfection ; but he knew that the Priesthood must already possess it ; that all Orders by their isolation and special way of life are separated from the Episcopate and from the cure of souls. All this forced upon his reason the self-evident truth that the *bonum universale Ecclesiæ*, the salvation of the universal flock, depends upon the universal Pastoral care ; that the universal Pastoral care is the office of the world-wide episcopate, including the universal priesthood ; that nothing less than this can do the work or execute the commission which our Divine Master gave to His Church : " Go ye therefore and make disciples of all nations." But the Church contains in itself the means of its own sanctification and the discipline of its own perfection; the priesthood is the divinely instituted means for its own perfect sanctification, and the instrument of the perfection of the whole body of the Church. St. Philip taught that the life of perfection needs no vows. St. Charles that the Priesthood and Pastoral Office were instituted in perfection without vows; and that the universal cure of souls demands an intimate union of the priesthood with the episcopate by obedience, whether by promise, by oblation, or if any so will also by vows; for such a vow would not separate the Priest from the Bishop, but would bind more closely to him; nor from the pastoral care, but would unite the pastor more intimately to the chief shepherd in each flock. No union can be conceived more intimate than this. It is a relation of authority, oversight, care, guidance, direction, defence, provision, and responsibility; that is to say in the Bishop, of government, in the Priest, of close personal care. No metaphor can express more precisely the idea of authority and of dependence, than that of a shepherd and his sheep. It implies mutual claims, bonds and obligations which unite them more nearly even than those of kindred. " I know mine, and mine know me." " The sheep hear his voice, and he calleth his own sheep by name; and leadeth them out. And when he hath led out his own sheep, he goeth before them; and the sheep follow him, because they know his voice." " The hireling and he that is not the shepherd, whose own sheep they are not (*cujus non sunt oves propriæ*), seeth the wolf coming and leaveth the sheep and fleeth." This is a divine vision which teaches the relation of property between the true shepherd and his flock. The sheep are his own, and the shepherd is theirs. They belong to one another; and have mutual rights in each other. It was this divine law which inspired the whole mind of St. Charles. Every saint represents some ray of the mind or life or work of our Divine Master. St. Charles represents the Good Shepherd; and this it is which has given to St. Charles a place of special authority. He is the saint of the Holy See, the source of all pastoral authority; of the episcopate which is the pastoral body; of the priesthood which shares in all the world the pastoral care of the episcopate. The name of St. Charles, therefore, reigns in the hearts of Bishops and Priests.

There has never been but one Church alone, but there have been many worlds. There has been a pagan world, a christian world, an imperial world, a dynastic world, a world of profound corruption, scourged and wrecked by a heretical world, soon, it seems, to be enveloped in a revolutionary world, anti-Catholic, anti-Christian, anti-social. The world at this day is warring not only against Catholic faith, but against Christianity; and not against the supernatural alone, but against human society; that is, the world is warring against itself. A world apostate from God must be suicidal. It destroys authority, law, morality, and the homes of men. How, then, can it stand? But through all this the Church moves on, imperishable in its life, and inexhaustible in spiritual light and power. The souls of men will ever need to be saved; and the salvation of souls will ever need the pastoral care.

The poor will never cease out of the land, and the pastors of souls will never cease to watch over them. The need and the care are both, while the world lasts, indefectible. The work of St. Charles was the renewal of the pastoral fervour of the Good Shepherd. It was no new way of life, drawn up by books and constitutions. It was the law and state founded by our great High Priest,—old as the faith, inherent in the priesthood, needed in all times, and vital in all the world. Wheresoever there are souls to be saved, there is the pastor's work; and there will be the life of St. Charles as the pattern, and the mind of St. Charles as the rule, of sacerdotal perfection. How profoundly he was penetrated and inflamed by the pastoral love of souls may be seen in the following words of his address to the Bishops and Priests in the second Provincial Council of Milan :—

" Fathers, this is our duty, and our office, placed as we are in the exalted seat of episcopal dignity, to look out for dangers as from a watch-tower, and to repel them when they threaten those who are resting under our charge and care. As parents we ought to have a fatherly oversight of our sons; as pastors never to take our eyes off the sheep which Jesus Christ has delivered by His holy death from the mouth of hell; and if any are being corrupted by the impurity of vice, to heal them with the sharpness of salt: if any be wandering in moral darkness, we ought to hold the light before them; for as the Supreme Creator of all things, when in the beginning He made the heavens which we behold, adorned them with a multitude of stars illuminated by the splendour of the sun to shine by night upon the earth, so in the spiritual renewal of this world He has placed in the Church, as in the firmament of heaven, prophets and apostles, pastors and doctors, who, like stars, illuminated by the light of Christ our Lord, the everlasting Sun, preside over the darkness of this clouded world, to drive away darkness from the minds of men by the splendour of a noble and holy discipline. These, then, the Wisdom of heaven has willed to be pastors, and to succeed in the place of the apostles as fathers; as the prophet says, ' *For thy fathers there are born unto thee sons.*' Why is it then that we do not imitate them as fathers, guides, and teachers? They in the first constituting of the Christian commonwealth, and in the greatest stress of difficulties, used to meet in council, and while they illuminated the face of the world involved in the darkness of error by the light of evangelical discipline, they also set to us the example how to restore order to the world."

Again, after describing the inflexible constancy of those who are on fire with a burning ardour for the salvation of souls, he adds, ". But if we act otherwise, at the fearful judgment of God, when we shall give an account of the souls entrusted to our charge and care, we shall hear their accusing cries, and the anger of the Judge sharply upbraiding us, and saying: If you were watchmen, why were you blind? if pastors, why did you let the flock committed to you wander? if the salt of the earth, how did you lose its savour? if you were the light, why did you not shine to them

that 'sat in darkness and the shadow of death?' if
apostles, why did you not use apostolic power, why did
you do all things for the eyes of men? if you were
the mouth of the Lord, why were you dumb? if you
knew yourselves to be unequal to this burden, why so
ambitious? if equal to it, why so careless and neglectful?"—*Orat. in* 2d *Conc. Prov.*, pp. 77, 80.

The mediæval world is passed away; the modern is
a missionary world, not outside of the Catholic unity
alone but within it,—among the Christian people,
jealous of the name, but many so unworthy of it.
The modern world is the world not of anchorites or of
recluses, but of apostles, pastors, and fishers of men. In
all the Catholic unity the episcopate and the priesthood
are roused into an unresting activity. It is the age of
pastors, and to every pastor's heart St. Charles is dear.

St. Charles intensely saw and grasped this master
truth: that while the priesthood is holy the laity will
follow in their footsteps; where the priesthood is
relaxed the people fall. He saw also that all raising
of the laity must begin by the raising of the priesthood. The Council of Trent would have taught him
this truth even if he had not seen it from his child-
hood, when he refused to appropriate ecclesiastical
revenues for which he rendered no service. His first
work, therefore, in Milan, was the reform of the
clergy. His chief sufferings and the risks of his life
came from the clergy who would not be reformed.
All this led him upward to the Great Exemplar, the
Good Shepherd, and the first pastors of the universal
flock. They were by their priesthood and its obliga-

tions in the state of perfection, united to their head, the Vicar of their Divine Master, serving the flock by the law of liberty, in charity and free obedience. And this divine reality, in all its beauty, lay hid under the burdens and trappings and privileges and possessions with which the priesthood and the episcopate were encumbered and corrupted.

The first great evil with which the Council of Trent had to contend was the non-residence of bishops, canons, and clergy. They were to a great extent drawing the revenues of dioceses and benefices, and living at a distance, immersed either in secular offices or in slothful indulgence. The decrees as to the residence of Bishops cut up this abuse by the roots. When St. Charles was appointed to the archbishopric of Milan no Archbishop had resided in that see for eighty years. His decision to leave Rome, and all the honours and offices of the Pontifical Court, was instantaneous. No remonstrances could restrain him. In his own person he set a prompt example of the Tridentine Reform. In September 1565 he entered Milan, and except to go to Rome, he never left his flock until November 1584, when he passed to his eternal rest.

When the plague broke out in 1576, the laity fled in multitudes, and of the clergy great numbers followed them. St. Charles called upon all priests who had the will to face the perils of the plague to come to him. He formed round himself a body of volunteers who offered themselves, and were ready, if need were, to lay down their lives for their Master's sake. This was a return to the early days when Bishop and Priest offered themselves a living sacrifice to God. So far the salt in Milan had regained its savour. The person and presence of St. Charles attracted men of like mind to himself. One by one they came to him, and offered themselves to serve him in the spirit of his own self-oblation to his Divine Master. They became, in the midst of a clergy, such as Giussano describes, a principle of the highest sacerdotal and pastoral perfection, working and assimilating others to itself. The law of their life was the imitation of our Divine Redeemer, "who by the Spirit offered Himself without spot to God." *Oblatus est quia ipse voluit.* His oblation was by His own will. His own will was the offering. He came not to do His own will, but the will of the Father. Not as I will, but as Thou wilt. This oblation or offering of the will is the most perfect obedience, and the surest test of perfection. It was this that the threefold enemy of the soul had striven to destroy in priests; and it was to revive this, as in the beginning, that St. Charles laboured. His whole life was in the spirit of the words of the Incarnate Son at His coming, "Ecce Venio," "Behold I come," and these were his last words in the hour of death.

In the year after the plague, that is 1577, St. Charles founded the congregation of the Oblates, or, as the word implies, of those who offered themselves to him of their own free will to obey him in the service of the Church of Milan. He gave to them a simple rule of life; he assigned to them the church and house of St. Sepolcro, where they live in community to this day.

They were priests of Milan who, for the more effectual exercise of the cure of souls and of all the various charges and offices of the diocese, were bound by an oblation and promise of obedience to their Bishop. After some years the oblation of obedience, which was at first confirmed by a promise, was further confirmed by a simple vow of obedience. But this vow did not separate them from their Bishop nor from the cure of souls. It bound them more closely than ever to him and to the pastoral office. The words of it were:—" To thee, and to thy successors, I promise and vow perpetual obedience in all things which shall be enjoined me . . . according to the prescribed rule of the Congregation of the Oblates."

It was manifestly the intention of St. Charles to diffuse this spirit of generous self-sacrifice throughout his whole clergy. He therefore instituted *consortia*, or societies of Oblates in all parts of the diocese. These *consortia* consisted of groups of the diocesan clergy, under a president, who was responsible to the Provost of St. Sepolcro, and he to the Archbishop.

The Church and clergy of Milan became the pattern of ecclesiastical order, and through all the vicissitudes of civil wars and revolutions, and the manifold evils of the last three hundred years, they preserve in a high degree the tradition of St. Charles.

The character of St. Charles will be best understood by reading his life. He was not a great theologian, or a great orator, or a great statesman. But he was a great pastor, a ruler, a lawgiver, a guide, and a judge in the Church of God. No man was more in the

world, and less of the world. He was immersed in
the world from his birth to his death, but the world
had nothing in him. He knew all the men who were
ruling the world in his day, and they knew him, but he
lived apart from them. His world was the sanctuary
and his flock. Nevertheless, he moved them, or de-
feated them as his duty demanded of him. He moved
the world because he did not rest upon it, and the
world could not move him because he rested upon
God.

It is not easy to form an estimate of his intellectual
faculties, for various and voluminous as are the letters,
pastorals, instructions, and outlines which remain
to us, they are too brief and occasional to give
any measure of his power. Nevertheless, they have
three special notes of a powerful mind—clearness,
solidity, and simplicity. They are full of patient
thought and industrious reading brought to bear without effort on the matter in hand, whether in synod, or
in preaching, or in conferences to the nuns of Milan.
Perhaps the chief intellectual power of his mind was
the legislative faculty. He had the discernment of a
master-builder, who can design the constructive lines,
calculate the dimensions, the masses, resistance, and
weights in a structure. The acts of his six Provincial Councils and his eleven diocesan Synods, in
which he had to encounter no little opposition and
much inert resistance, raised a fabric of ecclesiastical
legislation, which has given precedents to the episcopate of all countries. He was a great law-giver, and the
intellectual power of law-givers is to be measured not

by the writings but by the structures they leave behind them.

As to his moral powers; he was a great ruler, and
the power of rule is in the will.   His government over
himself was from his early years complete, and this
is the first condition of ruling other men.   His whole
episcopate was almost a continuous conflict with the
Spanish authorities of Milan, with inert colleagues, with
a relaxed clergy, mutinous religious, and a disorderly
populace.   To this must be added the injurious mis-
representations carried to Rome against him, and the
painful misjudgments formed there on imperfect or
false reports of his actions.   The letters written in
Rome at the time of his death show what he had to
endure.   It needed an inflexible firmness and a great
faith to bear this cross.   In the archives of Vienna
also, is a letter from Rome dated November 1584,
which says : "The death of Cardinal Borromeo, though
it has been felt universally with regret as is fitting, by
reason of the great and exemplary piety and goodness
of this holy man, nevertheless there are not wanting
some who feel a certain contentment because of the
relief they will receive thereby." [1]   Who can doubt it ?

It might be thought that a character of such force
and firmness would be wanting in tenderness of heart.
But all through his life are evidences of a delicate care
of others which is to be found only where charity has
ripened into all its fruits.   The distribution of two
patrimonies to the poor ; the two purses for alms, and
one only for his household ; his going barefoot at

---

[1] Hubner, Life of Sixtus V., vol. i. p. 67, note.

night lest he should wake his servants from their sleep; his endurance of the stench and misery of the homes of his poor, while his companions stood outside the threshold, lest he should give them offence; his sitting by the wayside to teach little children to pray; these and many other signs of an exquisite tenderness are to be traced throughout his life.

With such intensity of natural tenderness, what must have been his love of souls? He was eaten up with the threefold zeal for the house of God, for the priesthood of Jesus Christ, and for the souls for whom He died. He loved with a special affection those who had a love of souls; and we are told that to them he could refuse nothing. We have two beautiful examples of this love which are only a sample of the tissue of his whole pastoral life. During the pestilence in Milan, he came to a plague-stricken house of which the door was made fast. It was known that a poor mother and her infant were in an upper room. There was no access but by a ladder. St. Charles entered through the window, and finding the mother already dead, returned with the infant in his arms,—a deed worthy of a picture. The other and the last work of his love for souls was when death-stricken with fever, he embarked at Arona to return to Milan to die. In passing over the lake, he examined the boatmen who rowed him, in their knowledge of the faith and of their prayers. The good shepherd had long ago given his life for the sheep, and his self-oblation was now all but accomplished.

Such a life can be formed only by a faith which

lives in the unseen world, while it toils and suffers in
this ; and by prayer which is a second consciousness
at all hours, sustained and deepened by habitual
meditation on the Passion of our Redeemer.   The
Burial of Jesus in the Tomb was his constant meditation because it was the lowest humiliation of God, and
perhaps because it promised the only rest he looked
for in his waning life.

The impulse given by St. Charles to the pastoral
clergy of Milan spread to other parts of Italy and into
France.   The Bishop of Vercelli instituted a Congregation of Oblates ; and in France the Congregations
of the Missions, of St. Sulpice, of the Holy Ghost, and
the numberless diocesan congregations ; and, finally,
the Congregations of the Maristes, and of the Oblates
of Mary, all these with certain diversities are alike
in this: They are congregations of secular Priests
living by rule and in community.   It cannot be
doubted that this widespread movement was either
suggested, or directly promoted by the work and acts
of St. Charles.   The higher life of the diocesan clergy
has been nowhere more luminously manifested than in
the clergy of France.   It does no dishonour to the
priesthood of other countries to say that they stand at
the head of the clergy of the old European world.   The
revolution cut down the Church in France as with a
scythe, but it has risen again in renewed strength,
stripped of wealth and worldly greatness, but redeemed
from regalism and all its perils.   Its portion now is
poverty and conflict.   This was the state in which St.
Charles lived by free choice.   Surrounded by ecclesias-

tical state, with all the medieval traditions of privilege and benefices, tribunals and jurisdictions, though he was rich, for the sake of souls he made himself poor, and appealed by his life and labours to the zeal and self-sacrifice of his priests and people. It was so that St. Vincent of Paul, the Père Eudes, M. Olier, and others renewed the clergy of France.

It is a strange paradox that what is the first thing before us is often the last thing that is seen ; and what is the first thing to do is the last thing that is done. We might have thought that all would perceive the first work of our Divine Master to be the formation of the Apostles. And that the first work of reformation in the Church is the formation of the priesthood. St. Charles not only saw this, and promptly carried into effect the Tridentine Decree on Seminaries, but he perceived by his clear discernment that the formation of the pastors of the flock can only be surely effected by men experienced in the pastoral life. It is pastors who best know how to form pastors. In one of his MS. letters in 1579, to his agent in Rome, Speciano, preserved in the Ambrosian Library, he says that a seminary should be governed by those who have the same end and institution as the seminary itself. Every diocese should find and form its own clergy by its own priesthood, thereby becoming the source of sacerdotal and pastoral perfection to itself.

The movement of the seventeenth century in France which renewed the face of the Church was the creation of seminaries of which St. Charles had given the first example. Such is the chief work of the Church this day. The Lutheran Reformation stripped the Church in northern Europe, and the anti-Christian Revolution has stripped it in the west and south. It has to begin its work over again by the free oblations of the faithful, and in the poverty of its first days. It is a missionary among the people of the Old World, where once it was a mother and a queen. It is an apostle in the New World of the west and of the south, where as yet it has only laid the foundations of its home. But wheresoever it be, its chief work is always the same, the formation of the pastors of the flock. It is this which gives to St. Charles an undying and an universal influence over the Church throughout the world. He broke through the traditions of worldly ambition, avarice, inertness, which crushed and stifled the spiritual life of men, and revived in the midst of a sunken age the image and the reality of the Good Shepherd, surrounded by His apostles. Such is the first and chief work of the Church in this nineteenth century in the Old World and in the New. The Council of Trent has been reforming all things that are mutable to this day. The Council of the Vatican has taught what in the Church is immutable, its infallible authority in faith. The third centenary of St. Charles comes as a voice calling us to the greatest of our duties, the end for which all things are ordained, the care of the souls for whom Christ died, and the forming and multiplying of pastors, not hirelings or worldlings, but shepherds, willing to give their lives for the sheep.

NOTE.

THIS life was first published in the year 1610. Giovanni Pietro Giussano, its author, was born in Milan in the year 1553. At the age of nineteen, in the year 1572, after a course of study he took the degree of Doctor of Medicine. After following this profession for a few years he gave himself up into the hands of St. Charles and devoted himself to the ecclesiastical life. He was received by the Saint into his household, and became priest and oblate of St. Ambrose. On the death of the Saint he retired to Monza to write this life, being made by Cardinal Frederic Borromeo a conservator of the Ambrosian Library, and died at Monza in 1623. See *Argellati Bibliotheca scriptorum Mediolanensium.* The notes are selected from the abundant additions to the text of Giussano by Balthassar Oltrocchi of the oblates of St. Charles, contained in the Latin version of the same by Bartholomew De Rossi of the same congregation, and published at Milan in 1751.

CONTENTS.

BOOK I.

BOOK IL

Contents.

BOOK III.

VOL. I.   c

BOOK IV.

CHRONOLOGY OF THE LIFE OF ST. CHARLES.

---o---

From " Biografia di San Carlo Borromeo del Prof. Antonio Sala,"
Milan, 1858, *and " Histoire de Saint Charles Borromée," par M.*
l'Abbé Charles Sylvain. Bruges, 1884, 3 vols.

Birth of St. Charles	Oct.	2, 1538
Death of his mother, Margaret de' Medici, about .	...	1547
His father marries Thaddea dal Verme, widow of		
Lucrezio Gambara		1548
John Angelo de' Medici, his uncle, created Car-		
dinal by Pope Paul III.		1549
Count Julius Caesar Borromeo resigns in his favour		
the abbey of St. Gratinian at Arona. He puts		
on the cassock		1550
At the age of fourteen [1] he enters at the University		
of Pavia	Nov.	1552
His father marries Aurelia Vistarina, widow of		
Count Bolognini		1553
Death of Count Gilbert Borromeo, his father .	Aug.	1558
Takes the degree of doctor in canon and civil law .	} ...	1559
His uncle, Cardinal de' Medici, elected Pope .	} Dec.	
Created Cardinal	Jan. 31, }	
„ Administrator of the diocese of Milan	Feb. 8, }	1560
„ Secretary of State	...	...
Institutes the *Accademia* of the *Notti Vaticane* .	about this time	
The Council of Trent reopened . . .	Jan. 18, 1562	
He sends Mgr. Ferragatta as coadjutor to Milan .	April 23, 1562	
Marriage of his sister Anna to Prince Fabrizio		
Colonna	July	1562

---

[1] Giussano makes Charles sixteen years of age when he entered the
university (p. 8), but is evidently wrong. See St. Charles' own letter in
Sylvain's *Histoire de Saint Charles Borromée*, vol. i. p. 19.

Death of his elder brother, Count Frederic	Nov. 20,	1562
He sends the Jesuit Fathers to Milan	June	1563
Is ordained Priest	Aug. 15,	1563
The Council of Trent concluded	Dec. 4,	1563
Is consecrated Bishop	Dec. 7,	1563
Passes into the Order of Cardinal Priests	June 5,	1564
Founds the Borromean College at Pavia	June 19,	1564
Sends Mgr. Ormaneto as Vicar-General	July	1564
First Diocesan Synod held in the absence of St. Charles		1564
Beginning of the great Seminary of St. John Baptist	Nov.	1564
Resignation of Mgr. Ormaneto	Aug.	1565
St. Charles makes his entry into Milan	Sept. 23,	1565
First Provincial Council	Oct.	1565
Summoned to Rome to the death-bed of Pius IV.	Dec.	1565
Election of St. Pius V.	Jan. 7,	1566
Returns to Milan	April 5,	1566
Reform of his household for the second time	...	1566
Begins his reform of the Frati Umiliati	...	1566
Establishes his confraternities of Christian doctrine	...	1566
Makes a visitation of the city and diocese	...	1566
Transfers the church of San Fedele, the College of Brera, and the Abbey of Arona to the Jesuits	...	1567
Establishes the "House of Succour" and other pious foundations	...	1567
First controversies as to his archiepiscopal jurisdiction		1567
Visitation of the three Swiss valleys	Feb.	1568
Mission to Mantua	...	1568
Reforms in the Franciscan order	...	1568
Second Diocesan Synod	Aug.	1568
Second Provincial Council	April	1569
Edict of the Governor Albuquerque	Aug.	1569
Obduracy of the Canons of La Sala	...	1569
Attempt against his life by Farina	Oct. 26,	1569
Punishment of the assassin and his abettors	...	1570
Suppression of the order of the Umiliati	...	1570
Second visit to the Swiss valleys	...	1570
Famine in the Milanese province	...	1570
Death of the Governor Albuquerque	Aug.	1571
Battle of Lepanto	Oct. 7,	1571
Third Diocesan Synod, held in the absence of the Saint	April	1572
Death of St. Pius V.	May 1,	1572

ERRATA.

Page 94, line 4 from bottom, *note, for* "1571" *read* "1574."
Page 130, line 4 from bottom, *note, for* "Pius IV." *read* "Gregory XIII. in 1580."
Page 224, line 12 from bottom, *for* "Bernabò" *read* "Bernardo."
Page 354, line 4 from top, *for* "Luigi" *read* "Mgr. Charles."

LIFE OF ST. CHARLES BORROMEO.

𝕭𝖔𝖔𝖐 𝕴.

CHAPTER I.

OF THE BIRTH AND PARENTAGE OF ST. CHARLES.

1538.

Nowhere has the love of our Lord Jesus Christ for His Church been more manifest than in the diocese of Milan. Founded on the preaching of the Apostle, St. Barnabas, its first Bishop, it has never lacked holy pastors, who have been careful alike to preserve in its integrity the rule of faith delivered to them, and to repair the abuses of sin and time. Thirty-five of its Bishops have been canonized by the Church, and of these twenty sprung from the bosom of its illustrious families. Conspicuous amongst them was the great doctor, St. Ambrose, the principal patron and protector of the city.

But it was in later times that the love of our Lord has been shown more signally. Religion and piety had begun to decline, owing chiefly to the general

demoralisation caused by revolutions and the long
wars that had devastated Italy. The Church of Milan
had suffered more perhaps than any, when God, in His
mercy, gave to it a pastor who not only restored its
ancient glories, but also shone forth pre-eminent as a
model of sanctity to the priesthood and to the Christian commonwealth.

This was Charles Borromeo, who was born October 2,
1538, in the castle of Arona, the son of Gilbert Borromeo, Count of Arona, and of Margaret de Medici,
his wife.[1]

The parents of Charles were of noble birth, and
were eminent for their Christian lives. His father,
Count Gilbert, was a man of such prudence, that he
managed to retain possession of his estates, notwithstanding the wars between Charles V., Emperor of
Germany, and Francis I., King of France, and was
made by the former a colonel and one of the senators
of Milan. At home he set an example of piety, con-
fessing and communicating every week,[2] and reciting
daily the Divine Office on his knees, which were made
hard and callous by his long hours of prayer. Clothed
in sackcloth he frequently spent the hours of the
night in a little chapel he had built in a grotto on the
rock of Arona. To his tenants and vassals he was a
father, taking charge of orphans, and giving portions

---

[1] Sister of John James de Medici, Marquis of Melegnano, a famous
captain of the Emperor Charles V., and of John Angelo, Cardinal de
Medici, afterwards Pope Pius IV., who reigned from 1559 to 1565.

[2] The saint related that, in his boyhood, when the bell was rung at the
preface in high mass, by his father's orders he always went to church
with his tutor, in order to be present at the consecration.—O.

to poor girls; and he was so generous in almsgiving, that when his friends told him he would injure his children, he used to make answer: "If I take care of the poor, God will take care of my children." In a prophetic spirit he once said, "After my death my sons will be great men, and will not be in any need." It was his custom never to sit down to eat without first giving an alms to the poor.

The Countess Margaret was a model of Christian matrons. She shunned altogether the contagion of the world, never leaving her home save to go to mass every day in the neighbouring church, or for some other pious purpose. The modesty and humility of her bearing gave evidence of the interior union of her soul with God.

This pious couple had six children, two sons and four daughters, whom they brought up carefully in the fear of God. Frederic[1] was the elder of the two sons. He was raised to high dignities by his uncle, Pope Pius IV., and married Virginia della Rovere, sister of Francis, Duke of Urbino. The younger son was Charles, the subject of our history. The daughters were Isabella, who became a religious; Camilla, who espoused Cæsar Gonzaga, Prince of Molfetta; Jeronima, who wedded Fabricius Gesualdo, Prince of Venosa; and Anna, who was the wife of Prince Fabricius Colonna, afterwards Viceroy of Sicily. A half-sister, Hortensia, daughter of Thaddea dal Verme, second wife of Count Gilbert, married Count Hannibal d'Altaemps. All these children were good and virtuous. Anna

---

[1] Died November 20, 1562.

especially followed closely in the footsteps of her brother the Cardinal, and gave herself up entirely to God. She practised much self-denial in order to be able to give alms; and on her death at Palermo, in the year 1582, she was mourned by the poor as a mother.

CHAPTER II.

1538-1553.

CHARLES was born in the castle of Arona on the Lago Maggiore, situated forty miles from Milan, in the year 1538, on Wednesday, October 2nd, during the pontificate of Pope Paul III. The chamber in which his birth took place was called " the chamber of the three lakes," having a view of the lake in three directions; it was afterwards made an hospital for the sick. The birth of the saint was heralded by a miraculous appearance of brilliant light in the heavens, which lasted from two o'clock in the morning, the time of his birth, until daybreak. This circumstance was confirmed on oath by five eye-witnesses in the process of his canonization.

From his early years [1] Charles gave evidence of a great spirit of piety, and of a decided inclination towards the ecclesiastical state. His great delight was to make little altars and sing hymns. At an early age his father, perceiving his strong vocation, allowed him

---

[1] St. Charles had but weak health as a child, and spent his early years at Arona. He learnt Latin at Milan, under J. J. Merla, to whom he afterwards gave the benefice of Besana in Monte Brianzo. —O.

to receive the tonsure and to wear the cassock. This was entirely in accordance with his natural inclinations, as he thenceforward strove earnestly to act up to the dignity of his holy calling. When his companions, their studies over, hastened to amuse themselves in some light and thoughtless way, Charles would retreat to his little oratory, and for recreation would give himself up to prayer and converse with God. When of an age to be allowed to go out alone, he frequently visited the churches of Milan, especially the two churches of Our Lady, to whom he had a tender devotion. He was remarkable for his recollection, and avoided carefully whatever might distract his mind ever so little from the love of God, so that when feats of arms occasionally took place at the castle for the amusement of Count Frederic, his elder brother, he would always absent himself; and when tennis was played in the court of the palace, if he could not go away, he would betake himself wherever he thought he should be least noticed, so afraid was he of doing anything unworthy of the habit he wore. He was fond of music and singing as a recreation, but if he met with unbecoming words, he omitted them, and sang only the notes. Following the example of his father, Count Gilbert, Charles went every week to Confession and Communion as the medicine and nourishment of his soul.

Blameless as was the life of Charles, he did not escape persecution, for, instigated doubtless by the evil one, his companions, and even his father's servants, used to make game of his devotions and hinder him in

his pious practices. But the youth took all their railing in good part, and continued his way undisturbed
by opposition. There were some, however, who knew
how to appreciate his rare virtue, especially one venerable priest zealous for the furtherance of good discipline, Bonaventura Castiglione,[1] rector of the collegiate
church of St. Ambrose. Whenever he saw Charles,
he always stopped to speak to him, and when asked
the reason, he replied, "You do not know that young
man; he will be a reformer of the Church, and will do
great things." When Charles was twelve years old his
uncle, Julius Cæsar Borromeo, resigned in his favour
the abbey of St. Gratinianus and St. Felinus in Arona.
Mindful of the duties of those who enjoy ecclesiastical
revenues, Charles resolved to spend its income on the
poor. He, therefore, told his father that he had so resolved, because it was the patrimony of Christ, and as
such could not be expended in support of the family,
as he himself was only the steward, owing a strict
account to God. The good Count quite agreed with
his son, and allowed him to dispose of the revenues as
he would. Accordingly he laid them out on the poor,
with the exception of the sum required for his personal
expenses. Occasionally his father would borrow from
him, but he always kept a strict account of such outlay,
in order that the poor might not suffer.

[1] Born in Milan in 1487, was made apostolic commissary of the Holy
Inquisition, canon of Santa Maria della Scala in 1521, elected Provost of
the church of St. Ambrose in 1546, died in 1555.

CHAPTER III.

WHEN Charles was sixteen years of age, and had completed his humanities, his father sent him to the University of Pavia [1] to study civil and canon law. The morals of young men in such places of learning were at that time very corrupt, but Charles fortified himself against the snares of the devil by unwearied diligence in his studies. Besides regular attendance at the public lectures, he went every day to those of his tutor, Francis Alciato. [2] In a short time he made great progress, notwithstanding an impediment in his speech, owing to which he was sometimes considered devoid of capacity. In this respect he resembled the great St. Thomas Aquinas, who, for a like infirmity,

[1] St. Charles spent five years at the University of Pavia. Charles Francis Bonomo, afterwards Bishop of Vercelli, and a great friend of the saint, was a fellow-student.

[2] Francesco Alciato, born at Milan, 1522, was created a Cardinal at the recommendation of St. Charles by Pius IV. in 1560, and died at Rome, 1580. He was nephew of Andrea Alciato, the famous jurisconsult and emblematist, and was himself a man of considerable learning. St. Charles afterwards appointed him his deputy as Grand Penitentiary, and he was also Vice-Protector of Ireland.

was nicknamed by his fellow-students "the dumb ox."

Charles was distinguished not only for industry, but for virtue, which shone forth amidst the corruptions by which he was surrounded. He avoided all vain and frivolous talking, and fled from the slightest occasion of danger to holy purity. Although most kind and courteous to all, and much sought after by his fellow-students, he avoided particular friendships, as tending too often to dissipation of soul. Yet his sweetness of manner caused him to be loved by all; while there were not wanting men of discernment who already saw in him the promise of future greatness and sanctity. About this time Count Gilbert, his father, died, at the age of forty-seven, and Charles was called home to take charge of the family, an office which fell to him rather than to his elder brother, Frederic, on account of a prudence beyond his age. Doubtless divine Providence intended this to prepare him for the future government of a diocese; for the apostle St. Paul tells us that one of the qualities of a good bishop is the prudent government of his own household,[1] as he who fails in this will not be able to bear a greater burden.

Charles, after settling affairs at home to the satisfaction of all, began to show a zeal and capacity for ecclesiastical reform. The Abbey of St. Gratinian, at Arona, was served at this time by monks of the order of St. Benedict, who, from their irregular and undisciplined lives, showed themselves unworthy of their

[1] 1 Tim. iii. 5.

holy habit. When engaged in family affairs at Arona, Charles could not but hear of the bad example set by the monks, and resolved, young as he was, to try and repair the dishonour done to God, and to bring the monks to a sense of their disorders. By imprisonment and judicious punishments, he in a short time effected a reform, and brought them back to better observance of their rule.

Whilst Charles was thus occupied with the things of God, the enemy of souls, from hatred of his virtues, laid a snare to rob him of his chastity which he prized above all things. It was an age of licentiousness. Virtue in a young and rich man was looked upon with contempt, and vice was cloaked under the specious name of gallantry. Instigated by the devil, a dissolute man of some authority in his household, entered into a plot by which he hoped to destroy the virtue which was so obnoxious in his eyes. Under cover of night, when all was quiet, he introduced into the apartments of Charles a young woman of abandoned habits. No sooner had Charles cast his eyes upon her than he instantly fled as from the edge of a precipice, showing thus by his example, that the best means of preserving virtue is in immediate flight from occasions of sin. He cared nothing for the derision of men, but preferred an unstained conscience and the friendship of God to the vain judgments of the world.

Having completed the settlement of his affairs, Charles returned to Pavia, where he gave himself up with so much assiduity to his studies, that his health began to suffer, and he was compelled to rest for a while. Ordered some relaxation by the doctors, he chose music as a source of diversion; but even in this he was careful to mortify his natural tastes through a love of self-denial. He never entirely lost the effects of this attack of illness, but was afflicted for the remainder of his life with a cough, which the medical men affirm to be the effect of his extreme abstemiousness. Hence it became a sort of proverb that abstinence was the remedy of Cardinal Charles Borromeo.

Whilst he was pursuing his studies at Pavia, his uncle Cardinal de Medici renounced in his favour the Abbey of Romagnano and the Priory of Calvenzano. Charles accepted these charges with the firm intention of fulfilling to the utmost all the duties they entailed. Thenceforward he entertained the purpose of founding a college to enable poor students of good character to acquire, not only learning, but also to train them to holy living, and afterwards fully carried out this intention.

By his twenty-second year he had completed his course of study with the degree of doctor in civil and canon law. Towards the end of the year 1559 the Sacred College of Cardinals was in conclave for the election of a new Pontiff. An unusually large number of professors, students, and others had assembled to witness the admission of Charles to his degrees, when heaven itself seemed to declare approval; for, just as Francis Alciato, the senior lecturer, began his formal congratulations, the sky, until then dark and cloudy, was suddenly illumined by sunshine. This

auspicious omen was made use of by the orator, who
predicted that the future would in like manner be
illumined by him on whose head he was about to
place the doctor's cap.   With this saying of Alciato
many agreed, proclaiming that Charles would become
a great man in the Church of God.

CHAPTER IV.

ON the death of Pope Paul IV. the Sacred College of Cardinals unanimously elected as Pope, John Angelo de Medici, of Milan, the maternal uncle of Charles, under the title of Pius IV. This election took place on the day after Christmas Day, in the year 1559. Great were the rejoicings throughout Milan at the elevation of one of its citizens to the dignity of Vicar of Christ, and Charles was congratulated on all sides as nephew of the new Pontiff. But the soul of a saint is indifferent alike to honour and dishonour, neither puffed up by prosperity nor cast down by adversity. Charles, therefore, preserved his equanimity of spirit amid all the compliments he received; and the only particular notice he took of the occasion was to go to Holy Communion, together with his brother Frederic, making a special intention of uniting their wills with the holy will of God. He resolved to remain in Milan when his brother and other young noblemen went to Rome to tender their homage to the new

Pope. But a summons to Rome soon came for him. Pius IV., who loved his nephew, and appreciated his talents and sanctity, wished to make some use of him in the service of the Church. Charles was immediately made Protonotary and Referendary, and, on the last day of January 1560, Cardinal Deacon of the title of SS. Vitus and Modestus, which was after a time changed into that of St. Martin; and on the 8th of February he was appointed administrator of the See of Milan, at the age of twenty-two years and four months. It was by a special dispensation of His good providence that God raised up for Milan in her state of spiritual destitution so powerful a Father and Reformer.

The election of so young a prelate serves as a warning to men to abstain from judging the acts of lawful superiors, especially of the sovereign Pontiff, who is guided in an especial manner by the Holy Spirit. Viewed according to human wisdom, it might have seemed an imprudence on the part of the Holy Father thus to raise his nephew to a post of such responsibility in a time of unusual laxity. But the hand of God was soon visible in the wonderful effects which He deigned to work by means of the young Cardinal, not only in the diocese of Milan, but throughout Christendom; and many are of opinion that in exalting the uncle to the pontificate, God had also in view the raising up of the nephew for the reform of the Church.

Some have thus interpreted the wonderful sign which appeared during the infancy of Pius IV., as written in his life by Platina, and also recorded in the life of that Pontiff's brother, Giovanni Giacomo de Medici, by Messaglia. There suddenly appeared over the infant a brilliant flame that lit a lamp some distance off. The flame then disappeared, leaving the lamp still burning, which, however, soon itself vanished. The flame was understood to be the pontifical dignity to which the child was to be raised, who was afterwards to kindle the lamp of his nephew, to give light to the world as Cardinal and Archbishop. Charles was afterwards called "a lamp in Israel" by Gregory XIII., and "a great light of holy Church" by Clement VIII. It may truly be said that, like another Aaron, Charles was raised up, without expectation on his own part, to these honours.

The holy Father entrusted him with greater responsibilities, all of which he discharged with credit. He made him the head of the Consulta, giving him authority to sign in his name memorials, and ordinary faculties. He also entrusted him with the administration of high offices of state, to which many privileges were attached, none of which Charles sought for himself; indeed some honours which his uncle offered him he refused, and accepted others from obedience alone. Many of his relations and friends were displeased at this spirit of detachment in Charles, affecting to regard it as a want of charity, whilst secretly they were annoyed from fear of losing the advantages of his patronage.

In proportion as greatness sought him out, so did Charles abase himself the more with deep foundations

of humility; while it was from meditation and prayer
that he drew the wisdom which enabled him to direct
so many works.   Wealth, which would have been a
source of danger and relaxation to most, was in his
hands but an instrument for doing good deeds, and an
incentive to greater watchfulness in working out his
salvation.   Wonderful is God in His saints, for they
alone know how "sweetly and graciously He orders all
things "[1] for their sanctification.   Charles was wont to
say when speaking of the divine mercy, that God
had guided him not by the way of adversity, but by
that of prosperity, infusing into his soul a divine light
to know the vanity and worthlessness of earthly things
so as not to allow himself to be engrossed by them.
Using these earthly advantages merely as means to
advance the glory of God, his mind was ever fixed
on the true and solid joys which He has prepared in
heaven for those who love Him.

He was careful to testify his gratitude and love for
his uncle by the most exact fidelity in all the service
he required of him; ever keeping his intention pure,
and his heart disengaged from worldly interests.   The
glory of God and the good of souls were the end and
aim of all his actions; and he prayed earnestly for
more and more light and grace that one who was
called to govern others might not himself fall from
the right way.   In all things appertaining to the
government of the Church, he made a practice of
asking the advice of holy men of experience, and
prudently guided himself by their counsel.   He studied

[1] Wisdom viii. 1.

political works on the art of government, avoiding carefully all such as were founded on anti-Christian principles, destructive both to rulers and subjects. Having long intended to found seminaries and colleges for the furtherance of education and religion, he about this time made a beginning with a society of learned men, both ecclesiastics and seculars, who met at the Vatican to confer together on good morals and literature. By means of this society and the emulation in virtue which it encouraged, Charles hoped to combat the spirit of idleness so often found in the atmosphere of courts. He also had in view the revival of the ancient practice of Prelates and Bishops preaching in person to their flocks. It was of great advantage [1] to himself, as enabling him to overcome a natural defect in his speech, which made it difficult for him to preach. Many Bishops and Cardinals, following his example, began henceforward the practice of this apostolic office.

Charles found the study of the ancient Stoic philosophers to be useful as a means of sanctification and aiding him to subdue his passions. He often spoke with especial praise of the " Manual of Epictetus the Stoic " which was constantly in his hands. These academical meetings were known by the name of Notti Vaticane or Vatican Nights, because held in the

---

[1] St. Charles writes to the Cardinal of Mantua in 1575, from Bologna, as follows :—" Five or six Latin speeches are delivered every day, and I endeavour as I can to answer in the same language, but on unequal conditions, as I have, on the spur of the moment, without preparation, to answer an address which has been prepared. I find here how much I have been helped by our practice at the Accademia, for what we did there by way of recreation is now the occupation of serious moments."—O.

evening at the Palace of the Vatican, after the business of the day was over.   The academy became celebrated, and among its members were many noble and learned men, who became Bishops and Cardinals;[1] one afterwards Pope Gregory XIII.   The influence of Charles was greatly increased by means of these meetings, which brought into the light of day, the hidden love of his heart for virtue and virtuous men.   It was wonderful to see this young man in the flower of his age, and in high position, giving all his thoughts and affections to good works; and depriving himself of rest in order that public business should not suffer.   Thus he never lost a moment of time; he gave himself to the study of letters, not as some in high positions have done in order to cover their neglect of duty with the specious excuse of study, but for the purpose of gaining knowledge in order to govern wisely; and to rouse up Bishops and Prelates from idle repose for the good of Christendom.

Wholly detached from earthly interests, his heart fixed on God alone, Charles nevertheless thought it right to conform himself externally to the usages of the court.   By so doing he not only avoided singularity, but gained good-will, and was consequently able to do his work with greater facility.   His manner of living

[1] Among these were Alciato, Lodovico Simonetta, Carlo Visconti, Francis and Cæsar Gonzaga, Agostino Valerio, Bishop of Verona, Silvio Antoniano for a short time secretary of St. Charles, Tolomeo Galli, Archbishop of Siponto, who were all afterwards Cardinals ; Giovanni Delfino, Bishop of Torcello, Guido Ferreri, Bishop of Vercelli and Cardinal, a cousin of the Saint, Lodovico Taverna, Bishop of Lodi, Pier Antonio Lonati, Senator of Milan, Paolo Sfrondati, Baron of Valsassina, brother of Gregory XIV., &c.

and household he regulated according to the habits of the time, and was seen occasionally at receptions, especially those of his brother Cardinals, for whom, as a body, he had especial reverence. He was present at the wedding festivities on the marriage of his brother, Count Frederic, with Virginia della Rovere, daughter of Guidobaldo, Duke of Urbino.

It was evident, however, that he was not fond of such entertainments, and that his only motive was to give pleasure to others. The desire of his heart was to further good discipline in the Church, and he had a lively contempt for earthly grandeur.

Two virtues shone forth in Charles conspicuously. He, in the first place, knew how to accommodate himself to all sorts of persons, high and low, so that in truth it may be said of him, as of the Apostle: " I became all things to all men." [1] Next, though surrounded with occasions of sin, and independent of all control, he led a life of spotless integrity, and preserved his purity of heart and mind in a perfect degree. Witnesses who were living at the time have testified to the truth of the following incident. A certain prince, a relative, once invited him to his villa situated a few miles distant from Rome. This gentleman had determined to set a snare for the saint in order to tempt him to commit sin, and to this end, after a sumptuous repast, conducted the Cardinal to his apartments, into which, when all had retired for the night, he secretly introduced a Roman courtesan, famous for her beauty. Finding him alone she at once began to practise her

1 Cor. ix. 22.

arts in order to draw him into sin. No sooner did the Cardinal perceive the woman than he ran to the door, and loudly called out for those of his household, expressing strongly his anger at the intrusion. They removed the woman at his command, asserting that they were not to blame for her admission as they knew nothing about the affair. Attributing it then to his host, Charles, without a word, quitted the house before daybreak, to mark his indignation at the outrage. Such was the code of morality in high places, that a prince and his friends had felt no shame in concocting this plot.

At this time Charles was wholly pre-occupied with the cares of state and government. Well aware of his responsibilities he considered himself the guardian of a free people, not of slaves, and considered the common good above every other interest: being especially solicitous for the poor that they should not be in want, he kept the price of bread low.

The writer, when visiting a town of Romagna during the lifetime of the saint, expressed his joy on seeing the arms of Charles sculptured over the palace of the Governor. An old man said they had been placed there when St. Charles was the Legate of that province, during the Pontificate of his uncle, adding: " Would to God that we had him now. He would not allow grain to be exported as is done now, while the poor suffer."

Above all things Charles was careful as to the administration of justice ; and to this end he sent good judges into his provinces. If any of these proved unworthy of their charge, he at once removed them, even though interest was made for them by Cardinals, or other personages of high degree. These measures were carried out with so much gentleness that no one was offended. It was so in the case of a certain Governor of a city, who had been recommended for the post by a relative, who was a Cardinal and an intimate friend of Charles. As the people were not satisfied with his government the saint removed him, and would not give him any other appointment, and in this refusal, his relative, the Cardinal, allowed that Charles was quite right.

CHAPTER V.

NOTWITHSTANDING the heavy burdens laid upon him,
Charles never showed reluctance or weariness in the
service of the Sovereign Pontiff. Of unflinching up-
rightness in his actions, he was never known to swerve
in the least degree from his course from motives of
human respect. He was particularly careful in choosing persons to be proposed to the Pope for ecclesiastical
benefices, especially for the dignity of Cardinal, never
allowing himself to be swayed in the slightest degree
by motives of affection. He was so afraid of favouring
his relations, that he preferred to run the risk of seeming ungrateful and cold-hearted in their behalf. Conversing one day with one of his own kinsmen, who
served him faithfully in Rome, he said to him, "I
recognise your merits, and love you well; but it would
be against my conscience to requite you with church
preferments. If, however, you wish to serve God in
the ecclesiastical state, I will not fail to give you an
honourable post."

So great was the patience and sweetness of Charles amid various and complicated affairs, that he was never known to utter an ungracious or disdainful word, even to any one of his household. He gave audience to all who came with unwearied kindness. No amount of fatigue ever prevented him from attending to correspondence, or dictating to others as occasion required.

The Sovereign Pontiff, when he saw his marvellous aptitude for affairs, offered him the post of Grand Penitentiary,[1] which he accepted, not, it need hardly be said, from a love of honours, but in order that he might serve God in a post which needed reform. His disinclination to preferment was strongly shown by his refusal of the office of chamberlain, vacant on the death of Cardinal Santa Fiore.

Charles employed his influence as Grand Penitentiary in obtaining the execution of the bull for the reform of the office, in which the Pope affirms that he makes the revision by the advice of the Grand Penitentiary.

Nor did his honours end here, for he was chosen as Legate of Bologna, Romagna, and the March of Ancona, provinces of the Ecclesiastical States. He was also made Protector of the Kingdom of Portugal, of Belgium, and of the Catholic cantons of Switzerland. Under his protection were placed the Orders of St. Francis, the Carmelites, the Humiliati, the Regular Canons of the Holy Cross of Coimbra, the Knights of Jerusalem or Malta, and those of the Holy Cross of Christ in Portugal, whose Grand Master is the King,

---

[1] One of the last acts of Pius IV., who died December 10, 1565.

—of all which offices Charles was careful to fulfil the obligations.

In the meantime, while thus zealously serving God in these various charges, he was visited with a great sorrow, which, at the same time, proved of signal benefit to his soul. This was the death[1] of his brother, Count Frederic. During his last illness Charles never left his bedside, but tended him to the end with more than the affection of a brother. The death of one who was high in favour with the Holy Father was a great affliction to his relatives. On Charles himself it had a deeper effect than natural sorrow which finds relief in tears. Reflections on death and the instability of earthly things filled his mind; and as if by a light from heaven, he saw more clearly than ever the folly of seeking anything in this world but the will of God. Moved by the Holy Spirit, Charles sent for his confessor on the very night after the death of his brother, and by his counsel determined on henceforward observing a greater strictness in the spiritual life. This prompt determination was of great service in fortifying him for the battle which was to be waged against his holy desires.

By the death of Count Frederic, Charles remained sole heir to the hereditary wealth and estates ; and the Pope, on the urgent advice of other relatives, now suggested to him that he ought to marry as the head

---

[1] The author does not follow here the chronological order of events. Count Frederic Borromeo died November 20, 1562. St. Charles confessed to Mgr. Speciano that the death of his brother Frederic was a warning to him from heaven to bid farewell [to the perishing things of the world.

of his family. But Charles was proof against this proposal, which might have tempted ordinary young men. He was in no danger of giving up his resolution of consecrating himself entirely to the service of God, for he decided at once to extinguish all the hopes of his relatives, and for this purpose he received holy orders, and was ordained priest by Cardinal Frederic Cesa in the Church of Santa Maria Maggiore. This decisive step was a disappointment to his uncle the Pope, and his relatives. To the remonstrances of the Holy Father, Charles made this reply: " Do not be displeased with me, Holy Father. I am now wedded to the spouse whom I have so long desired." He now changed his diaconal title of San Martino ai Monti for that of Cardinal-Priest of St. Praxedes, in consequence of his ordination.

His ardent wish now fulfilled, he gave himself up to greater austerity of life and to fresh efforts to advance in the path of perfection. Fearful of being his own guide in the way to which God called him, he chose for his director in the spiritual life John Baptist Ribera, a devout priest of the Society of Jesus. This holy man, seeing from the dispositions of his penitent, that he was called to great sanctity, gave himself up to the direction of this soul as a direct charge from God. He made Charles go through the Exercises of St. Ignatius as a foundation for the practice of solid perfection. He visited him every day and conversed long with him upon the spiritual life. But the evil spirit, knowing well the harvest that God would reap through the sanctity of His servant

Charles, endeavoured to blight it in the very beginning.   He instigated the relations and household of
the Cardinal to make every effort to withdraw Charles
from his retired life to one more in accordance with
their idea of what befitted his station in the world.
They began to treat Father Ribera with scorn and
ridicule, even going so far as to endeavour to prevent
his access to the Cardinal.   Charles, however, perceived
their designs, and used himself to admit the Father by
a private door.

CHAPTER VI.

FOUNDATION OF THE BORROMEAN COLLEGE IN THE UNIVERSITY OF PAVIA.

1562.

ST. CHARLES, while a student at Pavia, entertained the design of sometime founding a college in that city for the benefit of virtuous youths who, being lovers of learning, lacked the means of pursuing their studies. Now that he was raised to the dignity of Cardinal, and had, moreover, the advantage of being the nephew of the Sovereign Pontiff, it was possible for him to carry this purpose into execution. His love for souls made him look with compassion on the perilous position of students who, away from the control of parents at a dangerous period of their lives, are exposed to the manifold temptations of life. He, therefore, made it a primary consideration in the discipline of the new college that the students should be trained in good morals and in the fear of God, in order to set an example of perseverance in a holy life.

As Charles conferred with the Holy Father concerning his new undertaking, he found him well satisfied with his zeal for education, and was promised the full measure of his protection and sympathy.

Having thus the highest approval, Charles lost no time in having a good design drawn out for the buildings on his own property in Pavia. He prevailed on his Holiness to allow certain benefices to be applied to the temporal maintenance of the new college, in which he intended that students should be boarded and lodged, with rules and statutes, and all regulations necessary for its good government. Through his exertions the college, dedicated to St. Justina,[1] Virgin and Martyr, rose rapidly, and from its noble proportions took rank at once among the finest buildings of the country.

When so far completed as to be habitable, the scholastic course was begun with a good number of students, who paid a pension, which was expended to the completion of the building. Among these students was the cousin of St. Charles, Count Frederic Borromeo, son of Julius Cæsar, brother of Gilbert, the father of the saint.. Count Frederic was afterwards Cardinal-Archbishop of Milan, and an imitator of the virtues of his cousin.

To this second Cardinal Borromeo [2] was left also the administration of the college; and he it was who gave it a constitution according to the spirit of its founder.

These constitutions, according to his intentions, were confirmed by a bull of Pope Sixtus V. It was the wish of St. Charles that this college, like the others which

1 Daughter of Vitalian, prince of Padua, founder of the family of Borromeo.

[2] Born, 1564; created cardinal, 1587; Archbishop of Milan, 1596; died 1632.

were founded by him, should remain under the care of the venerable congregation of the Oblates.

Most amply was the purpose of the saintly Archbishop fulfilled, for not only were the students noted for observance of good discipline at home, but gained reputation abroad for virtue and learning.

CHAPTER VII.

INDEFATIGABLE as was the saint in all matters relating to the temporal government of the Church, yet he never grudged any toil in the pastoral care and spiritual direction of souls. It seems indeed that he had been especially raised up in a time of need for the reformation of morals, the furtherance of discipline, and the extirpation of heresies in the Church. Thus we find him now giving counsel to the Holy Father, now suggesting to him precautions and remedies, according to the occasion ; at another time strengthening him in resolutions which he had formed,—in short, always engaged in good works. He was mainly instrumental in bringing about the reform described by Onofrio Panvinio in his life of Pius IV. Among his most important labours was the continuation and conclusion of the Council of Trent. In this holy work his prudence and zeal for the Catholic faith were more than ever conspicuous. The Council of Trent[1] had been begun some years previously, under the pontifi-

---

[1] Begun 1542, suspended 1555, re-opened 1562, concluded 1563.

cate of Paul III., to put down the heresy of Luther
and Calvin, which was then insinuating itself throughout great part of Christendom. The Council was
suspended for seven years at the death of Julius III.,
in consequence of various impediments.

The fatherly heart of Pius IV., grieved at the progress the new heresy was making among the children
of the Church in Germany, England, Hungary, France,
and parts of Switzerland and Piedmont, acquiesced
readily in the urgent appeals of his nephew, St.
Charles, for the convocation and completion of the
Council.

As a preliminary measure, Charles, with the assistance of many learned prelates, called together the
Cardinals, together with the ambassadors of various
princes, and discussed the propriety of re-opening the
Council. The Holy Father, by the advice of Charles,
ordered a solemn procession, himself going in person
barefooted from the Church of St. Peter in the Vatican
to the Minerva, accompanied by the Sacred College of
Cardinals, and by the Dukes of Florence and Urbino,
his relatives, who had come to Rome to kiss his feet.
He then dispensed the treasures of holy Church, granting a jubilee, and inviting all the faithful to make
fervent supplication to God for the success of the
Council. He sent to Trent five Cardinals, legates *a
latere*, as presidents of the Council in his name. First
among them, after the death of Ercole Gonzaga,[1] was

[1] Ercole Gonzaga of Mantua, Cardinal-President of the Council of
Trent, died there in March 1563.
  Giovanni Morone of Milan, born 1509, made Bishop of Modena by
Clement VII., Cardinal by Paul III. in 1548, President of the Council of

Giovanni Morone, and with him Lodovico Simonetta, both natives of Milan.

There were assembled two hundred and fifty Bishops, a great number of other prelates and theologians, as well as the ambassadors of the Christian princes. Thus, by God's grace, the labours of the Council were resumed, the seventeenth session being held on the 18th January 1562. The special superintendence of the acts of the Council was entrusted by the Sovereign Pontiff to his nephew Charles. To him therefore the legates of the Council rendered an exact account of all the doubts which arose, and the various decisions pronounced, all which are recorded in the " Letters of St. Charles." All these weighty matters were treated by the Cardinal with a congregation of eighteen learned men, and with the Holy Father himself; and the decisions of this Papal Commission were then forwarded to the legates with final instructions. Charles gave up everything to attend to this important affair, ever giving orders for the admission of messengers from the Council at any hour of the day or night.

Great was the strength of soul shown by the saint during this trying time. The devil sowed the seeds of discord among those assembled at the Council ; there were great diversities of opinion, and there seemed no remedy to the objections and impediments raised by

Trent by Pius IV. in 1563, was much employed in foreign missions, and died in 1580.

Lodovico Simonetta of Milan, Bishop of Pesaro, died 1563. The other Cardinal-Presidents were—Hosius, Bishop of Warmia ; D'Altaemps, Bishop of Constance ; and Navager, Bishop of Verona, chosen in the place of Cardinal Seripando, who died at Trent in 1563.

some of the Christian princes. The legates even wrote several times to Charles that the difficulties which arose seemed insuperable. Charles alone never lost hope. He consoled and encouraged his uncle the Pope, assuring him that God would not fail to conduct to a happy issue an affair so vital to the welfare of the faith. The labours of the Council continued uninterruptedly until the year 1563, when certain evil-disposed persons again raised the question of the expediency of its suspension, of which some princes were desirous. The legates gave a full account of these proceedings to Charles, in order that his authority might quell the storm.

The Sovereign Pontiff fell dangerously ill at this time. Self-interest might have induced many in the position of Charles to have kept this illness secret; but he, detached from all human considerations, thought only of the glory of God and the good of the universal Church. He sent at once to the legates of the Council, ordering them to hasten its conclusion, for fear that any accident, such as possibly the death of his uncle, might prevent its confirmation, and the fruit of all its labours thus be lost. The legates, in obedience, closed the twenty-fifth session held on two consecutive days, the 3d and 4th of December, 1563. Some matters still remained to be decided; but they resolved to leave these to the authority of the Sovereign Pontiff, as we read in the acts of the Council. Thus by the Divine blessing was this great undertaking at length brought to a conclusion, after having been many times interrupted. It became the instrument of reform to the whole Church. Through its means heresies were rooted out, and remedies applied to the abuses which had crept into Christian discipline.

CHAPTER VIII.

1564.

GREAT was the joy of St. Charles at the happy termination of the Council, and he now put forth all his energies to secure the execution of its holy decrees as a sure means of restoring the Church to the beauty of holiness. He studied them with the utmost minuteness, in order that he might have every detail carried out, classifying them according to subjects, and placing them in his oratory in three divisions. In the first, which he called "Sancta Sanctorum," he deposited the decrees concerning the Catholic faith and the Holy Sacraments; the second, called "Sancta," contained those relating to ecclesiastical reform; in the third were deposited those concerning the laity. In the first consistory held after the return of the Apostolic Legates from Trent, Charles proposed that a congregation of eight Cardinals should be formed for the purpose of deciding upon controversies that might arise in the interpretation of the decrees. This commission was appointed by Pius IV. *motu proprio* on the 5th August, 1564.

Charles also obtained from the Holy Father various provisions and constitutions concerning the residence of Bishops and Prelates, the profession of faith, and the time fixed for the execution of the decrees. He presided over the compilation of the Roman Catechism, and a reformed edition of the Roman Breviary and Missal, with the assistance of many theologians who were at Trent. Among these was Father Francesco Foreiro, a Portuguese Dominican monk of great learning and piety, who was much beloved by the King of Portugal and his uncle, Cardinal Henry, to whom St. Charles made many apologies for detaining the Father for the publication of the Catechism. On sending him back, Charles wrote to the King and the Cardinal in the following terms:—" By his diligence and industry, we have almost finished the Catechism, an excellent work, comprising nearly all the precepts of a devout and holy life." And replying to the Cardinal Hosius, Bishop of Warmia, one of the legates of the Council, on the 27th December, 1564, Charles wrote:—" We have now, by the assistance of learned men, finished the Catechism. In a short time we shall issue a new Missal and Breviary, which will satisfy, as we hope, the expectations of Catholics."

These were not the only fruits of the industry of St. Charles. He also revised and corrected some works of the Fathers, the texts of which had been corrupted by heretics, with the aid of Achilles Statius, a Portuguese, whom he kept in Rome after the Council for this purpose, as we see from the same letters to the King of Portugal.

Having had the management of the affairs of the Council, St. Charles considered that he was therefore bound to set the example of obedience to its decrees, and of zeal in their execution. Set up like a city on a hill in his position as nephew and coadjutor of the Sovereign Pontiff, the Vicar of Christ and universal Pastor of souls, his steps would, he knew, be followed by the prelates of Holy Church and by all Christian people, since there is nothing that furthers obedience so much as the example set by those in authority. But in his humility St. Charles began with himself and the reformation of his own life, since the decrees of the holy Council spurred him on with fresh fervour in the path of sanctity in which he was hastening. He gave up the innocent recreations which he had hitherto allowed himself; and with a cheerful countenance increased his austerities. He gave himself to prayer at least twice a day. He chastised his body with frequent disciplines and fastings. He frequently visited the churches, especially Santa Maria Maggiore, to which he went privately at nightfall, accompanied by some intimate friends, ascending the hill on his knees from the spot where stands the Church of St. Pudentiana. His almsgiving was abundant, both in Rome and Milan, and in the latter city he assisted not only the poor, but sent magnificent presents for the adornment of churches. It is estimated that he could not have spent upon himself any part of the income he received from bene-

fices in Rome.   In his clothing he put aside all pomp,
and gave up wearing robes of silk, putting on a simple
ecclesiastical garb.

After beginning with himself, the saint then directed
his attention to the reform of his household.   Judging
that it did not become a prelate to have a court chiefly
composed of laymen, he dismissed all the knights and
gentlemen who were in his suite with liberal bounties,
each according to his merit; retaining in his service
ecclesiastics only, and the needful domestics, and gave
them rules, forbidding the use of silken garments, and
all things unbecoming their condition, so that they
lived in this way a more ecclesiastical way of life.

For his own part, having given his heart to God,
prayer and contemplation were the greatest delight of
his soul.   In order to give himself with greater facility
to these holy exercises, he was in the habit, at certain
times, of retiring to a· little oratory he had built on a
hill, and adorned with representations of the sacred
Mysteries of the Life of our Lord.   Here he used to
be filled with the sweetness of the divine communications, and received inward illumination as to his conduct and manner of life.

Being more and more drawn to meditation and
prayer, Charles formed the design of giving up altogether the distraction of external affairs.   But fearful
of guiding himself in a matter of such importance he
sought counsel of Dom Bartholomew de Martyribus,[1]
Archbishop of Braga, whom, in the end of the year

---

[1] Born in Lisbon in 1514, raised in 1558 to the See of Braga, which he
resigned in 1582, and died in 1590.

1563, the providence of God led to Rome, after the
close of the labours of the Council. This prelate
was a Portuguese by birth, and received his surname
from the church in which he was baptized. He early
entered the Dominican order, where he was distinguished for learning as well as for merit. He was
united by a close friendship with a congenial spirit,
another very holy man—for eminent sanctity abounded
in the Peninsula in those days—a Spanish Dominican,
Lewis of Grenada,[1] who was confessor to the queen-
regent of Portugal. The latter offered to her director
the vacant archbishopric of Braga. Where mere
natural friendship perceives only matter for congratulation, spiritual friendship, on the other hand, sees nothing but cause for alarm. No sooner had the news
reached Bartholomew, than he wrote to his brother
Dominican, and represented to him the danger in
which his soul would be placed by his exaltation to
this dignity. The humble religious probably needed
not the advice; he declined the proffered see, but he
repaid the kindness of his friend by a service for which,
he might presume, the lowly monk would feel but
scant amount of gratitude. Being requested by the
regent to name some one whom he considered as most
worthy of so high and responsible an office, he
immediately recommended Dom Bartholomew of the
Martyrs as a man eminently qualified by his signal
merits to do good service to the Church. Doubtless

[1] Born in 1504 at Granada, died 1588. Author of the "Sinner's Guide,"
the "Stimulus of Pastors," and many other spiritual works. His works
were preferred by St. Charles to all others of the kind.

Lewis of Grenada thought so highly of his friend as to believe that he might accept with safety to his soul what he himself had modestly shrunk from undertaking.   Dom Bartholomew would readily have dispensed with the compliment; indeed, so terrible to him was the news of his promotion, that the very thought of the heavy burden with which he was threatened, produced a sudden tremor in all his limbs, and was the occasion, subsequently, of a serious illness.   He refused the perilous charge, and Lewis, after vainly employing every argument to overcome his reluctance, availed himself at last of his authority, as provincial of the order, to enforce his acceptance of the office, in virtue of holy obedience.

Bartholomew justified the high opinion entertained of him, both by his conduct as Bishop in his own diocese, and by the zeal and theological learning which he displayed at the Council of Trent, where he was one of those who insisted most strongly on the necessity of enforcing episcopal residence.   He was used to recall an example which had deeply touched him, of a young shepherd whom he once remarked, in the midst of a violent storm, refusing to shelter himself in a neighbouring cavern, lest the wolf should profit by his absence to attack his flock.   " What a lesson," exclaimed Bartholomew, " for the pastors of souls ! "   He was a man, in short, of a like spirit with Charles Borromeo.   Like him, too, feeling the awful responsibility of the episcopate, he desired to be released from the perilous burden, and retire once more to the safe obscurity of his monastery ; indeed, the hope of obtain-

ing the Pope's permission to resign his archbishopric
was one of the motives which led his steps to Rome.
He failed in obtaining the object of his wishes at that
time ; God had a work for him to do—the reform of
his diocese in accordance with the decrees of Trent ;
but if his journey was unattended with the success
he desired, it was not unproductive of one important
result.

The Cardinal and the Archbishop were mutually
known to each other through the share each had taken
in the affairs of the Council, but they had never
personally met until the day when the Pope admitted
Dom Bartholomew to an audience at the Vatican ;
where, after complimenting him on the zeal with which
he had laboured for the restoration of the Church's discipline, and the reform of Cardinals and Bishops, the
Holy Father turned to his nephew, and taking him by
the hand presented him to the prelate, with these
words, " I desire these things as ardently as yourself,
and here is a young man whom I place in your hands,
that you may commence the reformation of Cardinals
in his person."

" If," replied the Archbishop, " the princes of the
Church had all resembled the Cardinal Borromeo, so
far from proposing their reformation to the Council, I
should have proposed themselves as models for the
reform of the other ministers of Jesus Christ." He
added no more, perceiving how painful to the
modesty of Charles was the language of praise ; but
it was no empty compliment on his part; words of
flattery were indeed strangers to his lips. He warmly

esteemed and deeply respected one whom God had
inspired with the same pure zeal for His honour
which burnt so brightly in his own bosom, and not
less profound was the affectionate reverence with
which Charles on his side regarded the champion of
episcopal reform.   They were friends at once from that
truest and deepest of sympathies, the love of God.
Charles sought an early opportunity of a private interview with Dom Bartholomew, for the purpose of discovering to him the whole state of his heart, with the
scruples and difficulties which agitated him, and throwing himself completely upon his guidance in a manner
in which above all things he dreaded to follow his own
will   "We are alone here," he said, "in the presence
of God.   Deny me not my request.   Long have I
besought Him with many prayers and tears to enlighten me as to the course I ought to pursue.   I know
that He vouchsafes a special illumination to such as
have given themselves wholly to Him, and in whom
He abides as in His temples, whence also He returns
an answer to those that inquire of Him.   You see how
I am situated.   You know what life is at court and in
this city of Rome.   I am surrounded by innumerable
perils ; young, without experience, without other virtue
than the love and desire of it, is it not my duty to fly
from temptations which might one day overcome me ?
As nephew of the Sovereign Pontiff, all men magnify
the pretended services which I render to the Church,
but is this what God requires of me ?   What will it
avail me to gain the whole world if I lose my own
soul ?   God has lately given me a new attraction for

penance; He has given me the grace to prefer His fear and my own salvation to all things. I am thinking, therefore, of emancipating myself from all these ties, and retiring into a monastery, to live as if there were only God and myself in the world."

Here we have the clue to that love of retirement and disengagement from secular duties which in the eyes of the worldly is so incomprehensible and so worthy of censure. The saint, though full of the most ardent charity for his neighbour, is no mere philanthropist. His main object is not to make himself useful; his supreme end is God—to know Him, to love Him, to serve Him. Next to this, or rather included in this, is his love for the souls which God has made for Himself; and as first of all, and chiefly, God has committed to him the care of his own soul, that must be the great, the absorbing object of his care. One soul—one eternity; these words are for ever ringing in his ears. The love of his neighbour cannot, therefore, be separated from his love of God, still less set in the balance against it. The benevolence which allows a man to be careless of losing God, or even of one degree of His grace, is not charity, but a mere natural feeling such as works in the bosom of the busy men of this generation, and is compatible with the absence of all personal holiness, and of all respect for the first and greatest of commandments.

The Archbishop was filled with admiration at words so full of humility and of contempt of the world, and when Charles had ceased speaking, he remained silent awhile; he was engaged in beseeching the spirit of

God to dictate his answer. " I cannot," he said at last, " do otherwise than applaud so pious a desire, and I know also by experience the advantages and the security of life in the cloister. But the question is not which is the safest way, but what is that way which the will of God designs you to follow ? and it appears to me, judging by His conduct of you hitherto, and the graces He has been pleased to bestow upon you, that it is not His will that you should seek the retirement of a monastery. In leaving the world and entering religion, I forsook no duty ; but with you it would be otherwise. You cannot desert, without detriment to the Church's interests, the eminent and difficult post to which it has pleased the Sovereign Pontiff to raise you. If, indeed, you loved the world and the world's possessions, if you felt the least attachment or drawing of your heart towards its honours or its pleasures, then would I say at once, Fly. Undoubtedly we must not risk our own souls to save those of others ; but since God has given you the grace to be insensible to the vanities of the world, since it seems His will to make use of you for the reformation of His Church, I content myself with praising God while I praise his gifts in you ; and I entreat you also to give Him thanks and to humble yourself before Him, for having deigned to employ you and to fit you for so great a work. Abandon not the station to which He has called you, but accomplish that which you have so happily begun."

Charles had listened with profound attention ; and full of confidence in the spiritual discernment of the prelate whose advice he had sought, he promised that

he would renounce his design of following the inclinations of his heart, which prompted him to retire from
the world; but one weighty doubt still oppressed him.
He could not forget that he was an Archbishop, bound
by the stringent duty of residence; that he belonged
not to himself, but to the flock committed to his care.
"Many a time," he said, "have I implored the Pope
to grant me this favour, but he has hitherto always
opposed my departure."

Dom Bartholomew was not the man to combat so
just a desire, or to undervalue the duty of a bishop to
reside in his diocese; but he represented to Charles the
danger of precipitation, the advanced age of the Pontiff,
and his need at that critical juncture of devoted assistance and support. The urgent necessities of the Church
at large were to be considered before those of a particular diocese; he advised him, therefore, to adjourn for
a time his praiseworthy intention, and to watch for a
more favourable opportunity, which God, perhaps, might
afford him sooner than he expected. Charles, relieved
of all his doubts, threw himself into the arms of the
Archbishop of Braga; his path was now clear before
him, and most warmly did he thank his venerable
friend for the counsel he had given him, assuring him
that he believed it was a divine and special Providence
which had conducted to Rome so wise and holy a
counsellor, for the purpose of delivering him from the
weight that had oppressed him. Great, however, was
the surprise of our Cardinal at being informed soon
after by the Pope that Dom Bartholomew had sought
a private interview with him to beg permission to

retire from his archbishopric; and never, he said, had
an ambitious man more eagerly urged his suit for promotion than the Archbishop had pressed his petition
for leave to resign his high dignity—a request, however, to which his Holiness had not seen fit to accede.
Truly it seemed as if the worthy prelate was paying off
upon our saint the treatment he had himself received
at the hands of his friend Lewis of Grenada.   Charles
concealed his emotion, and praised the Archbishop's
humility, but he seized an early opportunity to expostulate with him on the apparent inconsistency of
his conduct.

   " What ! " he exclaimed, " you conjure the Pope to
relieve you from the distractions of business, and at the
same time you would precipitate me into the midst of
them ?   You think you cannot conscientiously retain
the charge of a diocese, and you counsel me to assume
the burden of one ; you, advanced in age and possessing
experience and capacity; I, a young man devoid of both!
Where is your esteem for the gospel rule, to love your
neighbour as yourself ?   Where is the tenderness of a
father, the affection of a brother, the sincerity of a
friend ? "

   The Archbishop listened to him with a smile of sweet
complacency, for he knew from how pure a source these
reproaches flowed, and then mildly and earnestly represented to him that God's conduct of one man often
differs widely from that by which he guides another.
He assured him that his friend's soul was as precious
in his eyes as his own, and he reminded him that the
reasons by which he had supported the advice he gave,

were drawn from the peculiarities of Charles's position, and the special manner in which God seemed to have dealt and to be dealing with him. With these and such-like words he silenced the Cardinal's remonstrances, and effectually removed his scruples; henceforward the two friends were inseparable. Short and precious to Charles were those few weeks of Dom Bartholomew's stay at Rome, when, as a humble disciple, he sat at the Archbishop's feet, seeking from his lips instruction in that which lay nearest to his heart, how to govern a diocese, and discharge the duties of a prelate; and when they parted, he received from his friend, at once as a token of regard and a memorial of their religious conferences, a much-valued gift, a treatise written with his own hand, entitled "The Stimulus of Pastors." This book became Charles's guide, when, to his deep regret, the living voice of the teacher could sound in his ears no more.

Thus he sought the company of those only who were lovers of holiness and virtue. With such he would often take counsel, in order to attain as far as possible to the perfection of the ecclesiastical state. Among these holy men were some Spanish priests, and others who had lately come from the Council of Trent.

The time had now arrived when St. Charles deemed it expedient to prepare himself more thoroughly for the office of a pastor. His high standard of the obligations of a pastor of souls, made him place among the chief of these the duty of preaching the Word of God to the flock, as inculcated by the Council of

Trent. Besides the academical discourses of which we
have spoken, he began to exercise himself in public
speaking. He commenced by giving spiritual conferences to some convents of nuns, and in the Church
of Santa Maria Maggiore, of which he was archpriest.
People listened to them with astonishment, as it was
not at that time customary for Cardinals to preach.
Moreover, well aware how necessary to the episcopal
office is the knowledge of doctrine not only to oppose
the false teaching of heretics, and to defend the flock
against them, but also to instruct them in the way of
their eternal salvation, St. Charles applied himself,
with the aid of professors,[1] to the study of theology,
commencing with logic and philosophy. It was wonderful to see him, overwhelmed as he was with so
many responsibilities, sitting like a humble student at
the feet of theologians, patiently learning from them,
and committing their lectures to writing. But what
cannot charity, and the desire of serving God perfectly,
do in a heart all on fire with His love ? St. Charles
afterwards put these academical exercises into a more
spiritual form, which he found useful as a pastor of
souls.

The progress of St. Charles in the holy life he had
laid down for himself was a source of edification to
the court ; and he was looked upon with awe by its
members, who began to shun license and giving bad
example, lest it should come to his knowledge. All
those who were aiming at perfection were, on the

---

[1] One of these was Jerome Vielmi, O.P.. Bishop of Argolis, one of the
theologians of the Council of Trent.

other hand, fortified by his example of sanctity. The Holy Father was especially pleased with his conduct, and his authority was greatly increased thereby. True it is that certain malicious men of the world, instigated by the devil, took exception at his spiritual life, calling him a hypocrite and impostor; but he, strong with the strength of God, opposed an unfailing constancy of soul to all that they had to say against him, so that their persecution did but add to his merits. Stimulated by the example of St. Charles, many members of the Academia took up sacred studies, in order to imitate him in learning, as well as in a holy life.

It pleased God about this time to try the patience of His servant by visiting him with a grievous infirmity, which was accompanied, however, with such heavenly consolations and interior illuminations, that, inflamed with divine love, Charles longed to quit this mortal life, in order that he might be united for ever to his Lord.

Charles had great devotion for the churches of Rome. He not only visited them frequently, but restored and adorned some of them at his own expense. At St. Martin on the Hills, his titular church as Cardinal Deacon, he rebuilt the dome. On the Church of St. Praxedes, his titular as Cardinal Priest, he spent large sums in repairs, as also upon the monastery adjoining. From being scarcely habitable, he made it such as it now is, and placed the sacred relics in a chapel worthy of them. At Santa Maria Maggiore, where he was Archpriest, he repaired the choir and porch, and added to the number of canons.   He spent a large sum in the erection of the Church of St. Martha, attached to a convent of nuns, whose Protector he was.   He induced the Sovereign Pontiff to build a church in the Baths of Diocletian, with a Carthusian monastery, under the title of St. Mary of the Angels. Other Cardinals followed his example, and from that time begun to restore and adorn their titular churches.

The prudence of St. Charles in all his undertakings gained for him esteem and love not only in Rome, but abroad.   The Catholic princes especially cherished a great affection for him.   Philip II. of Spain not only gave him a pension of nine thousand crowns from the Archbishopric of Toledo, but conferred upon him the Principality of Oria on the death of his brother, Count Frederic.

CHAPTER IX.

WHILST occupied in Rome with weighty affairs, St. Charles never for a moment forgot his diocese. He knew well how detrimental to the flock is the absence of its pastor, and he was most solicitous about the welfare not only of the city and diocese, but of that of the whole province, and kept himself diligently informed of all its needs. Often he begged of the Holy Father to allow him to take up his residence in his diocese. But it was in vain. The Pope could not accede to his request, for the presence of St. Charles in Rome was essential not only for the good of the Papal States, but for the welfare of the Church. He, therefore, dispensed St. Charles from the obligation of residence as ordained by the Council of Trent, and the saint in obedience contented himself with watching over his diocese at a distance, whilst he placed himself at the disposal of the Holy Father in Rome, resigning, however, his offices of government in order to be better able to attend to spiritual affairs.

His Vicar-General in Milan kept him diligently informed of all that took place there, and St. Charles from time to time sent him his directions : a large collection of which are extant, and testify to his solicitude for his Church.

Besides a Vicar-General, St. Charles sent Bishop Girolamo Ferragata to Milan, as his Auxiliary, giving him full powers to carry out whatever he might judge expedient for its welfare. This proved a great benefit to both clergy and people, for the industry of Monsignor Ferragata brought to light many things that needed reform. A great number of grown-up persons were confirmed by him, and it was found that the knowledge of the Sacrament of Confirmation had almost died out among the people. These facts led St. Charles to resolve on adopting yet more effectual means of improvement ; and he discussed the matter with some of his usual advisers, in particular with Gabriel Paleotto, Auditor of the Rota, and Agostino Valerio. The first named of those two Prelates had been especially sent to expedite the affairs of the Council of Trent by Pope Pius IV.

The decrees of the Council of Trent having now been published, St. Charles, though absent from his see, resolved that he would begin his projected reforms by holding the diocesan synod, commanded by the Council to be held annually. St. Charles therefore sought anxiously for a Vicar-General who could take his place and carry out his designs. A learned man was proposed to him in the person of Nicolò Ormaneto, parish priest in the diocese of Verona, who in time past had been Vicar-General to Giovanni Matteo Giberto, Bishop of Verona. This Bishop had assisted

Cardinal Reginald Pole when sent as legate *de latere* by Julius III., in 1553, to bless the reconciled kingdom of England, and Nicolò Ormaneto had laboured with him, and had especially devoted himself to raising the tone of theological studies in England. He had also been present at the Council of Trent. Subsequently he fled from worldly honours to the humble privacy of a parish priest, whence he was drawn forth once more to serve God with the permission of Cardinal Navagero, then Bishop of Verona, by St. Charles, who received him in Rome with great cordiality and discussed with him his projects of reform. Directions for carrying out the decrees of the Council of Trent for the erection of a seminary were drawn up. Many days were taken up with these conferences, and much surprise prevailed at Rome that the Cardinal, with so many weighty matters on hand, should devote so much time to a humble and unknown priest.

When St. Charles had sufficiently explained his intentions to Ormaneto, the latter proceeded to Milan invested with full authority as Vicar-General. Before this, St. Charles had some time previously sent thither Father Benedetto Palmio, a Jesuit father and preacher of repute, who was accompanied by others of the Society, in order to give missions to the people. As St. Charles had intended to introduce the Society into Milan, he obtained two Pontifical briefs for them; one to the Duke of Sessa, the governor, and the other to the Senate, in which the Pope exhorted them to provide a convenient house where the Fathers might dwell and exercise their functions. It was then that the Church of St. Vitus, near the Ticino gate, was assigned to them, together with a house taken on lease. Ormaneto reached Milan in July, 1564, and on beginning the work of reform was encouraged by finding much goodwill among the people in the midst of disorders and corruption, both of priests and people.

The Catholic King had given orders to the governors of his provinces to further by all means in their power the due observation of the decrees of the Council, and to this end to give every possible assistance to the Bishops in the exercise of their functions. The governor and senate of Milan were therefore of great assistance to Ormaneto, who wrote to the Cardinal telling him of the hopeful state of affairs, and likewise informing him of the publication of an edict, in which the governor had abstained from interference with ecclesiastics or the authority of their superiors.

On his arrival in Milan, Ormaneto had summoned the priests of the diocese, to the number of two thousand, to a diocesan synod, at which the decrees of Trent were published, and all made their profession of faith before the Vicar-General, who wished to have a personal knowledge thus of each one present. Various other matters were arranged for the execution of the decrees of Trent. On this occasion, Father Benedetto Palmio preached a sermon, followed by a discourse from the Vicar-General on the reform. These two sermons produced much fruit, and indeed this synod was altogether an auspicious beginning of a better state of discipline, for which the heart of St. Charles yearned.

The churches were the next care of the Vicar; he

visited all those of the city, and a great number in other parts of the diocese, eradicating abuses, and setting all things in order. He then turned his attention to the foundation of a seminary for clerics, and as a beginning brought together several young men, whom St. Charles maintained in a hired house, pending the erection of a suitable building. Nicolò Ormaneto also introduced a reform into several convents of nuns, and in all that he did he had all possible assistance from St. Charles, who, notwithstanding his weighty cares, found time to advise him continually by letters.

CHAPTER X.

NOTWITHSTANDING the efforts of Nicolò Ormaneto to carry out both in letter and in spirit the wishes of St. Charles for reform, the difficulties that arose daily in his path made him lose heart, and he wrote to beg the Cardinal to allow him to return to his parish; alleging his incompetency for the great undertaking in Milan, and adding, moreover, that it seemed to him impossible that a Church could be well governed in the absence of its own Bishop. On hearing this, St. Charles yearned more than ever to go to his flock, and again besought the Holy Father to allow him to do so, determining, in case of a refusal, to summon at least a Provincial Council at Milan, with the senior suffragan Bishop as President. Meanwhile, he wrote encouragingly to Ormaneto, desiring him to persevere until some decision was made.

His earnest entreaties prevailed so far with the Holy Father, that he gave him permission to hold the Council in person in Milan, to his great satisfaction. Before his departure, the Pope created him legate *ae latere*

throughout Italy in order to facilitate matters with
regard to his precedence over other Cardinals. The
saint with great care selected theologians to accompany him to the Council, and had long deliberations
with them on the various matters to be brought before
it, the manner of celebrating it, the summoning of the
Bishops, and the framework of the constitutions. He
also gathered round him on this occasion many eminent
canonists and members of religious orders, among whom
were Scipio Lancellotto,[1] John Baptist Castello,[2] and
Michael Tomaso,[3] all three distinguished for their ability
at the Council of Trent. The Cardinal also made choice
of the best theologians among his household, of whose
assistance he availed himself. Among these were three
eminent men of letters; Silvio Antoniano, afterwards
Cardinal, John Baptist Amalteo, and Giulio Poggiano.

St. Charles had already written fully to Monsignor
Ormaneto, entering into every detail of his journey, as
he was anxious to set a good example to Bishops
in every town through which he should pass. His
rooms he desired to be furnished with the utmost simplicity, and that two or three only should be reserved
for his own use; that all pomp should be avoided, and
earthenware used instead of gold or silver vessels; and
that his table should be frugal, with but a few dishes.
He also ordered the Bishops to be lodged in his palace
at his own expense. This was not only from motives
of hospitality as part of the duty of a Bishop, but also

---

[1] Auditor of the Rota, and Cardinal, died 1598.
[2] Afterwards Bishop of Rimini.
[3] Afterwards Bishop of Lerida, in Spain.

for greater convenience in treating with them upon synodal matters.[1]

Having concluded all these preparations, and received the blessing of the Sovereign Pontiff, St. Charles set out on the 1st September, 1565, accompanied by many Prelates and dignitaries. Great was the grief in Rome at his departure for what was feared would prove to be a long season.

St. Charles travelled quickly, longing to find himself once more in Milan; but yet he made time to visit churches and to venerate sacred relics on his way.

[1] On the 18th August, 1565, St. Charles writes to Ormaneto as follows :—"Let the Bishops know that I am coming to give notice of the Council. If any of the authorities of the city interfere because of rumours of plague in Switzerland and in Casale, you have a reason to give, as otherwise the Bishops might be prevented coming from these parts. As I shall be in Milan by the end of September in order that no time may be lost, the Provincial Council being fixed for the 19th October, the diocesan synod might in the meantime be held, for it is a year since the last, and I should be glad to see my clergy face to face. I have determined to invite all the Bishops to stay under my roof, for it is not fitting that they should go elsewhere, and it is my duty to be liberal since God has given me so much. I wish their apartments to be near each other, and that all should take their meals in common, as such familiar intercourse promotes friendship, and is convenient for taking counsel together. Let the ten Bishops be near each other, their apartments properly furnished and nothing wanting, their rooms provided with hangings, chairs, and beds. I shall bring nothing with me, but some silver vessels, linen, and five hundred earthenware plates. My household numbers a hundred. I am very anxious that there should be nothing extravagant, and that all pomp and show should be avoided. I shall receive the Prelates with all charity, but let them not expect anything sumptuous or splendid. Let their table be sufficiently but frugally provided, with nothing of silver excepting a water-jug and basin, the plates and dishes of ordinary ware. Keep for me two or three rooms with common carpets, without appearance of luxury, reserving for guests everything more commodious. I wish each Bishop to learn that hospitality of this kind only is allowable, as ecclesiastics have been especially noted for lavish expense and luxury, and I desire in this way to begin a method of life which I shall follow without fail from henceforth as Bishop."—O.

He remained three days at Bologna in his capacity of legate, to set in order certain matters of government. He also visited his abbey of Nonantola, and at a synod of its canons laid down rules for the reform of certain abuses.

All intent upon the things of God, St. Charles noted more especially in every city the influence of the Bishops, and the good or evil which resulted from their residence or non-residence in their sees; drawing therefrom motives for his own action, and facts to be laid before the Sovereign Pontiff. Throughout the whole of his journey he was received with great honour, both by princes and by private persons, all of whom were drawn to him by the good odour of his virtues.

CHAPTER XI.

ST. CHARLES MAKES HIS ENTRY INTO MILAN, AND CELE-
BRATES THE FIRST PROVINCIAL COUNCIL.

1565.

GREAT was the joy of the Milanese when it became
known that their pastor was coming to them. The
streets were decorated, and triumphal arches, adorned
with mottoes and symbols, attested their veneration
for him. His entry took place on Sunday, the 23rd
of September, 1565, when he was in his twenty-
sixth year. Having put on the pontifical vestments
in the church of St. Eustorgius, he made a progress
through the city, mounted on horseback, under a rich
canopy, accompanied by the clergy, the Duke d'Albuquerque, governor of Milan, the senate, magistrates,
and nobility, and an immense concourse of people.
Every countenance was radiant with joy, shouts of
gladness were heard on all sides, and there were not
wanting those who prophesied the future glory of their
Archbishop, proclaiming that it was sufficient to look
upon his holy face to be assured that in him they beheld a second St. Ambrose, who in like manner would
be raised to the honours of the altar—prophetic words

which have in our day been verified. It was noted as a marvellous fact that evil spirits were, during this procession, compelled to bear witness to the torment that the presence of the saint caused them, for there were some among the crowd who, possessed of the devil, howled and cried aloud in desperation and anger like wild beasts.

Having reached the cathedral, St. Charles prostrated himself in devout prayer before the Blessed Sacrament; and having given his benediction to the assembled multitude, retired to the Archbishop's house. On the following Sunday he sung High Mass in presence of a vast congregation, and addressed them from the text: "With desire I have desired to eat this passover with you."[1] In moving words he spoke of the love he bore them, and how he had longed to minister to their needs, preferring his own diocese to all the grandeur of Rome.

The Milanese nobles and citizens flocked to pay their respects to their Archbishop, who received all with loving-kindness and courtesy. Yet though his time was thus much engrossed, he commenced immediate preparations for the Council, and when the Bishops of the province arrived he assigned to each one his part in drawing up the decrees; as the head and guide of the whole work sparing himself no fatigue night or day, so ardent was his desire to effect the needed reforms throughout the province. The following were the Prelates who assembled at this synod :—Bernardino Scotto, Cardinal of Trani, Bishop of Piacenza, of the

[1] St. Luke xxii. 15.

order of regular clerks; Guido Ferrerio, Cardinal
Bishop of Vercelli, to whom the Cardinal's hat was
given in this Council by St. Charles in the name of
the Pope; Girolamo Vida, Bishop of Alba; Mauritio
Pietra of Vigevano, Cesare Gambara of Tortona,
Scipione da Asti of Casale, Pietro Costachiaro of
Acqui, Domenico Bollano of Brescia, Nicolò Sfrondato
of Cremona,[1] Girolamo Gallarato of Alessandria della
Paglia and Federigo Cornaro of Bergamo.   The first-
named of these, Cardinal Bernardino Scotto, made a
protest against being considered a subject of the diocese of Milan, although he voluntarily assisted at the
Council.   Five were prevented from attending through
various impediments, but were represented by their
procurators, viz., John Antonio Capisucco, Cardinal of
the title of Santa Croce, Bishop of Lodi; John Antonio Serbellone, Cardinal of the title of St. George,
Bishop of Novara; Gasparo Capria, Bishop of Asti;
John Ambrogio Fiesco of Savona, and the procurator
of the chapter of Ventimiglia, which diocese was at that
time vacant.   There were also present Cardinals Bobba
and Castiglione, who came, not as a matter of obligation, but out of a spirit of devotion to assist at this, the
first fruits of the Council of Trent.

The first session was opened with a solemn procession of all the prelates and clergy, accompanied by
the senate, governor and magistrates of the city; all
of whom assisted at the High Mass.   Father Benedetto Palmio preached a discourse on the necessity of

---

[1] Who was afterwards, in the year 1590, raised to the chair of St. Peter
under the name of Gregory XIV.

reform: and Cardinal Borromeo delivered a Latin oration on the need of Provincial Councils. The decrees of the holy Council of Trent were read and formally accepted, and the execution of them in the province committed to the care of the Bishops by St. Charles. A public profession of faith was made by the Bishops, and many decrees and ordinances were published on discipline and reform, having especial reference to Bishops. Great was the prudence, charity and zeal shown by St. Charles on this occasion, for the honour of God and the salvation of souls. He concluded the Council with a fervent exhortation to the Bishops to observe faithfully all that had been enjoined concerning the execution of the decrees. The zeal of the Archbishop was rewarded, for a very signal success attended this beginning of reform; and although there were some who doubted the possibility of so many details receiving due attention, yet St. Charles, who put his trust in God alone, was rejoiced by beholding its full accomplishment to the good of souls and benefit of the province. A large concourse of people, some from far distant places, had assembled to witness the celebration of this synod. General admiration was felt, not so much at the majesty of the proceedings as at the spectacle of a Cardinal, young in years and exalted in dignity, intent only upon the service of God, preaching himself the Word of God from the pulpit, and wholly bent upon reform of his diocese; convoking a Council for the promulgation of decrees which he himself was the first to obey. The fame of his sanctity began to spread on all

sides, and his example stimulated the oldest Bishops
to renewed zeal for souls, and for the welfare of
their sees, determining them to reside each in his
diocese.   The Sovereign Pontiff was filled with satisfaction at the success of his nephew, and when he
heard that St. Charles had preached during the celebration of High Mass, the Pope declared publicly that
it was fitting that he himself, as the Supreme Pastor
of souls, and Cardinals and Prelates having care of
souls, should follow the example of the Archbishop
of Milan.   The Holy Father expressed his approval
of all these good works in the following Brief which
he sent to Milan :—

Brief of Pius IV. to Cardinal Borromeo.

" Your letters have been most welcome to us, more
especially the last bearing date the 18th of this present month.   We rejoice at the success of the synod,
and the acceptation of the decrees of the Council of
Trent ; we are likewise gratified by the readiness of
the people to obey them, and by the goodwill of the
governor and other ministers of the most Serene
Catholic King, shown by their promises to help and
favour their execution.   We see clearly that God
Himself is furthering your pious designs, and exhort
you to persevere in giving good example and in
endeavouring to establish the reign of virtue.   You
will, in due time, be pleased to go to Trent, there to
meet and do honour to the Princesses ; you will also

carry out the other matters in accordance with what you know to be our will. We feel quite assured that in all things you will act with your accustomed prudence. May the Lord preserve you."

Rome, *October* 27, 1565.

CHAPTER XII.

1565.

THE Holy Father had commissioned St. Charles to go
to Trent, there to receive with due honours the sisters
of the Emperor Maximilian—Joanna, wife of Francis
de Medici, Prince of Florence, and Barbara, wife of
Alfonso d'Este, Duke of Ferrara. The Cardinal was
bid by his Holiness to make all possible speed to
Rome, where his presence was greatly needed, both for
the conduct of affairs and for the carrying out of the
decrees of the Council of Trent, regarding which many
appeals were made to the Pope.

Whilst waiting to start for Trent, the saint occupied
himself in the visitations of several churches, chapters,
and convents, in execution of the decrees of the Council.

Leaving Milan amidst general lamentation, St. Charles
set out for Trent, accompanied by the Cardinal of Vercelli and other prelates. On the way he made some
stay at Verona, and was received with great joy by
the newly consecrated Bishop, Agostino Valerio, whom
St. Charles much esteemed. Burning always with an

ever-increasing zeal for souls, the saint humbly sought information concerning the traditions of the Church of Verona, and the mode of government of the late Bishop Giberto, interrogating on these points some of the prelates of the Bishop's household. On his arrival at Trent he received the Princesses, and conducted them with the utmost courtesy, the one to Ferrara, and the other to Fiorenzuola in Tuscany. Here he was startled by the arrival of a courier with news of the serious illness of the Sovereign Pontiff, and taking post-horses he hastened to Rome. On questioning the doctors, and learning that there was no hope of recovery, he went to the bedside of the Pope, and told him with calmness that his hour was come to leave this world. Placing a crucifix before him, he said, " Most Holy Father, turn now all your thoughts to your heavenly home, place all your hope in our crucified Lord, who is our resurrection and our life. He is our Advocate, and the Sacrifice offered for our sins. He turns away none who, with true sorrow for the sins they have committed against Him, confess Him to be true God and true Man, and place all their confidence in Him. He is gracious and merciful, and takes compassion on true penitence and sorrow for sin. I therefore beg Him, since He has never refused to listen to your prayers, to grant you this grace according to His holy will."

The dying Pontiff united his prayers with those of his nephew, and thought of nothing, for the short space of time that remained to him, but the salvation of his soul and preparation for death. He was greatly comforted and helped by the prayers of the saint, who excluded all temporal matters from the bedside of his uncle, and with wonderful strength of soul administered the Sacraments of Extreme Unction and the Holy Viaticum with his own hand ; never leaving him night or day, until he breathed his last in the most edifying sentiments, on the 10th December, 1565, aged sixty-six years, eight months, and six days. He had reigned as Pope six years, less sixteen days. His last words were those of holy Simeon : " Nunc dimittis servum tuum, Domine,"—" Lord, now lettest thou thy servant depart in peace."

CHAPTER XIII.

THE CONCLAVE AND ELECTION OF THE NEW PONTIFF, PIUS V.; ST. CHARLES RETURNS TO MILAN.

1566.

THE Cardinal bore with fortitude the death of his uncle, seeing only in this, as in every other trial, the manifestation of the holy Will of God, to which he ever tried to conform himself. The election of the new Pontiff depended in great measure upon him, most of the Cardinals having been created by his uncle, and therefore well disposed to follow his suggestions. But with a soul far above all mere human considerations, St. Charles resolved to do all in his power to secure the election of a Pope who would be zealous for reform, and for the observation of the decrees of Trent.

This resolution of Cardinal Borromeo was vigorously combated by his friends and relations, who urged upon him the great advantage he might reap for himself by pursuing an opposite course, and that it would only be prudent in him to consider how he might further the interests of the Princes, who deserved his good offices. But St. Charles was deaf to all such reasoning, and answered that he was bound to do otherwise by the

holy canons, to which he was firmly resolved to adhere.
On entering the Conclave, being asked by Cardinal
Grassi as to whom they ought to elect Pope, he said,
" We shall choose him who will be chosen by God."

Whilst keeping his own counsel, from motives of
prudence, he carefully considered the various qualifications of the candidates for the Pontificate, and was
much inclined towards Cardinal Michael Ghislieri, of
Alessandria, of the order of St. Dominic, whom he
knew from personal experience to possess many of the
desired qualities, having frequently consulted him in
important matters.   But, on the other hand, there
were reasons against his election.   He had been
created Cardinal by Paul IV., and was, on that
account, an adherent of the House of Caraffa.   He had
also been looked upon with disfavour by his uncle,
Pius IV., and it was to be expected that he would be
naturally ill-disposed towards the friends of the last
Pope.   But these human considerations were of no
weight with St. Charles ; he had long ago trodden
under foot all private and personal interests, and
sought only the glory of God and the good of the
Church.   He gave his vote unreservedly in favour of
the Cardinal of Alessandria, who was elected Pope
by the Sacred College, and was crowned on the 7th
January, 1566, taking the name of Pius V., at the request of Cardinal Borromeo, in memory of his uncle.

This election was said by the world—always ignorant of the things of God—to have been the sole
and arbitrary choice of St. Charles, who had, it was
alleged, withdrawn himself from the ordinary mode of

procedure during the Conclave. But it was afterwards
recognised that he was guided throughout by the Holy
Spirit, for Pius V. proved a saintly and able Pontiff.
He carried out zealously the decrees of Trent, and was
a great reformer of ecclesiastical discipline. He greatly
esteemed and loved Cardinal Borromeo, who, on his
part, held Pius V. in great veneration. The wisdom
of St. Charles in this election was subsequently confirmed by public opinion, for at his death Pius V. was
by common consent reputed a saint.

The following letter to the Cardinal of Portugal
bears witness to the purity of intention exercised by
the saint in his choice of the Sovereign Pontiff, and
is a striking testimony in favour of the sanctity of
Pius V. :—

" To the Cardinal of Portugal.

" Although my grief at the death of my uncle the
Sovereign Pontiff was great and proportioned to the
paternal love he ever showed me and the veneration
I bore him in return, yet no sorrow, however bitter,
could ever distract me for a moment from my desire
to do everything for the benefit of the Holy See. To
my own private grief was added a twofold anxiety,
because whilst I recognised the obligation resting upon
me to act in union with the other Cardinals, I yet saw
that there were some matters connected with the
vacant see that were the special concern of my office.
The times were fraught with evils for the Church.
There were dangers to be guarded against on every
side, from the attacks of heretics as well as from the

avowed enemies of Christianity itself.   It seemed to
me that I ought to do all in my power to procure the
election of a Pontiff who would worthily replace him
who with so much prudence had known how to uphold the authority and dignity of the Apostolic See in
the hour of peril   According to established usage we
entered into Conclave for the election of a Pontiff, and
to this end I can affirm that all my thoughts, desires,
and faculties were exclusively directed.   Doubtless, it
is somewhat difficult for your Eminence and for the
other prelates to form your judgment on my course of
action.   In proceeding to the election of a Pope, it is
clear that I was bound to observe great care and diligence, and to exclude every consideration except
the service of religion and of the Faith.   This I did;
for all my efforts and wishes were directed solely
towards the good of the universal Church, and to the
exclusion of any kind of personal or private interest.

"Having known the Cardinal of Alessandria for a
considerable time, and conceived a high esteem for him
on account of his singular holiness and zeal, I judged
that no more fitting Pontiff than he could be found
to rule the Christian commonwealth wisely and
well.   I therefore took up his cause with all my
might; and with little delay he was elected Pope
to the great satisfaction of all   Nothing could
be so great a consolation to me in my grief for my
uncle, as the certainty that he is succeeded by one
who possesses all the qualities that your Eminence
sympathises with me in lamenting, and who with equal
courage and strength of soul will know how to main-

tain and uphold the authority of religion. Let us meanwhile mutually rejoice that we have in him a wise and prudent Pontiff whose holiness is so great that it seems incapable, indeed, of increase, though, doubtless, it will have fresh manifestations through the wise counsels of your Eminence.

" What you have written to me with so much prudence has been of the greatest consolation to me in my present trials ; for dear indeed to me is the true and solid affection you bear me, and the wisdom of your counsels, which I shall endeavour earnestly to carry out, feeling assured that in so doing I shall obtain light and consolation. Meanwhile, I pray our Lord to grant your Eminence health and prosperity."

ROME, *February 26,* 1566.

When the new Pontiff was fairly established in his see, Cardinal Borromeo put before him several important matters, which he thought demanded immediate consideration. Among these were the decrees of Trent, the new edition of the Ròman Breviary and Missal, and the publication of the Roman Catechism. These were considered by St. Charles most necessary . measures for the welfare of religion. He besought the Pope to confirm likewise with his Pontifical authority the decrees of his Provincial Council, so that he might, by virtue of the Papal confirmation, be able to cope with the difficulties that arose concerning their observance. These requests were most pleasing to the Holy Father, who at once acceded to them, confirming all the decrees in general by a bull, bearing date June

6th, 1566. He likewise confirmed some particular ordinances concerning regulars by three other bulls, dated respectively the 12th and 19th of April, and the 24th May, 1566. He added another of the 27th June of the same year, in which he bound all to the observance of the aforesaid decrees.

Having concluded his negotiations, St. Charles now craved permission to depart at once for his own see. But the new Pope stood in too much need of the counsels of the saint in the beginning of his Pontifical cares to part with him so soon, and showed great reluctance to accede to this request. The heart of St. Charles yearned, however, after the Church, which he looked upon as his spouse ; the grandeur of Rome, and the honour lavished on him by the Papal court and its princes was as nothing to him ; and though he might fairly have alleged that obedience to the Vicar of Christ dispensed him from residence, he only reiterated his request, urging that he considered it his duty to reside where the care of souls was committed to him. He added, moreover, that he had given a bad example to other Bishops, who might, on that account, absent themselves from their sees ; and that to secure the observation of the decrees of Trent in his province, it behoved him to be the first to obey the rule enjoining residence, so that his suffragan Bishops might follow his example. He at length obtained leave to depart from his Holiness, who exacted a promise that he would return the following autumn, from which engagement the saint was subsequently released.

The Sovereign Pontiff granted him many Faculties

for the government of his diocese, to which he added several Pontifical letters addressed to the princes of the province to secure their good-will and assistance in the work of reform. Before leaving Rome St. Charles made a change in his household, dismissing the greater number of his officials with liberal rewards for their services, and retaining only such as were likely to be of service to him in his diocese.

Having received the Apostolic benediction, he reached Milan again on the 5th of April, 1566.

Book II.

1566–1572.

CHAPTER I.

OF THE STATE OF THE CITY AND DIOCESE OF MILAN.

BEFORE relating the labours of this great pastor for the reformation of the Church of Milan, it will be well to describe its extent and miserable condition. Just as the skill of the physician is shown by the cure of desperate maladies, so the worth of a Bishop, the spiritual physician, is seen in healing the sickness of souls committed to his care.

The city of Milan was one of the largest in Italy. On the north, towards Germany, the diocese extended more than a hundred miles in length, and it included not only the State of Milan, but part of Venice, of the Duchy of Monteferrato, and of Switzerland. Lofty mountains surrounded a great part of it. Two thousand two hundred and twenty churches were under the jurisdiction of the Archbishop. Among these were fifty collegiate and eight hundred parish churches. The clergy numbered more than three thousand. The convents of women were seventy in number, without counting about twenty which were suppressed by St.

Charles. There were a hundred communities of men. The total number of souls contained in the diocese was computed to be at least six hundred thousand. The province comprised fifteen bishoprics, embracing not only the State of Milan, but the whole of Monteferrato, part of Venice and Piedmont, and the Genoese Republic, and extended along the shores of the Mediterranean to the borders of Provence. For more than eighty years Milan had been without a resident Archbishop, and left to the government of a single Vicar, but too often a man of lax discipline, who gave but a small portion of his time to the administration of the diocese. All this neglect, added to revolutions, wars, and other calamities of the times, had reduced the vineyard of the Lord to a deplorable condition. Not only was it barren of fruit, but the rank weeds of sin flourished in profusion for the chastisement of the wickedness of men. Ecclesiastical jurisdiction was almost entirely neglected, and in certain points was never exercised. It was altogether unknown in the valleys of Switzerland, clerics being liable to be cited before the lay tribunal. The lives and manners of the clergy were as scandalous as can be conceived, and gave the worst example, for their way of living was altogether worldly, and more sensual by far than that of laymen. They wore the secular dress, carried arms publicly, and lived for the most part in open and habitual concubinage, absenting themselves from their benefices, and neglecting all things appertaining to the service of God. The churches and sacred things were in consequence in a neglected and disgraceful state.

So great was the ignorance of many who had cure of souls, that they did not know even the sacramental form of confession, nor that there were such things as reserved cases and censures. In some parts of the diocese ignorance had reached such a pitch that priests having cure of souls never went to confession, believing that they were not bound to do so, because they confessed others. Many other lamentable abuses were seen in the lives of the clergy, whose office was thus rendered contemptible, and little short of hateful, in the eyes of the laity, so that it had become a common saying, " If you want to go to hell, become a priest."

Even the regulars were not exempt from these disorders. From the bad lives of both the secular and regular clergy, there sprang up among the people countless errors, corruptions, and heresies. Numbers having entirely lost all knowledge of God, abandoned, as a natural consequence, the observance of His holy law. The sacraments, especially Confession and Communion, were very lightly esteemed. Many persons neglected them for ten and fifteen years, or even longer. There were to be found men of ripe age who had never made a confession, and who did not even know the meaning of it; whilst those persons who desired to keep up an appearance of Christianity, approached the sacraments once a year from custom rather than true devotion. A very small number were indeed yet to be found, both among clergy and people, who were assiduous in attending the sacred mysteries, whose Christian lives shone out in contrast to those of the majority around them. So much ignorance of the things of God prevailed, especially among the poor, that they had no knowledge of the foundations and principles of the Catholic faith, and were unable to say the Lord's Prayer or the Hail Mary. They did not know the Articles of the Faith or the Precepts of the Church, and could scarcely make the sign of the cross. Holy days were profaned by plays, dances, games, banquetings, and other disorders, as also by servile works, and public fairs and markets. It was as if Festivals had been ordained for the express purpose of multiplying occasions of offending God. Holy places were treated with the utmost irreverence. The business of the markets was carried on in the churches even during the time of the Divine Offices. Men laughed and talked loudly in the assembly of the faithful, walking up and down, as though it were a public lounge. Worse still, in some parts of the diocese banquets and balls were held in the churches; while, at other times, they were used without any scruple for threshing grain, and other profane purposes. Religion was brought so low that men, in a state of semi-intoxication, would actually mock priests by feigning a wish to go to confession. They would even show themselves in the church with masks on, and, under pretence of making their offering, would seize upon the offerings of others. The majority altogether disregarded the observance of fasting days, especially during Lent, when not only milk food, but even flesh meat, was eaten openly and without scruple; and the bacchanalian orgies of the carnival were prolonged for several days of that holy season, during which public feasts, dances, and dis-

orders without number were carried on.   The public
scandals of adultery and of habitual concubinage were
of continual occurrence, together with thousands of
other vices and corruptions too numerous to mention.
In like manner there was a neglect of discipline and
strict observance in convents, the nuns allowing themselves the greatest liberty, coming in and going out
at their pleasure, and admitting seculars freely, there
being no observance of enclosure.   It were needless
and distressing to dwell at any length upon the public
entertainments, profane dances, and such like disorders
of these convents, together with grievous and deplorable scandals which resulted therefrom.

Such was the miserable condition of the Church of
Milan before God blessed it with the presence of St.
Charles.   Often would the saint weep bitterly when
on his visits to his diocese he witnessed with his own
eyes these miseries.   It was not, however, to be wondered at that weeds had overrun the vineyard, which
had been so long deprived of a careful husbandman.
Prelates and pastors may take warning from the sufferings entailed on their flocks by non-residence.   Strict,
indeed, will be the account they will have to render to
God of all the souls whom their neglect has buried
in hell.

CHAPTER II.

THESE disorders might well have been deemed incurable, since neither clergy nor laity seemed ready to submit to necessary remedies. It looked indeed as if no human power, however strong, could be equal to the work of reformation. But St. Charles never lost heart. The zealous pastor knew that he would be enabled to accomplish that which the Spirit of God had inspired him to attempt. Putting his whole confidence in the Divine assistance, he trusted that all his toils and labours would be abundantly blessed by His grace. He was greatly supported in this hope by the first fruits of the reform effected by Monsignor Ormaneto.

He began to work earnestly to free his vineyard from the weeds with which it was so thickly overgrown. The first remedy he resolved to apply was that of constant residence, for he was convinced that the work mainly depended on his personal presence. So firm was his determination on this point, that he was ready to resign his dignity of Cardinal if it had been any obstacle to his remaining in his diocese; and souls were more precious in his sight than rank and worldly greatness. To this resolution he added

another equally decided, which was, to be ready in case
of need to give his life, like the good Shepherd, for
his flock; to allow no rest to his body, and to grudge
no labour or fatigue in caring for the salvation of
souls. Earnest prayer was the means whereby he
sought assistance from God in his undertakings. It
was his habit to take counsel with Him in all his
affairs, and never to begin anything without this preparation. When the affair was unusually weighty, he
asked for the public prayers of the people, the clergy,
and religious houses. This was the source of the
great success of his work. The life of our Lord Jesus
Christ was the great model which he set before himself in order that by conforming his own life thereto,
he might perform his actions in the most perfect
manner. This divine Life is indeed the exemplar which
Bishops have to make the rule and pattern of all their
actions in the direction of the souls committed to their
care. Calling to mind the words with which St. Luke
begins the Acts of the Apostles : " Jesus began to do,
and to teach," St. Charles resolved, in the first place,
to attend to his own soul, by walking in the way of
perfection and holy living, as an obligation to which
he was bound by his episcopal character. In the next
place, he strove with all his might to do good to his
neighbour, remembering that it was the rule of the
Apostle St. Paul who said, in his Epistle to the Corin-
thians, " I chastise my body and bring it into subjection, lest perhaps, when I have preached to others, I
myself should become a castaway." [1]   In like manner

---

[1] 1 Cor. ix. 27.

he put before himself the example of the saints, especially such as were Bishops, his predecessors in the diocese of Milan, and strove to imitate their great deeds. Above all, he fixed his eyes on St. Ambrose, whom he had taken for his patron, and for this reason chose to be consecrated Bishop on the anniversary of the ordination of that saint.[1] It was observed that he not only paid that saint great honour, but that as far as possible he imitated him in everything as far as he could, so that the Cardinal of Verona calls him the faithful imitator of St. Ambrose;[2] and Cardinal Nicholas Sfrondato, Bishop of Cremona, who was afterwards Pope Gregory XIV., was in the habit of calling him the second Ambrose, a name also given to him by Cardinal Baronius in his Annals. St. Charles used to keep a picture of St. Ambrose before him, in order to stimulate his zeal in imitating this saint, and also had a great veneration for the portrait of Cardinal Fisher, Bishop of Rochester, martyred by Henry VIII., King of England. He took pains also to collect the lives and writings of other Bishops who had been illustrious in the Church of God, as in the instance of Matteo Giberto, Bishop of Verona.[3] Thus, great as had been the virtues which adorned him up to this time, they now shone forth with brighter lustre. He tried to practise perfectly the rule given by St. Paul to his disciple, the Bishop Titus: "In all things show thyself an example of good works."[4]

[1] December 7, 1563.
[2] *Vid.* "Life of St. Charles," by Cardinal Agostino Valerio, Bishop of Verona.
[3] *Vid.* Book I. p. 52.　　　　　　　　　　[4] Tit. ii. 7.

In this way St. Charles made progress in reforming
his diocese; for not only did the holiness of his life
make him pleasing to God, and worthy of His divine
aid, but likewise gave efficacy to his exhortations and
decrees. Certain regulations had been laid down at
his Provincial Council on the manner of life of Bishops,
and these he determined to carry out to the fullest
extent in his own person. In order to be more free
and disengaged from business, and to give himself
wholly to the care of souls, he resigned twelve benefices and pensions, placing some absolutely in the
hands of the Sovereign Pontiff, and applying others,
by leave of the Apostolic See, to the support of colleges
and pious works. Besides these ecclesiastical dignities,
there were other emoluments which he resigned,—as
the Principality of Oria, in the kingdom of Naples,
which brought him a yearly revenue of ten thousand
ducats. Three armed galleys, forming part of his
brother's inheritance, he sold, applying the proceeds to
pious uses. Lastly, that he might get rid of all super-
fluity, he parted with the valuable furniture which he
had brought from Rome. Part of this he presented to
his Metropolitan Church, and part he sold in Milan
and Venice for the benefit of the poor. Thus he only
reserved for himself the Archbishopric, with a charge
upon that of Toledo, in Spain, and an annual pension
upon his patrimony, of which he had made his uncles,
the Counts Borromeo, the administrators. He bestowed
the Marquisate of Romagnano on his relation, Frederic
Ferrerio, in order to be free from every worldly hindrance, and to give himself up wholly to the service

of God. Out of a revenue of about a hundred thousand crowns, he left himself twenty thousand, and would most gladly have resigned that sum also out of his love for holy poverty, had it not been necessary for the maintenance of his household, the exercise of hospitality and almsgiving, according to the office of a Bishop. He reduced his household furniture to very modest proportions, and, as time went on, deprived himself of it entirely. In consequence of this self-denial, his fame spread far and near, and was of no small help to him in the administration of his diocese.

P. 83.—*Giberto, Bishop of Verona.*

Giovanni Matteo Giberto was born in 1495 at Palermo. He was made Bishop of Verona in 1524 by Clement VII. In 1537 he accompanied Cardinal Pole on his unsuccessful mission to Henry VIII. of England. He died in 1543. His *Constitutiones Gibertinæ*, published in 1733 by Ballerini, are admirable, and anticipate the decrees of the Council of Trent.

CHAPTER III.

ONE of the marks of a good Bishop is to have a well-ordered and exemplary household, because as intimately associated with himself, it is open to the scrutiny of all. For this reason, St. Charles, not satisfied with making the reforms before mentioned, determined to go more into detail, so that gradually he brought his household into perfect order. He admitted no one who was not a suitable subject for the ecclesiastical state, those only excepted who were occupied in menial duties. Speaking on this matter, he was wont to say that a prelate ought not to have laymen as his assistants, and that Bishops and Cardinals ought to observe the good rule which has always been kept up in the Papal household, where all the officials are ecclesiastics, or at least all wear the ecclesiastical habit. He did not consider his own personal benefit in receiving subjects, but endeavoured to secure those only who would be able to be of service to the Church. All the members of his household, therefore, with the exception of the domestics, who were laymen, were either priests, or preparing for the priesthood, and

many were doctors in theology and law. They
amounted including his Vicars-General and the judges
of his ecclesiastical court with their assistants to about
a hundred in number. He was exceedingly particular
in choosing these members of his household; for great
numbers eagerly sought admission, some from personal
devotion to him, on account of his reputation for
sanctity, some to learn his methods and mode of
government; but he would only receive candidates of
good repute, who were above motives of self-interest
and had good credentials. He made it a rule not to
bestow preferments on his officials; if he found any
who were sordidly disposed, he dismissed them at
once. A secretary on one occasion having accepted
a benefice of small value from the Vicar-General
without the leave of St. Charles, was at once directed
to resign it. But as he stubbornly refused to do so,
St. Charles dismissed him, preferring to lose his services than to suffer a bad example to be set to his
household. But as this had been his only fault, he
continued to show him favour as one whom he
esteemed, and recommended him as secretary to a
Cardinal. To guard his household from temptation
St. Charles gave them liberal salaries, and often made
them suitable presents. Whenever he received anyone, however well recommended, he never failed to
test his qualifications: and this notwithstanding any
favourable impression he himself might have received
from the gift God had bestowed upon him of reading
character in the countenance. As, for example, if he
considered the new subject fitted for teaching, he

would set him to make a summary of the decrees of
the Council of Trent, classing them under different
heads.   If he stood in need of spiritual training, he
would make him study good authors, as Granada and
the like; he would also try him in acts of virtue,
particularly in humility, which he desired to see
practised by all.   For this reason he never considered
the noble birth or good education of any candidate,
but insisted on his discharging humble offices, such
as writing out instructions, acting as train-bearer,
carrying baggage on a journey, or bearing his archiepiscopal cross which he considered as a most honourable office.   Occasionally he would keep a person near
him for some time without assigning him any particular duty in order to try his patience.   Sometimes,
before receiving candidates into his household, he sent
them into retreat for several days in his seminaries,
putting them under obedience to make special trial
of themselves, and to follow the spiritual exercises,
so as to lay a solid foundation for the ecclesiastical
life.   Thus, as gold in the furnace, he put all to the
proof; and if in the process any were found wanting
in humility, patience, or other virtue, he declined his
services courteously, being resolved to admit no one
into his house who was led merely by ambition, or
likely to give bad example.

Those members of his household who had taken
good degrees were employed by him in the administration of the diocese; and no matter what their offices
might be, all had some part assigned to them in the
business of visitations, inspections, and the like.   In

due time he preferred them, according to their deserts and good conduct, and advanced them gradually in this way to the higher posts and benefices involving residence, provided they did not ask for them. His watchfulness over them was so great that he knew the daily occupations of all, and did not give them leisure for a moment's idleness.

St. Charles drew up excellent rules for the management of his household both in temporal and spiritual matters; which are to be found at length in the "Acts of the Church of Milan." Briefly they are as follows:—He appointed a superior over all the members of the household to whom he gave the title of "*Preposito*," or "Provost," a name sanctioned in Holy Scripture,[1] in preference to that of *Maggiordomo*, or master of the household, which is in use in the houses of seculars; he directed that he should be a priest, and placed under him a *Vicar*, whose duty it was to look after the daily routine of the house; an "*Economo*," or Procurator, and stewards, who had the charge of lands and revenues. He had twelve chamberlains, all priests and doctors, two of whom men of judgment and experience, he kept always with him as witnesses of all his actions, which he considered a very great advantage for a Bishop. In addition, he had two private Monitors, whom he allowed, or rather ordered, to reprove him with all plainness for whatever faults they might see in him, in order that he might correct them. This he afterwards recommended in his sixth Provincial Council, as a

[1] Judges xx. 28, præpositus domus, *et passim.*

rule for all Bishops of his Province, having found it
to be a very efficacious means for making progress
in virtue and holiness of life. Another priest he
appointed Spiritual Prefect, whose office it was to
manage all the spiritual affairs of the household, and
to provide for all its requirements in this respect.
Another again was entrusted with all matters relating
to hospitality, whose title was Prefect of the Guest
Rooms, and it was his business to receive, and show
attention to the prelates and other strangers who were
constantly staying in the house. There were two
Almoners, a public and a private one, of proved charity
and compassion for the poor of Jesus Christ; and an
Infirmarian to whom was committed the charge of
the sick. In like manner the lower offices of the
house were filled only by those of exemplary life.

In spiritual matters the priests of his household
were bound to go to Confession at least once a week,
and to say Mass every day. All others were bound
to go to Confession at least once a month, to hear
Mass every day, and to give the spiritual Prefect a
written certificate of having fulfilled these duties from
their confessor. Those bound to recite the Divine
Office, who were not precluded by residence or occupation elsewhere, met every morning in the Cardinal's
antechamber at the second stroke of the cathedral bell,
and there, together with him, if he was not prevented,
they said Matins and Prime, preceded by at least a
quarter of an hour's mental prayer as preparation for
this duty of praise: the rest of the office being said
at appointed hours. The others, not thus bound,

assembled at the same time, in the archiepiscopal chapel and after mental prayer, recited the office of the Blessed Virgin as far as Vespers; which was said afterwards together with Compline, at a suitable time. After supper all met in the Chapel for Examination of Conscience, after which the points for the next morning's meditation were given out, either by the Spiritual Prefect, or by some one deputed for the office: then after being sprinkled with holy water, each one retired to his room in silence as in a religious house; it being strictly forbidden to stay out or even to go out at night without express permission either from the Cardinal or the Provost. In the winter, when it is usual to gather round the fire after supper, was the time fixed for the Spiritual Conference, so as to avoid idleness by profitable conversation. At these conferences, every one told with simplicity and modesty the subject of his meditation, and what fruit he had gathered from it. St. Charles was generally present at these conferences, in order to make them more useful by discoursing upon them.

Instructions in Christian doctrine were given by appointed persons to the inferior servants, who met in the Chapel at stated hours to hear them. All the clerics were bound to be present at the Divine Offices in the Cathedral on Festivals, wearing cottas; but the Vicars-General, and other officers of the tribunal who also attended, wore only their usual habit. They were also bound to assist at sermons and at processions, whether in the church or in the city. Their dress was exceedingly plain, silk and other costly stuffs being prohibited. The ecclesiastics wore cassocks, according to their rank as directed in the decrees of the Councils. Those who were laymen dressed entirely in black, without lace or any useless ornament, and were not allowed to carry or keep by them any kind of arms or musical instruments: neither were they permitted to converse in their own rooms with any one, whether members of the household or strangers, nor to amuse themselves by singing together; music being allowed only on Feast Days in the Chapel during the time of prayer; even this custom was afterwards abolished by the express order of the Cardinal. He had the Lives of the Saints and other spiritual books kept on the tables in his antechambers, and in the sacristy of the Cathedral, for the use both of his household and of any persons who might be waiting, so as to give them the opportunity of spending their time profitably, and of avoiding idle conversations. He afterwards issued a decree in the Fourth Provincial Council, recommending this practice to his suffragan Bishops. All, including his Vicars-General, had their repasts in common in a refectory built by him for the purpose. During the meal, spiritual books were read aloud, unless one of the priests of the seminary preached a sermon, when silence and attention were required from all. The Cardinal himself, in the earlier years of his episcopate, took his repasts in common with the others in this refectory, until he imposed on himself the rule of fasting on bread and water. The dishes were distributed in equal portions, each receiving his own share, which,

while strictly within the bounds of ecclesiastical
moderation, was amply sufficient. After dinner and
supper, they all went to the chapel to return thanks
to God, and to recite the Litanies. Wednesdays were
days of abstinence, and Fridays were fasting days.
Not only were the vigils of Days of Obligation observed
as fasting days, but also the vigils of Days of Devotion, and of the feasts of the canonised Archbishops
of Milan. These amounted to thirty-six, including
St. Bernard, who was elected but declined the dignity.
The Lenten fast began on Quinquagesima Sunday.
During Advent which, according to the Ambrosian
rite, begins on the first Sunday after the Feast of St.
Martin, they abstained from flesh-meat and from milk-
food, thus imitating their master at a distance: for he,
at these seasons, chastised his body by fasting on bread
and water. They also imitated him in the matter of
the discipline, which they took together on Fridays, in
honour of the Sacred Passion of our Lord Jesus Christ.
Such indeed was the abstinence practised in this holy
house, that flesh-meat was eaten in it during not more
than three months of the year. He was very careful
to provide for all needs of his household, and every
member had his room furnished according to his rank
and position. The sick were liberally provided with
physicians, surgeons, medicine and good nursing, free
of charge. His care for them was so great that he
used to visit them himself when they were laid up:
not only did he console them by pious exhortations,
but he saw for himself that all their bodily and
spiritual needs were supplied. Whenever any one had

to travel, the Cardinal provided him with a horse, and
with money to procure all things necessary for his
journey, even when it was undertaken for private
business.

By these means he brought his household to such a
state of regularity and order that it was not inferior
to any religious house of strict observance.   A Bishop
and celebrated preacher, having seen the devotion,
modesty, and exact observance practised in it, said that
he wished all the world could see the court of the
Cardinal of St. Praxedes, as it might truly be said to
surpass the monasteries of Regulars in good discipline
and obedience.[1]   All his household were loved by him
and treated as his sons and brothers : and he strove
earnestly to inspire them with the same mutual love
for each other.   With this object in view he was in
the habit of visiting them personally at stated times,
conversing with the least among them, in order to
find out whether there existed any difference or bitter
feeling, so as to remove it with as little delay as
possible.   These visits enabled him also to learn
whether his rules were observed by all, and whether
all wants were supplied.   He would likewise inspect
all the rooms to see that his orders were fully carried out.
These visits were a great check to any disorders that
might arise, especially as he used to make the round
of the rooms at unexpected seasons, giving no one

---

[1] When Cæsar Gonzaga, his brother-in-law, was stopping in his house
in June 1571, the Cardinal being away from home gave the following
directions to his steward, " Do not disturb the usual order of the house
on his account, and let him be told to be at home by the Ave, as the
doors must then be shut."

time to hide anything unbecoming that might be there. Once a month the Cardinal presided at a meeting to ascertain and provide whatever might be needed for the spiritual and temporal management of the house. At this meeting were present the various heads of the different departments, and those who held any authority. He insisted on his household being well cared for in all respects, and gave strict orders to that effect to the provost or superior. He took care that all should be fully occupied each in his own department, so that not only was idleness, the root of all evil, banished, but every one had their hands full. Hard and severe as their condition appeared, seeing that they had scarcely breathing time for their many duties, yet they were full of joy and cheerfulness in the midst of their labours, as they had continually before their eyes the example of their master, who toiled day and night indefatigably in the service of God.

The Church gained great advantage from this well-managed household. His palace was in after times publicly proclaimed to have been a training-school for Bishops and Prelates. Many of these were employed by the Holy See as nuncios to the Courts of Europe, and in other important offices. More than twenty were selected to fill illustrious sees on account of the bright example they had shown while members of the Cardinal's household. Among these were: Silvio Cardinal Antoniano, secretary of the Consistory and Chamberlain to Clement VIII.; Nicolò Ormaneto, Bishop of Padua, nuncio at the Court of Spain; John Baptist Castello, Bishop of Rimini, nuncio in France;

Jerome Federici, Bishop of Lodi, governor of Rome and nuncio in Savoy; John Francis Bonomo, Bishop of Vercelli, nuncio at the Court of the Emperor in Switzerland and in Flanders; Cæsar Speciano, Bishop of Cremona and nuncio both in Spain and to the Emperor Rudolph II.; Owen Lewis, Bishop of Cassano and nuncio in Switzerland;[1] Bernardine Morra, Bishop of Aversa, secretary of the Congregation of Bishops and President of that of Apostolical Reforms; Nicholas Mascardo, Bishop of Brugnetto; John Fontana, Bishop of Ferrara; Charles Bascapè, Bishop of Novara, and Antonio Seneca, Bishop of Anagni, secretary of the Congregation of Indulgences and one of the Examiners of Bishops-elect at Rome.

P. 89.—"*Private Monitors.*"

Girolamo Castano and Lodovico Moneta were at one time appointed to this office. Castano related that he was once severely taken to task by the Cardinal because he had left only Lodovico Moneta with him on the occasion of an audience given by the saint to his cousin's wife.

---

[1] Dr. Owen Lewis was a man of great learning, ability, and experience in ecclesiastical affairs. Born in 1534, he became a fellow of New College, Oxford, and Regius Professor of Canon Law at Oxford and Douay, 1568. An intimate friend of Cardinal Allen, he was of great assistance to him in the establishment of his Seminaries. In 1580 we hear of him as one of the Vicars-General of St. Charles, and the saint is said to have died in his arms. Pope Sixtus V., on the nomination of Philip II. of Spain, made him Bishop of Cassano in Calabria, February 3, 1588. Gregory XIV. sent him as nuncio to the Swiss Cantons to arrange an intricate affair in 1591. Clement VIII. appointed him one of the Apostolic Visitors of the city of Rome, and was only prevented by his death in October 1595 from making him a Cardinal to take the place of Cardinal Allen, who died in 1594. He was buried in the chapel of the English College at Rome. See "Records of English Catholics," vols. i. and ii. London, Nutt, 1877, 1882.

CHAPTER IV.

HIS ADMINISTRATION OF HIS DIOCESE.

THE extent of the diocese of Milan required a great number of officials for its government. The saint, ever anxious for the greater good of the souls committed to his care, carefully sought out men who were fitted for these charges, and brought several with him from Rome, as well as from other places, whenever he met with suitable persons. In so doing he was regardless of expense, for, besides paying for their journeys, keeping them in his house, and providing them with the ecclesiastical habit, he even in some instances defrayed the cost of their studies, till they obtained the degree of doctor. In fine, he spared neither labour nor expense when it was a question of procuring a supply of good administrators and labourers in the vineyard. When he had found them, he was as tenacious in keeping as he had been diligent in seeking them, so that, lavish as he was of everything else that he possessed, it was with the utmost difficulty that he could be prevailed upon to deprive the diocese of a well-qualified ecclesiastic. Some of these bound themselves voluntarily to his service ; among whom was Ludovico

Moneta, a Milanese of great holiness of life, who never
would accept any Church preferment or salary, but lived
sparingly on his own patrimony, spending very little on
himself in order to give more to the poor.   This venerable priest, knowing the holiness of St. Charles, was
devoted to him, serving him indefatigably for many
years in various offices, besides being his constant com-
panion in all his journeys and labours.   St. Charles
always held him in the highest esteem, and consulted
him on all matters, finding him not only eminent for
sincerity and holiness, but distinguished also by great
prudence and judgment, with a wide and varied experience.   He survived the saint fourteen years, dying
in the good old age of seventy-eight years, and left
behind him a reputation for sanctity scarcely inferior
to that of the saint himself.   He was buried in the
Church of Our Lady of Grace at Milan, and was followed to the grave by great numbers, especially of the
poor.

The Cardinal distributed the work of the diocese
among the officers whom he had chosen with much
care and zeal, and special regard to the talent and
capacity of each one.   His prudence and discernment in this matter were more and more conspicuous
as time brought him maturity of judgment.   His attention was first directed to the various needs of his
diocese.   It was of primary importance to have a
Vicar-General of exemplary life and mildness of character, well versed in law and ecclesiastical discipline,
and he was careful that this office should always be
held by men of eminence.   Two Assessors, the one

for civil, and the other for criminal causes, were associated with the Vicar-General.

There was also a Treasurer, and an Auditor whose business it was to attend to causes pertaining to the temporal government of the diocese. For these offices he always chose those who were not natives of Milan, in order that not being fettered by the petitions of friends and relations, or by any human respect or interest, they might be more free to render strict justice. All these were members of the Cardinal's household, living at his expense, and under the rules he had drawn up. He gave them handsome salaries, forbidding them to accept the smallest present, in order that justice might be administered without any motive of self-interest. Speaking on this subject, he was wont to say, that if he ever chanced to receive the most trifling present, he felt drawn to the giver, and for this reason it was his practice to decline them. For the same reason, he forbade the members of his household to recommend persons to any of the judges or other officers, or to use their influence in any lawsuits or trials. All these dignitaries met together to decide the civil and criminal causes, in company with others duly qualified belonging to his household, or to the city, all being ecclesiastics.

The Chancellor of the diocese used to be a layman, who was at liberty to receive registration fees and the like; but when St. Charles made the other reforms in this department, he revived the old custom of having a clerical Chancellor, who was a Canon in ordinary of the Cathedral Chapter, and of the order of deacons.[1]   The salary of this office was a hundred crowns a year, besides table expenses.   A certain number of coadjutors were appointed under him, and he was also assisted by three notaries for criminal causes, all of whom had suitable salaries, besides their board as belonging to the household, and wearing the ecclesiastical habit.   In the course of these reforms, he cut down the taxes of the Chancellor's Court to the smallest possible proportions, and insisted on many matters being settled gratis, especially such as concerned spiritual causes and ecclesiastical discipline. He had the regulations of this court printed and inserted in the " Acts of the Church of Milan." The money realised by the fees and charges was paid over to a treasurer appointed to receive them.   There was an officer for the especial protection of prisoners, another for the defence of the poor in their lawsuits and causes ; together with a commissary of police, a custodian of prisons, and eight attendants for the service of his court, all receiving ample salaries.   The fines exacted by these officials were placed in the hands of an ecclesiastical trustee, whose duty it was to distribute the money so collected among different pious works, according to the decision of the Archbishop, or of the Vicar-General.

Not content with having made these rules, and put his tribunals in order, St. Charles frequently inspected all the departments of administration, in order to see

---

[1] There are documents which show that St. Galdinus was Archiepiscopal Chancellor and Canon in ordinary of Milan, and subsequently Cardinal and Archbishop, circâ 1170.

whether the different officers discharged their duties satisfactorily, so that justice was duly administered, and lawsuits expeditiously settled. He corrected with due charity any fault which he perceived in his deputies, and dismissed them if it was a case of serious neglect of duty. With the same object, he visited the prisons occasionally in person, and at other times he deputed some trustworthy person to ascertain their condition, whether the prisoners were properly attended to in spiritual and temporal matters ; and he appointed a spiritual prefect to take charge of their souls. He had an altar erected opposite the prison windows that they might hear Mass daily; and he was particular in arranging for their morning and night prayers, and for their reception of the sacraments.

The Cardinal, by means of these numerous coad-jutors, attended diligently to the souls committed to his care. Besides his Vicar-General, he had two Visitors-General, one for the city, and the other for the rest of the diocese, both of whom he chose with great care. He also appointed as Visitors of the city six priests as Prefects, the city being divided into six districts according to the number of the gates, one being assigned to the care of each prefect. The same arrangement was made for the diocese, which was divided into six provinces, over each of which, in like manner, was placed a priest with the title of visitor. Their duties consisted in visiting the churches and ecclesiastics of their district or pro-vince, for which office they had special authority and jurisdiction. They all met once a week in presence

of the Cardinal, to discuss these matters of reform and
discipline, which meeting was called the " Congregation
of Discipline." Besides this there were three other
general meetings for the same object, one before the
assembling of the diocesan synods, the second before
the visitation of the diocese, and the third before the
general meeting of the Vicars-Foran or rural deans.

Sixty Vicars-Foran were appointed for the general
government of the diocese. These were either the
rectors of the parishes into which the diocese was
divided, or other ecclesiastics chosen according to
their fitness. These vicars were bound to visit the
churches of their vicariate at stated times, to provide for the execution of the orders given at these
visits for different reforms, and to summon the clergy
of the parish to the monthly meeting at which cases
of conscience were decided, and things necessary for
the cure of souls discussed. Every one who attended
these meetings was bound to present to the vicar an
attestation of having been to confession once a week
during the month. These vicars were invested with
a limited jurisdiction in civil causes, and were very
careful to exact a strict observance of ecclesiastical
discipline, and of the archiepiscopal decrees, both from
clergy and laity. They were all bound to meet in
presence of the Archbishop on the twelfth day before
Septuagesima Sunday, previous to the assembling of
the diocesan synod, after having each visited his
own vicariate in order to report its condition at this
meeting, so that particular regulations, if necessary,
might be made at the synod for each district.

St. Charles had special regulations for communities of religious women. He appointed a vicar and a certain number of visitors for spiritual matters, and other deputies and guardians for temporal concerns. The former was charged with the duty of visiting the convents at stated times, once a year at least, and taking particular care of them. All the religious houses were distributed, so that each had his particular charge. These visitors also met once a week before the Archbishop, the meeting being called " The Congregation for the Care of Religious Houses," in order to discuss all matters relating thereto with a view to promote reform, and the observance of good discipline. In the same way, the temporal business of the convents was transacted by the deputies, some of whom were ecclesiastics, and the rest laymen.

Relieved on the one hand from the burden of temporal cares, and well supported in spiritual things, these servants of God were thus powerfully aided to run with vigour in the way of perfection to which they were bound by their vows.

There were many other officers besides those already mentioned, such as prefects of the clergy, synodal witnesses, secret monitors, punctators, and others, amounting, it is calculated, to the number of four hundred. These were eyes, feet, and hands to the Archbishop, who effected great things by their means, and brought the Church of Milan into a flourishing state. Just as all the members of the body derive their life and vigour from the heart, so did all these officers receive their strength from the authority and

prudence of their head.   He inspired them with courage, wisdom, and desire for good works, giving them
excellent instructions, and encouraging them in their
labours by his own example.   He was as it were the
mainspring, moving all the rest with order, and keeping them continually watchful and diligent in all that
concerned the service of God, and the salvation of souls.
He taught them exactly all that they were bound to do,
each in his own charge and office.   This was the source
of the excellence which was noted in so many persons
trained in his school.   On one occasion, when conversing with some of his suffragan bishops, he said that he
was so happy as to have at least thirty persons employed
in his diocese, who were all well qualified to be at the
head of any department, however important.

Note on p. 97.—" Labourers in the Vineyard."

Mgr. Speciano, the saint's agent in Rome, and afterwards Bishop of
Cremona, says that the Cardinal never went to Rome without bringing
back with him men of merit and distinction for employment in his
diocese.   Pope Pius IV. in 1560 commissioned his nephew to take note
of all men of piety and learning, in order to use them in the service of
the Church.   St. Philip Neri, who was always looking out for good
priests, rejoiced in this gift of St. Charles, and spoke of him playfully as
"a most rapacious robber to carry off good men;" and on another occasion, when the Cardinal had set his heart on bringing to Milan the celebrated Father Cæsar Baronius, of the Congregation of the Oratory,
refused his permission, telling him "he was a daring robber of good souls,
and a man who would strip one altar to adorn another."   See Oltrocchi's
notes, and "Life of St. Philip Neri," by Mgr. Capecelatro.   Burns &
Oates.   1882.

CHAPTER V.

THE state of the Church of Milan at this time might
be compared to that of a vineyard overgrown with
brambles and thorns. Abuses and sins were so rife
that the good seed was almost choked. This state of
affairs was well known to St. Charles, both through
the information of Mgr. Ormaneto, and from his own
observations. The saint realised with grief that the
chief cause of these miseries was the bad conduct of
the clergy, who, by their ignorance, and yet more by
their scandalous lives, were totally unfitted for the cure
of souls. He saw that the only remedy for the evil
lay in the foundation of seminaries for the training of
clerics who, by holiness and learning, would be fitted
for the sacred ministry. The Council of Trent had
recommended the erection of such seminaries, and St.
Charles had some time previously sketched out his plan,
as yet imperfect from the lack alike of fitting subjects
and sufficient means for its execution. He saw that the
assistance he needed was threefold. First, were needed
good men to sustain the burden of the management;

secondly, a number of fresh priests to fill the vacant parishes; thirdly, there was need of some means whereby the clergy might supply their lack of learning, and be encouraged in the practice of priestly virtues, in order to labour more fruitfully in the vineyard. It was his especial aim to supply these pressing needs, and he directed his plans accordingly.

The first and principal of these seminaries was established in Milan, under the patronage of St. John the Baptist, to accommodate a hundred and fifty students, who, having gone through their studies of grammar, gave good promise of completing the full course of philosophy and theology. Another seminary, the *Canonica*, was adapted for sixty students, who were instructed in moral theology, the Sacred Scriptures, and the Roman Catechism, that they might be fitted for the direction of souls. The Collegiate Church of Santa Maria Falcorina, with an adjoining house for canons, had become reduced in funds, and was converted by St. Charles into a third seminary for the reformation of such priests who, from their irregularity of life and lack of knowledge, had become unfitted for the sacred ministry. They in like manner received instruction in moral theology and the Roman Catechism, and when they had gained sufficient knowledge of their duties, were allowed to return to their benefices.

Large as these three seminaries were, they yet proved insufficient to accommodate the number of clerics necessary for carrying out the plans of the saint in their full extent. He therefore found it necessary to establish three more seminaries; the first at Santa Maria di

Celana, in the parish of Brivio; the second at Santa Maria della Noce, in Marliano; and the third at San Fermo, in Incino. Clerical students who had not completed their course of grammar were divided according to age among these three houses, whence they were afterwards, in due time, transferred to Milan, where they took their places in the principal seminary or the *Canonica*, according to their proficiency, and by these means provision was made for three hundred more clerics. Of these seminaries that of St. John the Baptist was the chief, the others being dependent upon it.

The necessary furniture and alterations in the buildings entailed a considerable outlay, which was defrayed by the Cardinal chiefly from his own private means. The students were only expected to find their clothing and their books; if any were too poor to do even this, all their needs were supplied. None found a more ready welcome than poor students from the remote valleys and mountain districts. Good parish priests were very much needed in those parts, where it was scarcely possible for any to dwell except natives of the country, few of whom ever evinced a vocation to the priesthood. St. Charles sought out the peasant boys of intelligence who were in service in Milan, and, when they showed capacity, trained them to be parish priests, and, in some cases, made good theologians of them, to supply the mountainous districts in this way with fervent pastors.

The expenses of the seminaries had been defrayed, in the first instance, by the Cardinal, but, as the de-

mands increased, he put in effect the recommendation
of the Council of Trent, and levied a rate for their
maintenance upon the ecclesiastical benefices of the
diocese, being himself the first to set the example of
willingly paying his contribution.   In this way was
raised a fixed income of more than six thousand crowns
a year.

St. Charles never refused admission into his seminaries to the rich, but always gave the preference to
the poor, who could not obtain an education elsewhere.
Likewise he admitted into them such priests of his
diocese who, being desirous of assistance in their studies,
sought yet more a renewal of fervour and strictness of
life.   Those who had been brought up in his seminaries
were especially welcome.   Many of these became rectors and professors of seminaries in other parts, where
they laboured with abundant fruit.   The Constitutions
of the seminaries were drawn up with prudence, in
conformity with the orders of the Council of Trent.
Four ecclesiastical delegates were appointed as a committee of supervision, two of whom were chosen from the
Chapter of the Metropolitan Church and two from among
the other clergy, and were intrusted with the management of the revenues and the temporal concerns of the
institute, on which St. Charles held a weekly consultation with them, or as often as occasion demanded.
The domestic and spiritual government of each seminary was presided over by a rector of piety and prudence, assisted by several coadjutors.   Such was the
mode of government of the chief seminary, and of all
the various branch establishments.   Each house was

provided with a rule adapted to its special object and circumstances. These regulations are preserved in the " Acts of the Church of Milan."

For some years St. Charles committed the direction of his seminaries to members of the Society of Jesus, whom he also employed in many other offices in his diocese. After a time, with their consent, he transferred the seminaries to the Congregation of the Oblates, in order to know the characters of the students, and so judge better of their several qualifications for the various posts. He took especial care that their spiritual father should be a man experienced in the direction of souls, and in the guidance of youth to the punctual practice of daily mental prayer and examination of conscience, together with the frequentation of the sacraments and the mortification of self. St. Charles provided also that the students should be trained in the true way of preaching the Word of God. To this end the clerics were accustomed to preach in turns in the refectory during meals.

The first care of St. Charles on the admission of a new candidate was that the edifice of his spiritual life should rest on a solid foundation. He directed that the neophyte should be kept apart from the other students for some days of retirement and meditation under the guidance of his confessor; and that the old man might be entirely put off, a general confession was made of the past life. These spiritual exercises were renewed every year at the beginning of each course of studies, and likewise before they were admitted to the priesthood. These wise provisions were attended with great advantage. The system was afterwards rendered still more complete by the erection in the *Canonica* of a range of cells after the fashion of a Capuchin monastery. Over the door of this building was cut the word "*Asceterium*" in Greek characters, to denote that it was a place set apart for meditation and the spiritual life, which St. Charles valued far above mere culture of the intellect. He would often impress upon the young seminarists and those who had the charge of them that knowledge is of little worth unless it is based on the solid foundation of the fear of God. Great care was exercised also in providing the seminaries with good professors, especially the principal college, where the full course of theology was studied. They were freed from all other occupations and engagements, in order that they might watch constantly over the youths under them, and be present at all their disputations and recitations. Once a week a lecture was given on the Roman Catechism and the doctrine of the Holy Sacraments and Christian life.

Some of the more advanced of the students, who had been remarked for their regularity and zeal in the observance of discipline, were appointed with the title of prefect to watch over the rest in each dormitory, both by day and night, within and without the house. This proved a powerful means of influencing the rest for good, and of keeping them from evil. In addition to these helps to spiritual and intellectual culture, the Cardinal provided them with means of instruction in plain song and harmony, and the rites and ceremonies of the Church.

For the maintenance of regularity and discipline in the internal arrangements of his seminaries, there was appointed by him a second congregation of ecclesiastics with the title of "spiritual delegates," who were commissioned to superintend the interior management of the seminaries. They met once a week to confer upon the order of studies, the observance of the rule, and the introduction of fresh regulations.

All these provisions seemed to the saint but small in comparison with the importance of the persons concerned, seeing they were to be ministers of God and pastors of souls. He felt it incumbent on him to become acquainted with the most minute particulars of the working of his system, and to watch over the whole as the dearest of his obligations. Thus he was always present to receive new-comers, and, by conversing with them, he made himself acquainted with their character, so that he might be better able to make his selection from among those who applied. After they were admitted he always retained a distinct recollection of each, remembering their faces and names in a manner that was astonishing, considering the great number he saw. He made a visitation of the seminary twice a year, at Easter, and at the beginning of September. On these occasions all the students were examined in the presence of the Cardinal and of the spiritual delegates. St. Charles kept a note of the principal circumstances of each, such as their age, the circumstances of their parents, their expectations, talents, proficiency in their studies, aptitude for learning, memory, and the rest. According to the progress

they made, they were promoted to higher classes, some
being sent to follow the courses of philosophy and theology in the College of Jesuit Fathers which he established at Brera; while others went to the *Canonica*
to study moral theology.   When the whole course of
training had been gone through, St. Charles made final
selection of those who appeared most fitted for the
higher offices in the diocese, and conferred on them
the degree of Doctor, in virtue of the special faculty
which he had received from the Apostolic See; en-
dowing them with theological prebendaries, or with
some other appointment conveying a title to orders.
Those who had studied moral theology in like manner
he provided with cure of souls according to their capacities.   It bears witness to the charity of the saint
that none were ever dismissed from the seminary without some provision having been made for them, except
in extreme cases of unworthiness.

Besides the annual examination as to proficiency
in study, St. Charles often inquired minutely of the
rectors and those who held office concerning the character and deportment of each student; then satisfying
himself by personal interviews with each individual of
the exactness of the report made of them, he investigated their progress in the spiritual life and religious
exercises.   This scrutiny enabled him not only to assist
those whose souls were thus laid open to him, but also
to discern their different qualifications.   With words of
charity he would then urge them on to the study of
perfection and to progress in virtue.   He also took
advantage of these personal interviews to inquire into

their individual needs, in which he used to assist them
as a father; and, by well-directed questions, he learnt
from them how the temporal concerns of the different
seminaries were conducted. If, unhappily, a cleric
was found to be leading an irregular or immoral life,
the saint with great charity would do his best to bring
him back to his duties with tender admonitions.
If this failed, he had recourse to the imposition of
penance, or sent him from one seminary to another,
or to the house of some good priest, keeping his
eye still upon him. In fine, he was so compassionate
towards these weaknesses that he left no means un-
tried to save such persons from danger of falling, and
in doubtful cases, leaned rather to the side of mercy
and compassion than to that of strict justice. Thus
he saved many souls who would otherwise have been
lost. He would often temper the zeal of superiors in
administering correction, taking care to do it in such
a way as not to diminish their authority, but rather
to edify them and inspire them with his own spirit of
gentle conciliation. His visits to the seminary were
made with such thoroughness as well as punctuality,
that they always lasted a fortnight, during which he
never suffered himself to be disturbed by any other
business. He left nothing undone, and found time
during his visit to hold a special meeting of inquiry
into temporal matters. To this meeting the temporal
delegates were convened, and with their assistance
the Cardinal ascertained that all was going on in
order, according to his regulations. Besides these long
visits, he often paid shorter ones as occasion arose,

and threw life and interest by his presence into the studies and exercises. All prelates who came to Milan were taken to see them as places of spiritual recreation, there being interest enough attaching to the varied discourses, Latin orations, disputations, and other devotional and literary exercises of the students. The idea of the Cardinal was, however, rather to induce other Bishops to found similar institutions in their own dioceses by showing them the abundant fruits they might look for in reward for their labours. The refreshments given to these visitors were always provided at his own cost, in order not to burden the means of the college.

As time went on, it became certain that the glory of God was very much increased by the abundant harvest that sprung from the good seed sown by the saint. For, although at first students were few on account of the report that gained credit that the place was like a prison and that the health of the inmates was endangered by the severity of the rules, yet, after a short time, the number that applied was so great that admittance was perforce refused to many. Noble families in the city as well as in the country esteemed it an honour if the Cardinal accepted their sons. But he would never consent to anything that might prejudice those who had a greater claim upon him. Therefore every year before the September visitation of the seminaries, he required the rural deans to give him a list of the number of candidates in their district, and the condition of each one. From this list he selected the required number, always taking care that every part of his diocese should have a share in the benefit of the institute; if he showed any favour it was to the poorer districts, especially the mountain parishes, the poverty of which deserved greater consideration.

The institution of the seminaries may be considered without doubt to have been one of the most potent means employed by St. Charles for the restoration of Christian discipline. These schools of Divine wisdom are still indeed, as in the days of St. Charles, sending forth to the vineyard many holy priests eminent in their love for learning and discipline. The religious orders have gained subjects from the seminaries of the holy Cardinal of Milan: for the spiritual exercises enjoined by him taught many souls the emptiness of the things of time, so that preferring a life of greater perfection they have entered monasteries where they have shone as models of perfection. Distinguished preachers, prelates and theologians have sprung from the seminaries of the saint; and so many left the seminary to enter the Society of Jesus, that the Cardinal was anxious lest his diocese should suffer by this diminution of her ministers. Accordingly he deemed it advisable to procure a Brief from Gregory XIII. prohibiting his clerics from being admitted into the Society until four years after they had left the seminary.

Note on p. 106.—" The Principal or Great Seminary."

This was opened in October 1565, the *Canonica* in October 1571, after the suppression of the order of the Frati Humiliati.

P. 107.—"*San Fermo.*"

There is an anachronism here, as it appears that this college was not opened till 1591 by the saint's successor, Archbishop Gaspar Visconti. Father Giussano omits mention of the seminary established by St. Charles at Arona in the Abbey of St. Gratinian in the year 1570.

"*Needs of the Seminarists.*"

There is extant a letter of Father J. P. Bimio, of the Oblates of St. Ambrose, begging the Cardinal for a supply of shoes and stockings for the students.

"*Poor Scholars from the Valleys.*"

Among these was Father Marc Aurelio Grattarola, a native of Val Sassa who was thrice elected Superior of the Oblates of St. Ambrose, and had charge for ten years of the process of the saint's canonisation. He is the author of "*Successi maravigliosi della veneratione di S. Carlo,*" published at Milan, 1604.

P. 109.—"*The Great Seminary transferred to the Oblates of St. Ambrose.*"

This was done by the saint in 1579, when Fathers Andrew Pionnio and Domenico Ferro took over the administration.

"*The True Way of Preaching.*"

Mgr. Valerio, Bishop of Verona, at the desire of St. Charles drew up for the students a manual of Ecclesiastical Rhetoric, the MS. of which is still in the library of the Seminary.

P. 115.—"*Brief of Gregory XIII.*"

This prohibition had been laid on the Society by a Brief of St. Pius V. dated July 23, 1570. See Sala's *Documenti circa S. Carlo Borromeo,* Milan, 1857, tom. i. p. 245. It was renewed by Gregory XIII. by Brief of September 4, 1577, five Milanese students having in the meantime been admitted into the Society.

CHAPTER VI.

A.D. 1566.

THE foundation-stone was now laid, and the general outline planned of the work which St. Charles had undertaken for the glory of God. Fitting instruments for the carrying out of his design were at hand, and he resolved, like a good husbandman, to rest not night or day until he had uprooted all the weeds that cumbered the ground, in the shape of abuses and evil customs that had crept into the diocese. The canons of his first Provincial Council, confirmed by Pius V., were now printed. They contained many decrees respecting the restoration of divine worship, the defence of the faith, the administration of the Sacraments, and the reform of clergy and people. St. Charles sent copies to his particular friends among the Bishops and Archbishops of Europe, writing himself on the subject to the Cardinal of Portugal, the Archbishop of Braga, the Cardinals of Lorraine in France and of Warmia in Poland, the Archbishop of Salzburg in Germany, and others. His wish was to lead them to undertake similar reforms in their own dioceses, and

to give them information about the Provincial Council
of Milan, which, as yet, was the solitary response to
the recommendations of the Council of Trent on the
subject.

One of the matters to which St. Charles applied his
mind was most important in his eyes, viz., the teaching of Catholic doctrine.   It had been sadly neglected
for some time past, especially in the province of Milan,
where the purity of the faith was endangered by the
proximity of heretical sects, and also unhappily by the
loose habits and conduct of the clergy and people,
which is wont to give rise to heresy.   Such tenden-
cies had already appeared in the province, and certain
preachers were suspected of being tainted with the
infection.   Rules were, in consequence, laid down by
St. Charles for his Vicars-general in order to deal with
the evil, and he urged the Father Inquisitor to be
watchful, and promised him every assistance, with a
sum of two hundred crowns annually from his own
purse, to enable him to maintain a sufficient staff
to carry on the work.   This provision was, after his
death, ordered to be paid in perpetuity by a decree
of the Apostolic See, requiring that the Archbishops
of the diocese for the time being should pay the
whole of the said sum.   St. Charles likewise appointed
certain censors to examine books already in circula-
tion, and forbade printers, under pain of severe penalties and censures, to issue any work without a license
from the Father Inquisitor.   These measures were an
effectual bar to the long-prevailing custom of issuing
profane books with impunity.   The Congregation of

the Holy Office founded by him consisted of the Archbishop, the Inquisitors with their Vicars and Fiscals,
besides other ecclesiastical councillors, theologians,
canonists, and laymen learned in the law; all of
whom, being selected with care, rewarded his vigilance by the great benefit which resulted from their
labours for the suppression of the prevailing licentiousness. He established also the Congregation of
the Index, whose office it was to exercise supervision
over the press for the suppression or correction of
dangerous or doubtful works tending to heresy or suspected of false doctrines. Regulations for the guidance of printers and booksellers contributed to the
effectual eradication of all publications injurious to
faith or morals.[1]

St. Charles instructed rural deans and parish priests
to be on their guard against foreigners, especially
such as came from countries suspected of heterodoxy.
There were known to be coming from France workmen
and hawkers, going about selling trifling wares, who
carried prohibited books concealed in their packs; they
were, by order of the Cardinal, subjected to strict examination, for in this way not only heretical opinions,
but books containing superstitious and profane rites
were let loose on the country. When any of these
persons were discovered, they were, by order of the
Cardinal, brought at once before his tribunal. By
this prudent foresight numbers of the simple-minded
were saved from contamination. All persons belonging to the diocese were forbidden to visit heretical

Acts of the Church of Milan, Part III.

countries, or to hold intercourse with them without express leave in writing, commending the bearer to the especial care of his parish priest. Finally, this watchful shepherd required all teachers of youth to make a public profession of their faith, and to preserve their charges from contagion by making use only of approved books.

It may be said that St. Charles neglected nothing in order to defeat the enemy of souls and preserve inviolate the purity of the Catholic Faith in his diocese.

Note on p. 117.—The Cardinal of Portugal, &c.

Henry, Archbishop of Evora, uncle of Sebastian, King of Portugal, was made Cardinal in 1546 by Pope Paul III. After the death of King Sebastian, in Morocco, in 1578, he succeeded to the throne at the age of sixty-seven. His councillors exhorted him to marry on account of there being many aspirants to the throne. Application was made for a dispensation to Pope Gregory XIII., who refused to grant it, and the Cardinal-King formally withdrew the petition. He died in 1580, after a short reign of two years. See Book VIII., chapter XXIV.

Charles, Cardinal of Lorraine, born 1525, Archbishop of Rheims, died at Avignon, 1574.

Stanislaus Hosius, Bishop of Warmia, was one of the Cardinal Presidents of the Council of Trent and Grand Penitentiary, died 1579, and was buried in Santa Maria Trastevere in Rome.

P. 119.—"Supervision of the Press."

From a letter to his Vicar-General Ormaneto, in 1566, it appears that the saint once discharged this office in person, and that his visit was not much liked by the booksellers, whose volumes he one day turned over without giving any notice. He confiscated heretical works, but at his own expense provided the dealers with Catholic books in their stead, according to the testimony of Ottaviano Abbiato Forrero his chaplain, afterwards Arch-priest of the Duomo and Oblate of St. Ambrose.

CHAPTER VII.

HIS WORK OF REFORM—THE SOCIETY OF JESUS IN MILAN.

1566.

NEXT in order to the care of the saint for the integrity of the faith came his earnest desire for the reformation of the clergy.   None knew better than he that the morals of the people depend materially upon the character of their pastors.   He held, too, that it behoves a prelate in authority over others to have a thorough knowledge of his priests, and to facilitate this he kept a record of all particulars concerning each one in his diocese, their name, surname, and standing; whether they did the duties devolving upon them, what benefices they held, and what qualifications they had, and the examinations they had passed.   All additions or changes throughout the year were recorded, and precautions taken to ensure accuracy.   The information he thus gained was of the utmost use to him in his visitations, as it enabled him to select from among his clergy those who would be able to co-operate with him in the carrying out of his measures, and give assistance to those who needed it.   He summoned to Milan many priests of the diocese who were imperfect in the knowledge requisite for their duties, and gave them the benefit of a special instructor, who gave them lectures in ecclesiastical discipline and in the principles of spiritual direction.

By these means he remedied in a short space of time the ignorance and scandalous life that prevailed among ecclesiastics; and though his priests were more than three thousand in number, he yet had such an accurate knowledge of them that on hearing the name of any individual, he at once remembered all about him, his name, his character, and his particular duties—a marvellous fact considering the multitude and diversity of the Cardinal's engagements.

He was in the habit also of visiting his priests at their own residences without giving them any notice of his intention. He found this a good means of putting a stop to various irregularities. Four hours sufficed him in this way to visit all the presbyteries in Milan.

One of the first steps taken by St. Charles for the reform of the clergy was a censure of all who neglected to wear the cassock proper to their calling.

Those priests who were possessed of several benefices were ordered to resign all but one; in which St. Charles enjoined them to take up their residence, as much dishonour to the Church and scandal to the laity had resulted from non-residence. In this matter he found it necessary to adopt unusual severity, as the evil with which he had to cope was most inveterate; and the subjects with whom he had to deal were too hardened and obstinate to receive his admonitions in a right spirit, if he had only acted with his character-istic gentleness. Much against his inclination he was obliged to resort to punishment in order to put an end to scandals. Little by little he led on his clergy to a strict observance of the decrees of the Provincial Council. To give still greater effect to his enactments, he commenced at this time the visitation of the city and diocese.

The saint, after doing all he could for the clergy, directed his attention to the reform of the religious communities of women, which indeed stood in great need of supervision. He visited the convents, and enjoined upon them the execution of the decrees of Trent, those of his own Synod, and the constitutions of the Sovereign Pontiffs. But the enemy of souls raised up a storm of opposition, especially in convents directed by Regulars, under the pretext of asserting all immunities and exemptions in their integrity, which was but a cloak for the assumption of undue liberty. The families even of the nuns took part in the disputes, and determined to resist to the utmost the execution of the decrees and reforms. Evil advisers abounded, and opposition was met with in the most unexpected quarters. The matter soon assumed such importance that the Town Council took cog-nisance of it, and proposed to despatch an envoy to the Supreme Pontiff to beg him to interpose his authority to prevent the threatened changes. But by the mercy of God this step was rendered unnecessary. St. Charles exercised so much tact and patience that not only was peace re-established, but the very opposition his views had encountered tended to bring out in still clearer relief the singlemindedness of his motives. All were forced to acknowledge that his efforts sprung solely from his zeal for the glory of God and the salvation of souls.

Having thus put an end to all contradictions, the Cardinal carried out in course of time all his measures of reform. He suppressed several religious houses throughout the city and diocese on account of various inconveniences, and transferred the nuns to other convents. In some cases he put in force the special powers conferred upon him by the Holy See of withdrawing the direction from the Regulars to place them under the immediate jurisdiction of the Ordinary. His principal object was the enforcement of observance of strict enclosure in each convent, and punctual observation of the rules. By providing them with visitors and confessors experienced in the spiritual life, in a short space of time a great and edifying change became apparent in the discipline and habits of these convents, and they were indeed reformed in newness of life.

Whilst thus occupied with religious persons, the Cardinal was not unmindful of the need in which the laity were of his reforming hand on account of the open licentiousness which prevailed among many. He turned his attention first to the teaching of the truths of faith and Christian doctrine : he impressed this duty upon all the clergy, but especially on the parish priests having the care of souls, and provided them with lay assistants and other aids. Burning with zeal and love for souls, the holy Cardinal not only preached himself, but set a practical example of fervour in these pastoral labours by administering the Word of God and the Sacraments. On the Feast of Pentecost large numbers received the Sacrament of Confirmation from his hands. With regard to the reception of this Sacrament, he directed that the recipient should have attained at least the age of eight, and should go to Confession and Communion on the day, if of age to receive Communion, and should take the name of some saint. He always administered the Sacrament as soon as possible after early Mass, to give it greater honour, and ensure its reception with more devotion. A sermon on the efficacy and requisite preparation preceded the celebration of the rite. Never had the people witnessed so much zeal in the service of God as was evinced by their Cardinal; and he had his reward in their increased love and reverence for holy things.

But the indefatigable pastor was still full of anxiety concerning the welfare of his flock. He had long grieved over the scarcity of labourers, and the abundant harvest which rewarded his own efforts made him the more solicitous that husbandmen should be found to assist in the good work. There was at that time in Milan an eminent and zealous preacher, Father Benedetto Palmio, Provincial of the Society of Jesus in Lombardy. In 1563 this Father had been sent to Milan by St. Charles, who now consulted him as to the foundation of a Jesuit College in Milan. With the consent of the General of the Order, the establish-

ment was begun without delay, and from the outset
it was supplied with Fathers of singular devotion
and zeal for the glory of God. St. Charles assigned
to them the church of San Fedele, transferring its cure
of souls to that of San Stefano, and provided them with
furniture and all other necessaries for their house. He
employed these Fathers in the direction of his newly-
founded seminaries, in the guidance of souls, and other
works. Filled with the spirit of Divine charity, these
holy men were fervent in preaching, diligent in hearing
confessions, and assiduous in every duty of the sacred
ministry, giving proof in all that they did of great
prudence and sound doctrine. The saint also availed
himself largely of the services of the congregation of
Regular Clerks of St. Paul, called Barnabites, whom
he found already established at Milan.

Desiring to make his own house a model of piety
and devotion to all his people, the Cardinal, in
addition to the practice of the usual religious exercises, instituted in his chapel public night prayers,
inviting many of the people of Milan to assist every
evening at prayers said in common, spiritual conferences, and singing of the Divine praises to the accom-
paniment of sacred music. By these means many were
drawn to a love of piety, and a relish for the things of
God. These gatherings were often attended by the
nobles of the city, many of whom were won to a
holier life by the grace and sweetness of the counsels
with which he sought to benefit their souls. Surprising indeed was the reformation wrought in a short time
among his flock, but the evil was too deeply rooted to

be entirely overcome by gentle measures, and he was obliged to legislate with greater authority.

Already some steps towards the restoration of Christian discipline had been made by Monsignor Ormaneto, who had laid special stress upon the fulfilment of the Easter duty of Confession and Communion, and the profession of faith in presence of the parish priest. He was strenuously supported by the Duke of Sessa, governor of Milan, who made his own household set the example of so doing. The Marquis of Pescara did likewise, making the refusal to comply with the injunction tantamount to instant dismissal from his service. These examples produced a great effect upon the rest of the people, and roused many from the lethargy in which they were plunged, to a consciousness of the importance of the things of God. The good pastor deemed it now opportune to require the observance of the precept, and he therefore required all parish priests to draw up a list of those who had failed to come to their spiritual duties ; and to take note of all who were leading irregular lives, that he might provide for their reformation and correction. Very great were the scandals that reigned with impunity, and among the worst of these vices was the public concubinage that provoked the especial wrath of God. St. Charles resolved to drive out this cankerworm of society, and published an edict against it on the 21st August 1566, enforcing also other decrees of the Council of Trent, and of his Provincial Synod on the reformation of morals, the observance of festivals and fasts, and the suppression of theatrical performances and other abuses on days of obligation. In all these measures he did not shrink from the severity demanded by the corruption of the age.

But the enemy of souls, enraged at the escape of so many from his power, now put forth all his malice to defeat the endeavours of the saint to win them to the yoke of Christ. He craftily aimed at undermining the authority which had enabled St. Charles to carry out his measures, through the cheerful submission of his people, suggesting doubts of the good intentions of the Cardinal, of his sanctity and of the prudence of his administration, and instigating evil-minded persons to circulate reports to the effect that the Cardinal had overstepped the limits of his authority, and was exercising intolerable severity.

The multitude, easily led by specious pretences, gave ear to these charges. Some said that his abundant almsdeeds, his austerity and other good works, sprung from ambition and vainglory, and a wish to pass for a saint. Others accused him of want of judgment, of ignorance of the true principles of government, and incapacity to govern even himself, whilst he took council with incapable and ignorant men who misled him. These calumnies chilled the fervour which his labours had kindled, and withdrew many from following one whose piety was thus stigmatised as hollow and hypocritical. His decrees and his authority began to be openly contemned and disputed. Even some of his own friends drew back from him, and doubted whether he had acted wisely in thus incurring the odium of a licentious and unscrupulous populace.

One prelate of high position even thought fit to address some words of warning to him, couched, however, in terms of fraternal moderation.

When the reality of the holiness of St. Charles was thus called in question, its true and solid nature was never more apparent than amidst this storm of invective. Of small moment was it to his humble soul that he himself should be misrepresented and despised. Like his Master, he sought not his own glory. But deeply he grieved at the dishonour done to episcopal authority, and above all at the interruption of the labours he had in hand for the salvation of souls. Not for one moment, however, did his trust in God falter. Well he knew that such trials are the lot of all the servants of God, and that those who labour for the salvation of others are often distinguished by a greater share in the cross of their Lord.

Undauntedly he went on his way, turning a deaf ear to the vain judgments of the men of this world. He might have taken as his motto the words of the Apostle St. Paul: "To me it is of the least account to be judged by you or by the day of man."[1]

Nevertheless he lost no opportunity of contradicting the falsehoods that were afloat, for he considered that they greatly impeded his efforts for the good of souls. He opened his whole heart to the prelate who had written so severely to him, humbly asking for his counsel, and thanking him for having admonished him with so much zeal and charity, and admitting that there was some foundation for the charge of severity

[1] 1 Cor. iv. 3.

which had been brought against him.   But he justified his seeming rigour by the fact that it had been rendered necessary owing to the sad condition of the diocese, which had obliged the employment of severe measures for the salvation of the souls that he loved too tenderly to spare the pruning-knife their miseries required.

St. Charles thought it right to render this account of himself; but, far from holding tenaciously to his own opinions, or despising the judgments of superiors, he prayed his monitor, by the good-will which he had shown, to assist him with his advice upon the best course to be pursued in future.   He knew well that none can be self-sufficient and despise the help of others, and that often those most need advice who have refused to be admonished.   The prelate to whom he wrote did him justice, and encouraged him to proceed with his reforms without regarding the efforts of the Evil One to defeat the work of grace.

P. 125.—"*Jesuit Fathers.*"

Among other Jesuit Fathers who laboured in the diocese were F. Francesco Adorno, Achille Gagliardi, Leonetti, Perusco, Emanuelle Sà, Pietro Ribadeneira, Jacopo Paz, Alfonso Sgariglia and many others.

P. 126.—"*Barnabites.*"

So called from their church of St. Barnabas in Milan.   Of this order the Blessed Alexander Sauli, Bishop of Aleria in Corsica, of which island he was called the Apostle, was confessor of St. Charles: Mgr. Carlo Bascapé, Bishop of Novara, wrote his life in Latin, published in 1592. F. Dominic Boero was sent by him into Switzerland, and the Fathers Besozzi, Marta, Asinari, Homodei and Michieli filled various offices of trust.

P. 129.—"*Prelate of High Position.*"

This prelate is supposed to be St. Charles's great friend Gabriel Paleotto, Bishop of Bologna, made Cardinal by Pius IV.   He had been professor of law at Bologna, the Cardinal's theologian at the Council of Trent, one of the lights of the day.   He died in 1597 at the age of seventy-three, with the reputation of never having sullied his baptismal innocence.

CHAPTER VIII

THE principal means employed by St. Charles in his work of reform were, after the foundation of seminaries and the celebration of provincial and diocesan councils, the continued visitation of his diocese, either in person or by proxy. By this means he learnt the needs of the clergy and people; and his synods enabled him to provide for them by various decrees.

The saint was most punctual in the celebration of the councils at the appointed times, as also in his visitations, in which he persevered to the last days of his life, deeming these two measures of greater importance for the welfare of his flock than any of his other pastoral functions. He would often say that he counted all the other labours of his vicars-general as nothing in comparison with their visitations.

Overwhelmed as he was with a variety of business, he yet found time formally to visit in person the whole of his diocese twice in the year. Churches, oratories, convents, monasteries, hospitals, were each and all subjected in this way to the watchful care of their pastor, and no amount of difficulty in the way of travelling to remote localities could daunt his zeal.

He cherished with great care the schools of Christian doctrine, which he always examined himself, considering them of the first importance for the training of the faithful in the practice of Christian duties, and teaching them to spend the festivals of the Church in a holy manner, by abstaining from the profane games and unseemly diversions in which they had been wont to indulge.

His journeyings in making these inspections were most fatiguing, his way often lying across rocky passes and steep mountains, up which he might be seen toiling, staff in hand, alternately frozen with the cold or exhausted by heat. In most places the path was impracticable to horses, and he was obliged, therefore, to travel many a mile on foot like a simple mountaineer. Often in his humility and charity he would insist on relieving his companions of the heaviest portion of the baggage, and we have also on record that when the path lay across a craggy rock or beside a precipice so steep that the natives themselves were accustomed to preserve their feet from slipping by iron spikes on their shoes, St. Charles, in the ardour of his zeal, would hasten on, supporting himself with his hands on the ground—on all fours, as the saying is.

His travels often brought him to districts where no bishop had ever been before, and to the edification of the beholders on these occasions, he would allow himself no rest after his toilsome journey, but, after spending some time in prayer in the church, would at once open the business of the visitation. So soon as he had fulfilled the object of his journey in one place, he set out at once for the next. Thus it often happened that for many days together he was travelling from place to place. Only in the larger towns, where the amount of business demanded it, did he ever spend more than one day.

It was his invariable custom to take up his abode in the presbytery of the place, even when comfortable apartments might have been at his service in the houses of the rich. Thus he often passed the night lying on bare boards, or, it may be, on a little straw, having given up his bed to one of his household; he practised similar self-denial with regard to food, leaving the best for them and contenting himself with a handful of chestnuts and a little milk, or the coarse diet of the country. If he showed any preference, it was always for the poorest fare. His attendants were strictly forbidden to bring with them any food, furniture, or other comforts, and on one occasion the Cardinal severely reprimanded a person of his suite who had brought with him a metal spoon, disliking the wooden ones in use among the inhabitants of the Leventina valley.

The hottest season of the year was that usually chosen for the visitations, in order to reap a spiritual harvest in the time commonly spent in inaction and repose. In like manner the sultry hours of the midday siesta were those chosen by St. Charles for his journeys. He never took more than six horses with him in rich parishes, in order to spare expense; and where his hosts were poor, he always defrayed the outlay himself, on the plea that it behoved a Bishop to spend his own when he visited the poor of his flock.   The simplicity he enjoined obviated the necessity for any extra beasts of burden, as each member of his suite, even though he were a person of quality, carried his own baggage with him on his horse.   Sometimes, however, the Cardinal made use of a second horse to carry a couple of cases of books for study, but of this we shall have occasion to speak hereafter.   The same simplicity appeared in his regulations concerning diet. He would never suffer more than three dishes to be served up.   These consisted of fruit, soup, and a dish of meat.   More simple yet was his own fare, for when the others were helped, he himself would withdraw to partake of bread and water.

In proportion as the austerity with which he treated himself increased, so did the heart of the saint expand the more in love to God, in zeal for the embellishment of His house, and in liberality towards the poor.

St. Charles was careful to carry out the outward ceremonial of his visitations with befitting dignity and devotion.   His public entry into a town, solemn consecration of a church, pontifical Mass, and other functions, were all characterised by solemnity and attention to ritual, even in the remote mountain districts, so that all could see that the thoughts of the holy Prelate were wholly centred in God, and his heart filled with a burning desire to give honour to His Divine Majesty in all places and circumstances.   The people were greatly edified by the decorum and solemnity thus given to the public worship of God.   From increased reverence for Him, they were led on to greater veneration for His house and ministers; so that of their own accord they received the vicars of St. Charles on their visitations with like honours. When the latter made their reports to the Cardinal, he was wont to warn them against self-gratulation in the words of our Divine Lord to His apostles, when they took praise to themselves because devils were subject to them, saying: "Rejoice not that spirits are subject unto you, but rejoice in this, that your names are written in heaven."[1] So deeply were the people impressed with the reverential treatment of holy things by St. Charles that they were scandalised whenever less reverence was shown by other prelates.

The visitations were conducted as follows. On the arrival of the Cardinal the people of the town came out to meet him, and led him in procession to the church, where he spent some time in prayer. If it were in the morning he then said Mass, preaching after the Gospel: if in the evening, he ascended the pulpit at once and preached to the people, doing the same more than once on the succeeding day. He always began with a sermon on visiting a convent, school, confraternity, or other religious house. The subject of these discourses was always confined to the object of the visitation, pointing out its intention and importance, and the benefits to be derived from it. St. Charles was in the habit, moreover, of learning previously from the parish priest, the particular sins and abuses that prevailed; he then addressed himself especially to the denunciation of such evils, as an

[1] St. Luke x. 17, 20.

experienced physician arranges his remedies according
to the various maladies of his patients. Most wonderful were the effects of his preaching, especially of the
admonitions which he administered in private to the
more notorious sinners, whom he never failed to con-
vert to penance and newness of life.

Another great work of his visitation was the
administration of the Holy Communion which was
his constant practice in every place. Priests with
special faculties for reserved cases of conscience were
sent on in advance of the Cardinal, to stir up the
people to confession, and the resident clergy were asked
to increase their efforts to the same end. This was
followed by a general Communion on the day of the
visitation, given by the Cardinal himself. The people
hastened to receive Communion from the hands of
their Pastor, some even coming from a distance, and
following him about from place to place in order to
have this consolation repeated. The heart of the
good shepherd rejoiced on these occasions which were
to him as the gathering in of the lost sheep of the
flock.

Immediately after the general Communion, St.
Charles administered Confirmation, as he wished it
to .be received fasting, and only after confession, for
greater reverence to the Sacrament.

The daily repetition of these labours was fatiguing,
but the Saint never showed any signs of weariness;
neither did he complain of the excessive heat of the
overcrowded churches, which became at times quite
intolerable, from the fact that in the mountain dis-

tricts the people brought into the church the smell of the cattle that herded with them in their dwellings. The attendants of the Cardinal were often compelled to go out of the church at intervals, for the sake of breathing the fresh air for a few moments. But the servant of God persevered without ever flagging: his love for God and zeal for souls far outweighed any physical inconvenience.

But more laborious even than these labours was the work of consecrating churches and altars. The deplorable and ruinous condition of most of the churches in his diocese, called for their restoration, which in some instances was so complete that the church had to be reconsecrated. On one occasion it was observed that the Cardinal during eighteen days of visitation had gone through fourteen consecrations. But it was not the number of churches consecrated so much as the austerity of the preparation he made for their consecration that was remarkable. He fasted on bread and water the day preceding, and spent the night in watching before the holy relics on the altar. The actual ceremony occupied eight hours, including the High Mass, the sermon, and administration of the Sacraments. Bells, chalices, and other sacred things were often blessed at the same time, the whole cere-mony often lasting till past mid-day. This stress of work never made him less exact in the rest of his visitation, — of the Blessed Sacrament, sacred relics, holy oils, the altars, the condition of the clergy, the state of other churches in the district, and all the matters belonging to the visitation of a Bishop.

On concluding the visitation of one district, the Cardinal would retire to some quiet place where he could carry out and communicate to his clergy the directions suggested to him in its course. He conferred with them in general, giving his orders for reforms; and he also conferred with each priest privately, admonishing or advising each one according to his particular needs, of which he had previously taken care to be duly informed. It was his practice to make the time of these gatherings correspond with the usual monthly meeting of the clergy of each district, that more life and interest might be infused into the ordinary routine by his presence.

It would sometimes happen that during the absence of St. Charles on a visitation, he had to return to his cathedral to hold an ordination or keep some festival day. On such occasions the Cardinal never failed to attend, returning, when the ceremony was over, to the place of his visitation.

These outward results were not the only fruit of the zeal of St. Charles at these times. He was accustomed to use his influence in putting an end to feuds among the people, and effecting a reconciliation. He restored religious worship by reclaiming alienated possessions of the Church, and rousing the clergy to greater diligence in their ministry, and their flocks to a deeper sense of the reverence they owed their pastors. He upheld ecclesiastical jurisdiction, and brought sinners to repentance, enforced the due fulfilment of pious bequests, erected new parochial churches, united benefices, transferred convents and other titular churches to more convenient situations, and put an end to numbers of abuses. His great consolation in these works was the opportunity given him of becoming acquainted with all the sheep of his fold, in order that he might bind up the wounds of their souls, feed them with the Bread of Heaven, and provide even for their temporal necessities with the tenderness of a father. Besides the general statement of the souls in each parish which was sent to him yearly, he was in the habit of noting in a book entitled " *The temporal needs of such and such a district,*" the names of those who were in danger of committing sin through poverty, in order to help them if possible, of those who were living in a state of sin that he might restore them, and of the perverse and impenitent that he might correct them. When the time of his visitation came round, he would then make diligent inquiry about their cases, and would not lose sight of such souls until he had placed them out of danger.

During the first years of his episcopate, the Cardinal made his visitations on horseback, but afterwards his fervour inspired him to travel on foot after the example of our Divine Lord and His apostles. He commenced this practice on the occasion of his visit to the parish of Vimercato, but was obliged to desist through an attack of lameness. Edifying indeed was the sight of the Cardinal walking from place to place, followed by his loving people, who accompanied him from devotion as if he were a new apostle of the Lord.

St. Charles was equally watchful over the visitations of his vicars. He had an exact account of all that they did, taking care that they were continually employed in the duties that devolved upon them; and encouraged them with every possible counsel and assistance. It may indeed be said that the Church of Milan was thus subjected to a perpetual visitation. When the untiring self-devotion of the saint is considered, the wonderful transformation which he wrought appears as the natural consequence of such zeal. He made the wilderness to blossom as a rose, and the uncultivated field to bloom as a garden bringing forth all manner of fruits and flowers.

P. 137—"*The work of consecrating churches.*"

F. Possevin in his life of the saint records that three hundred churches and altars were consecrated by him. It was said that there was hardly a church in the diocese which had not been either rebuilt, repaired or adorned in some way by him.

CHAPTER IX.

REFORMS IN THE CATHEDRAL CHAPTER.

St. Charles commenced his visitation with that of his Metropolitan Church of Milan, as the first in order of importance. Many reforms were found necessary, which he effected in course of time. As the object of his special solicitude, he saw that his cathedral would be a model to all the chief churches of his province, on account of the devotion of the Chapter to his least wishes.

Many beneficed clergy of different ranks comprised the Chapter. There were first the Ordinary Canons, having the privilege of wearing the red or purple cape according to the season, like the Cardinals at Rome. Besides these there were notaries, and those known by the name of Decumani and Mazzaconici,[1] who wore the black cape; lectors and obedientiaries, who were accustomed to attend the Canons at ecclesiastical functions. There were also various custodians, with their chief officer called *Cimiliarca.*[2] Notwithstanding this numerous body of clergy, the Church was badly served.

---

[1] *i.e.*, Minor Canons. Vid. Du Cange.

[2] Κειμηλιάρχης, treasurer.

But few remained in residence, and the decorum of the divine worship was much neglected. One reason for this was that some of the Canons held other benefices in which they resided, while others held two Canonries in the same church, as the offices of "decuman" and "obedientiary" were posts of but little emolument, and, indeed, the income of the canonries themselves was small. There was often found no one to sing the offices of the Church, which all fell into disuse with the exception of Terce, Mass, and Vespers: even for these it was usually found necessary to hire an extra chaplain. Many other abuses had sprung up in consequence of wars and calamitous times. On his first visitation the Cardinal discerned both the evils and their remedies, and had indeed recognised in the lifetime of his uncle Pius IV. that the slender stipend allotted to the Canons in residence gave rise to abuses. He had then obtained that an annual sum of twelve hundred crowns should be assigned to them from the revenue of the Abbey of Miramonte. Other sums were in like manner procured by the Cardinal, who received from the Holy See authorization to prescribe statutes and rules for securing regular residence. He suppressed certain canonries, and amalgamated their incomes with the general fund, so that the endowments of all were considerably increased.

He then required the Canons to resign other benefices which were incompatible with residence, and laid down rules for the Chapter, by authority of the Holy See, binding them to constant residence, and to unite in reciting all the Canonical hours in choir under pain of losing their share in the distribution. To this was added the obligation, which had long fallen into abeyance, of saying the Office of Our Lady in common on the days and times prescribed by the general rubrics, and by particular decrees. To strengthen these rules, the Cardinal ordered that the Archbishop for the time being should nominate another Punctator besides the one chosen by the Chapter, to take note of those absent from choir, and also of all personal failings in the recitation of the Divine office. In conformity with the recommendation of the Council of Trent, the canonical prebends were divided into the three orders of priests, deacons, and subdeacons, to whom were assigned according to their rank, distinct places in choir and in processions, and such like occasions. In pursuance of the same recommendations, two prebends were founded, one for a canon theologian to which was attached the duty of instructing the people in the truths of faith on festivals ; and on the two last days in the week of delivering a lecture to the clergy on some theological subject in the archiepiscopal chapel. The second for a canon penitentiary, who had four coadjutors, or minor penitentiaries, with faculties for reserved cases. St. Charles assigned separate stipends to these offices, intending afterwards to give them a more definite form. In the meantime, the penitentiaries were required to attend at the cathedral to hear confession, and they were also called upon to meet together with other doctors and canonists, to consult upon cases of conscience which had arisen in the course of the week throughout the whole province. This was called the Congregation of the Penitentiary, and it proved of great benefit to confessors. He instituted also a third prebend, which he called doctoral, with the obligation attached to it of reading canon law to the clergy at least twice a week in the archiepiscopal chapel. All these different foundations proved of importance, and great good was wrought by their means throughout the diocese.

The Archbishop had greatly at heart the due celebration of Divine worship with the dignity and decorum prescribed in the Church. He was most solicitous that the most minute rites and ceremonies should be strictly observed; and to this end he appointed a master of ceremonies with an assistant to be present in the choir during the Divine Office. These officers were resident, having their share in the emoluments of residence, and their own prebends. In course of time it became evident that there were not a sufficient number of subordinate officers for the requirements of the church. St. Charles therefore substituted a college of twelve doorkeepers, or custodians, who were appointed to serve under a sacristan, for the inferior offices of the choir. Their duties were to preserve decorum in the church, and prevent talking therein, to open and shut the doors, and watch over the separation of the sexes in church. They were also to ring the bells, for the Cardinal would not have any part of the service of the Church, however small, done by a layman. The duties of these custodians were substantially those of the minor orders of the clergy, save that they served the High Altar alone. Two priests were appointed sacristans, with separate sacristies and distinct functions. To the first belonged the care of the silver vessels and all the furniture of the high altar. The second had charge of the other sacristy containing the furniture and ornaments of the minor altars, and he also had the regulation of the private masses which were to be said at the hours most convenient to the people, according to the order published by the prefect of the choir each week.

The attention of the Cardinal was also given to the musical arrangements of the church. He increased the number of musicians, dividing the best singers into different choirs, and allowing them sufficient stipends. He ordered all the music to be of a devout and ecclesiastical character, and that due effect should be given to the words so that they might be perfectly understood. He intended thereby that his people should be incited to devotion by the music rather than to mere admiration. This made him prohibit the use of all instruments employed in secular music, retaining the organ alone. This order was established by a decree of the Council, so as to make it binding throughout the province. And as the cantors were to be ecclesiastics, he dismissed all seculars, and retained only clerics of good character. He made it a rule also that they should always wear cottas in church, deeming it fitting that the ministers of the altar should be vested in the outward symbol of the purity that should be their distinctive characteristic. Hearing that some of the beneficed clergy belonging to the cathedral were wont to join with the singers of the church, he forbade the practice, in order that they should not be absent from their places in choir.

The reform thus wrought by St. Charles in the celebration of divine worship, had its effect upon his people. They now flocked to the services of the church, for their devotion to the worship of God rose in proportion as they saw it worthily celebrated.

Ever eager to do good to souls, the holy Cardinal took advantage of their presence in such numbers to instruct them in Christian doctrine. He ordered that a sermon should be preached after the Gospel whenever there was High Mass, and also in the afternoon after Vespers, by preachers of special learning and holiness, in order to win souls to a knowledge of the truth, and to the practice of virtue. To these were added frequent processions and other spiritual exercises, litanies sung to music, and the like. By these means he hoped to keep the people occupied with holy things on festivals of the Church, and so to withdraw them from theatres and such like profane amusements. His efforts were crowned with success. The cathedral, lately so deserted, was now served with becoming splendour, and the services conducted with devotion. A great spirit of fervour manifested itself among the people, and it was not unusual for some to remain in the Church during the whole of a Feast Day, leaving it only at the dinner hour. The crowd of devout worshippers was so great that it was necessary, in order to obtain a seat, to be in good time for any service; although the church was one of the largest in Europe. Such dispositions in his flock could not but fill with joy the heart of the good Shepherd, and he was ever adding fresh incitements to devotion in order to stimulate their appetite for the services of the Church.

His own example was not the least attraction in itself. When the people saw their pastor assisting with angelic fervour at the services, they were so filled with devotion, that they found it difficult to tear themselves away from the church in order to attend to their temporal affairs.

The Cardinal had an apartment prepared for himself in the Canons' house, with a passage from his own residence, so that he was enabled to join the Canons in their Matins at break of day, and thus satisfy his desire to be in choir. He was wont to tell his Canons that it was his delight to be with them.

CHAPTER X.

THE CATHEDRAL OR DUOMO OF MILAN.

WHILST thus occupied in perfecting the spiritual beauty of his Church and its offices, St. Charles was by no means unmindful of the claims that the material structure had on his attention. It was one of the finest religious edifices in Europe, both from its size, its bold and magnificent design, as from the marbles and sculptures which adorned it. Large sums in the course of years were expended on its maintenance, and a council of administration was found necessary, called the Chapter of the fabric of the cathedral, consisting of the Archbishop, his Vicar-General, three Canons in ordinary, and a procurator, three collegiate doctors, and twelve knights who were attached to the Church, and wore the short mantle. The duty of this Chapter was to take due care of the repairs of the cathedral.

Before the time of St. Charles, the subject of Divine worship was little understood by the people, and more attention was paid to worldly pomp and vain show than to the service of God, its true End. Thus while without this magnificent temple was adorned with beautifully chiselled statues, it was like any secular

building within, hardly retaining the form or proportions of a church. There was no choir, no chapels,
and but very few altars, all totally neglected. In place
of devotional pictures and images of saints, the whole
interior was encumbered with pompous monuments of
the nobles and dukes of Milan, ostentatiously placed,
and the walls were hung round with banners display-
ing the arms of the principal families of the city, so
that the Cathedral bore the appearance of a public
exhibition rather than that of a House of God. Worse
still, as two doors on opposite sides of the sacred
building afforded a convenient passage from one street
to another, it became the custom for the people to pass
through with their merchandise, and even their beasts
of burden, to the dishonour and desecration of the
House of God.

The saint, filled as he was with zeal for the glory of
God, could not witness these profanations without grief
and indignation. He resolved to put an end to them
at once, and to restore the interior of the cathedral to
simplicity and beauty. In accordance with a decree
of the Council of Trent, he swept away all the trophies
of worldly pomp which filled the Church. Although
by the decree monuments of stone and metal were
allowed, he would not spare even the bronze monu-
ment of his uncle, the Marquis of Melegnano, brother
of the Sovereign Pontiff, Pius IV., but put it away as
an example to others. He had the choir arranged entirely afresh, according to his own design and judgment,
which was very good in architectural matters. He
raised the high altar so as to be visible to all the

people. It had been consecrated by Pope Martin V., and under it reposed eleven bodies of the Holy Innocents. He had it surrounded by the seats for the choir in three degrees, the highest being for the Canons. Upon these was sculptured in relief the life of St. Ambrose, Doctor, and Patron of the Church and city of Milan.

The seats of the second rank were for the clergy who held other benefices or offices in the cathedral. The third row of seats was assigned to the clerics of the seminary. The archiepiscopal throne occupied its proper place, raised upon several steps, and was richly decorated. This first part of the choir was enclosed by a balustrade of marble.

The Cardinal forbade any layman, however exalted in position, to assist at the Divine Office in this part of the sanctuary, which was railed off, and set apart solely for the ministers of the altar. In this he imitated his predecessor, St. Ambrose, who, for the same reason, shut the gates of this very choir against the intrusion of the Emperor Theodosius. Neither would he permit any ecclesiastic to take his place there unless vested in a cotta, as was befitting the reverence due to the holy place.

He had another portion of the church below the choir railed off, and furnished with raised seats for laymen of high station, magistrates and nobles. This he did advisedly, deeming it right that magistrates and persons in authority should occupy a more elevated and conspicuous situation than others. A proper seat was set apart in this place for the Governor of the city. The two organs were brought into the choir, as great inconvenience had arisen from their being at a distance, and seats were arranged beneath them for the singers.

Two pulpits were placed against the last pillars of the choir, facing the people. They were of beautiful design, gilded and adorned with sculptures. Each was supported upon four figures wrought in bronze; that on the right-hand side having the emblems of the four Evangelists, while the other was upheld by the four Doctors of the Church. The new position enabled both clergy and people to hear sermons without leaving their places. One was set apart for the exclusive use of the Archbishop, as a token that preaching was a part of his pastoral office, and worthy of a special place and prominence.

When the restoration of the choir was complete, the Cardinal turned his attention to the part of the church immediately below it, called the "Scurolo" or Confession. He restored the ornaments in stucco, and erected an altar in the midst, with bodies of saints and other relics, which he had collected from different places. Round it were seats for the accommodation of the Canons when reciting their Matins in winter. He obtained for this altar the same privilege as was enjoyed by the altar of St. Gregory at Rome, namely, that of liberating a soul from Purgatory at each Mass that was said there. It became an object of great devotion to the people, who were drawn thither by the example of their Archbishop, who frequently said Mass there, and spent hours of prayer at the shrine.

The next care of the Archbishop was the arrangement of the other altars and chapels throughout the
church in the beauty and order in which we now see
them.   Each altar was surmounted by a lofty canopy,
out of reverence for the sacred mysteries there
celebrated, and was protected with iron railings from
too near approach, in accordance with conciliar decrees
afterwards made.   The two side doors of which
we have spoken were walled up, and two additional
altars erected in their place, dedicated, one to Our
Lady " of the tree," over which was placed the picture
of the Annunciation from Florence, which had been
given to the Cardinal by Francesco de Medici, Grand
Duke of Tuscany ; the other altar possessed the sacred
relics of St. John Buono, Archbishop of Milan.
These altars in the part formerly so desecrated are
now objects of great devotion with the people. .

To show his desire that the administration of the
Sacraments should have especial honour in his church,
St. Charles had a magnificent baptistery erected near
the principal entrance.   The font of porphyry was
placed under a cupola supported upon four marble
pillars, and surrounded by an ornamental railing.
In ancient times it had been customary for the Archbishop himself to baptize at stated times.   This
custom was revived by the saint who, twice a year,
on the vigils of Easter and Pentecost, administered
Baptism with his own hands.   This baptistery was
only provisional, as the Cardinal intended to erect a
chapel outside the church exclusively for the administration of the Sacrament of regeneration.

The way from the Archbishop's house to the cathedral was most inconvenient, as it lay through the public streets. When St. Charles erected the Canons' lodging, he made a way of communication by a subterranean passage which enabled the Archbishop and Chapter to go under cover to the church at all hours.

The burial place for the Archbishop and Canons was marked out at the foot of the first tier of steps leading up to the choir. That for priests was on the right, the deacons and sub-deacons on the left, and the Archbishop in the centre. But his intention was not fulfilled, for he was the first himself to die, and the ground where he was laid was deemed too sacred to be the resting-place of any other, for it was at once venerated as the glorious shrine of a saint of God.

To leave no part of his work incomplete, St. Charles provided that every altar should have a sufficiency of sacred vessels, and other furniture required for Mass and other offices, and spared no expense in order that everything might correspond with the dignity of the church.

He then arranged the body of the cathedral more according to the canons, and to guard against distractions during the services, fixed a strong wooden screen in the nave for the separation of the men from the women.

Finally, that the irregularities in administering the funds for repairs might not recur, he made rules for the future disposition of these funds, apportioning them according to the ascertained cost of the maintenance of each part of the fabric.

Thus little by little, did the church assume an entirely new aspect. The majesty with which the services were conducted attracted the faithful; and what was of infinitely greater importance, their hearts were drawn thereby to the love of God and heavenly things.

CHAPTER XI.

1566.

HAVING thus restored order in his cathedral, the Cardinal with fatherly solicitude, turned his attention to the other churches of Milan. After enforcing residence in the collegiate churches, he found it necessary to suppress some poor benefices, or to unite them to others, closing some of the parochial churches, and affiliating the parish to some other church better situated for the convenience of the people, and the necessary maintenance of the clergy. The income of the latter was augmented in some poor parishes by grants from the revenues of the Abbey of Miramonte, already largely drawn upon for the needs of the cathedral Chapter. By these means he made provision for the residence of the clergy in their benefices.

During his visitation of the collegiate and parochial churches, he did not overlook the various confraternities, and the societies of penitents. Among these latter abuses and neglect of discipline had to be set in order, and their constitutions and management to be better organised.

Pious societies of laymen were instituted in some churches, and especially in those which had no cure of souls. To these confraternities, St. Charles gave excellent rules to enable the members to make progress in virtue. They were distinguished from the penitents by a habit of different colour, and their edifying lives soon drew many others to follow them in the paths of benevolence and well-doing. A work he had much at heart was the confraternity of St. John the Beheaded, the members of which accompanied criminals to the place of execution, and remained with them to the last. Many nobles and chief men of the city were persuaded by St. Charles to join this work of charity, and, before long, officers of state and the Governor himself applied to have their names inscribed among the brethren. Men who wasted their time before were now to be seen engaged in these labours of mercy, and spared no efforts in order to dispose the poor criminals to receive the Sacraments worthily, and to make a good end. To secure time for their ministrations, it was ordered that two days should always elapse between the passing of a capital sentence and its execution. As soon as a prisoner was condemned to death he was taken to the Oratory of the prison, where the brethren of the confraternity announced his fate to him, exhorting him to accept it with patience and submission, for the love of God, and in penance for his crimes. In consequence of these regulations, no criminal is now executed on the day on which he received Holy Communion; and as soon as sentence is passed, he is given into the care of a priest of the society, or some other confessor, who makes it his duty to prepare him for the Sacraments of Confession and Communion. The whole confraternity also attend up to the last moments of the condemned, who is assisted and encouraged by the presence and prayers of these good persons.

The singing of the Litanies on the Rogation days was observed by the Church of Milan. But as the three days' fast, according to the institution of St. Mamertus, Bishop of Vienne in France, had been adopted here, the Ambrosian Rite transferred the time of reciting the Litanies to the week after Ascension, so as not to infringe upon the custom of not fasting during the Forty Days of Eastertide. But unhappily this observance had been so abused, that it had become rather an occasion of offending God than of drawing down His mercy. The fast had been long omitted, and debauchery and excess prevailed instead. The procession had lost its religious and devotional character, and only presented a scene of confusion and disorder. St. Charles was deeply grieved at these scandals, and took measures to put an end to the abuse by ordering the strict observance of the prescribed fast, and requiring the clergy to assemble at break of day in the great church, where ashes were put upon their heads by the Archbishop. The procession was then celebrated in a spirit of penitence, and of devout preparation for the coming of the Holy Ghost at Pentecost.

The presence of their Archbishop inspired the people

with so lively a sense of religion, that there was hence-forth a complete absence of former excesses.

The fast was observed, and the people followed in the procession with every mark of devout recollection, in the garb of penitents, and with books or rosaries in their hands.

St. Charles himself on these three days took only bread and water, although it was his habit to preach after High Mass in the cathedral on each day. Not-withstanding the early hour, and the inconvenience from the crowding of the people, he was in the church with the Canons at daybreak to say Mass, after which came the distribution of ashes, followed by the proces-sion, which often lasted till one or two o'clock in the day. The clergy were all bound to attend the pro-cession unless lawfully hindered, and the Cardinal used to wait to see them pass by, two and two.

Another abuse of not less importance had long pre-vailed among the people through the laxity of former prelates. It was an ancient custom in the city for public oblations to be made from the six regions into which it was divided towards the expenses of the fabric of the cathedral on the six Sundays after Pente-cost. This had been suffered to degenerate into a kind of afternoon burlesque, attracting crowds of idlers, who came to it as to some profane spectacle. It were out of place to narrate all the desecration of the holy house of God that took place on these occasions. The pruning hand of St. Charles found means to eradicate these abuses as he had done so many others. In the first place, he had the oblations brought in the morning during the High Mass instead of in the afternoon as formerly. The people were required to come in procession, preceded by the clergy of each district in cassock and cotta, the great banner of the town, with the figure of St. Ambrose, being borne in front. These regulations have been strictly observed ever since, so that the oblations are now made with due piety and reverence.

When all was brought into order in the city, St. Charles in this same year, 1566, made a visitation of other parts of the diocese, in which his labours caused him much bodily suffering, while the sad state of religion inflicted grief of mind. The burning fire of zeal which consumed him, soon, however, worked wonders in a short space of time. Sinners were converted to God, discipline was restored among the clergy and the churches rendered more worthy of the presence of God.

Repeating over again the same measures of reform he had carried out in Milan, the Archbishop enforced the residence of Canons, and united foundations in thinly-populated districts, so as to make one efficient body, or transferred them from scattered and deserted parts to the large towns.

Thus, from Castel Seprio, situated amid dense woods, he translated a college of Canons to the town of Carnago; also, from Olgiato Olona, a place of little importance, to Busto Arsizio: again from Gagliano to Cantù, and another from the village of Castello to Lecco.

At Abbiategrasso he founded a collegiate church,

and united others to it. He arranged for the support of the Canons, either by increasing their scanty revenues from ecclesiastical benefices which he suppressed, or by giving them the third part of the revenues of the prebendaries, as is permitted by the Council of Trent. He ordered all to observe residence, punishing those that were refractory by depriving them of their canonries. All who held more than one preferment were required by his decrees to retain one only. In some cases he was met by the exhibition of a faculty to hold both, which had been obtained from the Holy See, but his persuasions and forcible reasoning never failed to obtain a voluntary resignation.

He proceeded in the same way also with the parochial churches, obliging the parish priests to reside on their cure, and to live at the presbytery. In places where there were no presbyteries, or such as could not be occupied, the Archbishop obtained contributions from the flocks to repair the buildings, and in some cases to build fresh houses. He did the same for the residence of the Canons, for he was determined to leave his clergy no excuse for associating with lay people, nor for absenting themselves from their duties. Where the emolument received by a priest was insufficient, and there was no means of increasing it by the application of Church property, he called upon the people to come forward and enable their pastor to live in a manner befitting his sacred calling.

Property belonging to the Church was in many cases in the hands of laymen. This St. Charles required them to give up, prevailing upon them to

resign titles and other ecclesiastical revenues which
they had in their possession in contravention of the
decrees of the Council and applying them to the Church,
to which they of right belonged. Thus was the residence of the clergy enforced everywhere, so that there
was scarcely any parish, even in the remote and inaccessible districts, which had not its church and priest.
Many new parishes were formed and assistants granted
to those clergy who were overworked.

A corresponding improvement resulted in the life
and manners of the people, with a deeper appreciation
of the things of God. The practice of preaching to the
people and instructing them in the Word of God was
earnestly inculcated by the saint, together with the
frequent administration of the Sacraments, and the
observance of all the solemnities and ceremonial of the
worship of God. He was indefatigable in stirring up
the clergy to greater zeal, and he strove to enkindle in
their hearts the burning charity that filled his own
soul. He was constantly exhorting them to give due
effect to the decrees of the Council of Trent and the
provincial synods. All these labours were blessed with
great success; the people grew daily in veneration for
the things of God, and in reverence for their good
pastor and for all his wishes in their regard.

During his visit to Besozzo, which is about forty
miles from the city, St. Charles learnt that the relics of
St. Nicus were somewhere in the neighbourhood, and
that a chapel dedicated in his honour was held in
great veneration by the surrounding peasantry. The
feast of St. Nicus was always celebrated with great

solemnity on the 18th April.   The saint's body was
found in a stone coffin under the altar.   These sacred
remains were reverently gathered up and deposited
in a shrine, placed under the altar of the chapel,
which was fittingly restored.   To ensure its being
taken care of, St. Charles instituted a society of pious
men under the title of Penitents, giving them a rule
and certain religious exercises in order to keep up the
chapel.   By their devotion it has been enlarged, and
at this time has become a considerable church.

CHAPTER XII.

DURING his visitation St. Charles took especial note of the private lives of the clergy and people. He found the laity sunk in abuses of every kind, men living openly in concubinage and adultery, and thus giving great public scandal. He resolved, if possible, to change this state of things for the better, looking upon these sins as offences against the sanctity of God rather than as mere social evils. To this end he made use at first of the power of the Word of God, trying to draw sinners to repentance by remonstrance and warnings. But the evil was too deeply engrained, and too openly and persistently indulged, to yield to these measures. He was therefore obliged to resort to the courts of justice he had lately established, and to exercise his jurisdiction by committing to prison some of the more flagrant and obdurate offenders. This proceeding occasioned great excitement among the people, particularly among the rich, and the question was clamorously raised whether he was not trenching on the jurisdiction of the Crown. The long years of

party faction and civil commotion through which the
State had passed, together with the absence of the
Archbishop from his see, had caused the authority of
the Church in such matters to be forgotten, so that it
was now looked upon as an unbearable restraint upon
the liberties of the upper classes.

Some of the royal officials even considered that it
was incumbent on them to protect the subjects of his
Catholic Majesty against the lawful jurisdiction of
the Archbishop.   Herein they were instigated by the
devil, who, envious of the good done to souls, sought
by all the means in his power, to impede the work of
reform.   With a great show of zeal for the prerogatives
of their royal master, these men set themselves with
all their might against the enactments of the Cardinal.
They did not dare to issue any public mandate or edict
of contravention in regular form, on account of the
authority he wielded and the universal esteem in which
he was held for his holiness of life.   But they intimated to the officers of the Cardinal that they would
incur severe penalties if they imprisoned any more
laymen, or carried arms, which was forbidden by order
of the Governor, adding that they would not suffer the
least infringement of the royal rights.   These doings
being reported to the Cardinal, he recommended the
whole matter to God in his prayers, and, according
to the advice of men of experience, laid the matter
before the Sovereign Pontiff, undertaking to accept
whatever decision the Pope might make, in the hope
that the opposing faction would do the same.

Meanwhile he tried by persuasion to bring his opponents to an amicable settlement of the dispute. Finding, however, that they had appealed to the King, he felt bound to inform his Majesty of the reasons which had actuated him, viz., that the honour of God and the salvation of souls were his sole motives, and that he had but fulfilled the obligations of his office. To this the King replied in courteous terms, that the matter belonged entirely to the jurisdiction of the Supreme Pontiff, and that he would abide by the decision of the Holy See. This resolution he repeated to the Governor, desiring him not to encroach upon the rights of the Church whilst upholding the prerogatives of the Crown.

To the Pope, therefore, the matter was referred, and Giovanni Paolo Chiesa,[1] a senator of Milan, was deputed to represent the King. The Holy Father delegated certain Cardinals and learned Doctors to examine into the matter, and wrote to St. Charles to maintain possession of his rights until judgment should be given.

The Cardinals entered at great length into the question, and as the case appeared likely to last a considerable time, Monsignor Chiesa applied for permission to return to Milan. It was granted, and the Pope entrusted him with two Briefs to the Cardinal and the Governor, exhorting them to watch carefully and religiously over the rights of the Church.

The following is the Brief addressed to the Senate:—

---

[1] Born at Tortona 1521, a learned jurist, and long a practising lawyer, he attracted the notice of St. Pius V., and was made Apostolic Protonotary, and in 1568 Cardinal. He died 9th January 1575.

Pius V. to the Senate of Milan.

" Beloved children,—We have gladly availed ourselves of the return to Milan of your colleague, Giovanni Paolo Chiesa, to render our testimony to his diligence in your business, which, from its importance, cannot be speedily concluded. We will⁹ take care that it shall not occupy more time than necessity demands, but both sides must be maturely weighed. Meanwhile, we call upon you in the Lord, with all affection to uphold your Archbishop and the Bishops of the Province, and to assist them in the fulfilment of their pastoral office ; for nothing tends more to establish the credit of the secular power than the security and dignity of ecclesiastical jurisdiction. Whatever adds to the stability and vigour of the spiritual power strengthens the secular government; and the reverence and submission paid by princes and magistrates to ecclesiastical superiors wins the loyalty of subjects, so that it cannot be denied that ecclesiastical jurisdiction is the only firm foundation of states. Would to God that this truth were not daily proved by examples of the sad consequences resulting from the opposite policy. But your predecessors have not been wanting in their duty; on the contrary, their pious example has stirred up other cities and provinces to imitate them.

" We are moved by the paternal affection we bear you to encourage you to uphold with all your might the sacred jurisdiction of the Church ; to the end that your pastors may take heart, and render to the Lord more abundant fruits of their labours in the harvest of His flock."

This pontifical Brief was received with due honour both by Governor and Senate. It was hoped that matters might now be arranged satisfactorily, but unfortunately such was not the case. Some of the royal agents, making great account of the fact that they were in possession of authority, determined to put down the ecclesiastical court, and keep power in their own hands. All, however, were not unanimous in so novel a proceeding. There were many who would have been content to await the decision of Rome now that the appeal had been made; but the latter were not numerous enough to consider themselves safe in opposing such a delicate matter as the defence of royal prerogatives. Hesitation would be thought to savour of treason. The result was an order to Georgio Visconti, the Captain of Justice, to imprison the Bargello, or sheriff, of the Archbishop, on the charge of having borne arms contrary to the royal edict. It was hoped that this would suffice to render the person of any layman inviolate. The order was carried out in all haste. The unlucky sheriff was hung up thrice in the public square, and then driven out of the city under penalty of being sent to the galleys if he returned.

This occurrence was a fresh sorrow to the heart of the Cardinal. He beheld his authority disregarded, the sovereignty of the Apostolic See set at nought, and new impediments in the way of his reform. Nor was this all. Those very persons who should have seconded his exertions in the service of God, rose up against him, and endangered the salvation of their own souls. His faith, however, never wavered, for he trusted in God and in the goodness of his cause, and was supported by the opinions of men of piety and learning, well versed in canon and civil law. Filled with zeal which would have led him, if need were, to martyrdom in defence of the liberties of Holy Church, and strong in the conviction that he was actuated solely by his pastoral duty, the Archbishop pronounced sentence of excommunication against the captain of justice, the royal attorney-general, a notary, and the governor of the prison where his sheriff had been detained, as aiders and abettors. Without delay this sentence was published throughout the city, and a citation was affixed to the door of the Senate-house, calling upon the President and senators to show cause why the sentence should not be carried out.

The Duke of Albuquerque, the Governor, was much annoyed at the punishment inflicted on the sheriff, entirely without his cognisance. He was religiously inclined himself, and he was likewise well acquainted with the good dispositions of his royal master, who always respected the rights of the Church. His pious indignation at the occurrence was testified by his imprisonment of certain bailiffs who had taken upon themselves to tear down the notices which had been posted at the Archbishop's house, and at the churches. He also refused to admit into his presence a judge who had sent an ecclesiastic to prison because copies of the Cardinal's citation were found upon him.

The Senate denied that they had issued any order for the punishment of a sheriff of the Archbishop's tribunal, affirming that he had been punished as a transgressor of the royal proclamation, and that they were not aware that he was an officer of the Archbishop's tribunal. While making the same excuse to the Sovereign Pontiff, they laid the blame of the disturbance upon the Cardinal. The Holy Father was greatly displeased at the whole affair, and still more by the letter of the Senate to which he vouchsafed no reply, but wrote to the Duke of Albuquerque admonishing him to see that due satisfaction was made to the Church. He required also that the president of the Senate and two senators who had taken part in the act by counsel or authority, should appear at Rome within thirty days to make answer for themselves. He also by a special messenger summoned to Rome the officials whom the Cardinal had excommunicated. The papal courier arrived on 1st September, 1567, and was received with honour by the Governor, and by the Grand Chancellor of Spain, who declared that the letters of the Sovereign Pontiff should be received with the same veneration as though they came from the very hand of St. Peter. The Governor afforded every assistance in his power to the envoy, appointing his own confessor to wait on him, and furnishing him with his recommendation whenever necessary.

Hereupon the enemy of souls raised once more a storm against the saint, exciting men to assail his reputation for sanctity, so as to hinder the influence he exercised over the people for good. He was now accused of harbouring ambitious designs, and attempting to make himself master of the city. It was said that by his late measures he had been paving the way for obtaining this object, and that his reference to the Pope was only a feint for the purpose of drawing off suspicion from his own aims.

The Governor was highly incensed by these slanderous reports, for he knew that the holy Cardinal was incapable of entertaining any such idea. To testify his abhorrence of these attacks, he put under restraint a person of rank who had made himself notorious by spreading the scandal.

Conscious of his innocence, the saint pursued with patience the even tenor of his way, seeking not to justify himself, but solicitous only for the welfare of his flock. He went on with the reforms he had undertaken, and kept up the constant practice of all the functions and obligations of his office. It might well, indeed, have been a cause of discouragement to him to see that the calumnies circulated against him, impeded his efforts for good; and that many gentlemen who had formerly visited him, now held aloof. But all these things he accepted as mortifications, and purified his soul more and more in the love of God, and in detachment from the world.

The persons cited by the Sovereign Pontiff had been, in the first instance, required to present themselves in Rome within the time above named; but subsequently a later day was fixed, to admit of the arrival of the Marquis of Seralvio, who had been deputed by Philip

II. to represent him at the Papal Court, and to settle
the dispute. The Marquis arrived at Milan early in
1568, and immediately requested an audience of the
Cardinal, with whom he consulted at length upon the
matter at issue. At the commencement of the discussion, the Marquis was inclined to consider that St.
Charles had laid himself open to a charge of undue
severity, by his treatment of the senators; and that
he had been unwise in applying to the Pope, and thus
prejudicing him, instead of leaving the matter in the
hands of the King, who would have settled the difference. The Marquis considered also that his Majesty
had a right to expect that such a course would have
been taken, out of consideration for the favour he had
always shown the Cardinal, and his appreciation of his
merits, which would have led him to support his
rights to the utmost. In conclusion he begged him to
treat the affair as a loving father would, in order that
it might be brought peaceably to an end, and at least
to write to his Holiness beseeching him to recall his
citation, and thus settle the dispute without requiring
the presence of the senators at Rome.

St. Charles replied with humility and firmness that
it did not become him to interpose in the course the
Holy Father had thought proper to adopt; neither did
he see that there was any other open to him, since
grave injury had been offered to the rights of the
Church. For himself he was afraid that his Holiness
might blame him for delay in the matter. As to the
slight he was supposed to have put upon his Catholic
Majesty, this was not borne out by the fact, since,

before referring to Rome, he had patiently waited for
a long time, in the hope that his opponents might
come to a better mind.   Afterwards he had communi- ·
cated in the most conciliatory spirit with the Governor
and senators, seeking in this way to put an end to the
contradictions which had been raised against the
exercise of the power of the Church.   But all his
efforts had proved useless.   Moreover, violence had
been offered to the prerogatives, not of the See of
Milan alone, but to those of the universal Church,
and to the authority of the Supreme Pontiff.   These
outrages had rendered it necessary for him to apply
to his Holiness as the supreme Judge and Father of
the faithful.   He had not thought by this to incur
the displeasure of his Majesty, whose great qualities
he had always appreciated by submitting himself and
his concerns to him in all lawful matters, to his royal
will and pleasure.   He himself could not, however,
be expected out of gratitude to his Majesty to waive
the rights of the Church in the slightest degree.
The devotion of the King to the Church was well
known to him, and especially his consideration for
the See of Milan, as shown by his constant readiness to employ himself in her defence.   He added
that, although the advice which it had been suggested
he should offer to the Holy Father would not have
been becoming, he had written a fitting letter to the
Pope which he entrusted to the Marquis to be delivered
to his Holiness.

Letter of St. Charles to Pope Pius V.

"Most Holy Father,—It is but lately that I had occasion to give your Holiness a particular account of all things concerning the jurisdiction of the Church of Milan. I have now commissioned Monsignor Ormaneto to report what has taken place between myself and the Marquis of Seralvio, now on his way to Rome. The Marquis having urged me to write to your Holiness to arrange the dispute, and not to require the attendance of the senators who have been cited to appear in Rome, I have felt bound briefly to express my opinion, as I have already expressed it by word of mouth to the Marquis. With regard to the senators, I have only to say that I seek no redress whatever for the personal affront offered to myself. Concerning the remainder of their offence I would leave it entirely to your Holiness to do what is necessary to vindicate the majesty of the Church of which your Holiness is the head, whilst I am but one of its least members. Concerning the rights of the Church of Milan, I declare here most solemnly that I have no other desire than to preserve them in their integ-. rity, and transmit them to my successors, in order that future Archbishops may exercise their powers without let or hindrance from the secular arm. This being so, it is enough for me that I have been enabled to send your Holiness the proofs of the just rights and prerogatives of this see. Around your Holiness stand men of wisdom and sound doctrine, who took part in the Council of Trent, and have already pronounced judgment in such causes. In a word, as the Church is guided by the Holy Ghost, I can only await your decision, and hold myself in readiness to accept it as necessarily just and holy with cheerfulness and submission."

CHAPTER XIII.

1567.

IT might be thought that a matter of so great consequence as this question of ecclesiastical jurisdiction would have sufficed to engross the whole time and attention of the Cardinal, so as to have prevented his leaving the city. It was not so, however, nor did he even so much as intermit any of his usual functions, or labours for the souls of his flock. With regard to the affair that was pending, the Cardinal left all issues wholly and entirely to the decision of the Supreme Pontiff.

In the height of the dispute he went on the visitation of the three Swiss valleys which stood, he knew, in great need of his personal supervision. He started in the beginning of October 1567, when the weather is already wintry in those districts, which lie at the foot of Mount St. Gothard, which separates Italy from Germany, about a hundred miles distant from Milan. He would not defer his visit to a more favourable time of year, for he yearned after these

few sheep, among whom, for lack of episcopal supervision, Christian discipline had well nigh died out.

These three valleys, Leventina, Bregno and La
Riviera, were not altogether under Swiss dominion,
but were subject to the three cantons of Uri, Schwytz,
and Unterwalden. They had before belonged in
matters temporal as well as spiritual to four Canons
of the Church of Milan, to whom they gave the title
of Counts. They passed from their possession in the
course of a war between the Swiss and a former
Duke of Milan, who, desirous of making peace, consented to cede the rights of the Canons over them,
giving the latter in compensation certain revenues
in the territory of Castel Seprio, and allowing them
to retain ecclesiastical jurisdiction over the valleys.
Even this, however, they were unable to defend against
the pretensions of certain usurpers, and retained only
the right of nomination to benefices. The ecclesiastical
jurisdiction over this territory devolved, therefore, upon
the Cardinal, situated as it was within the confines
of his diocese. One great obstacle, however, greatly
impeded the enforcement of his discipline, viz., the
absence of representative of the temporal power for
the time being. St. Charles previously to his visitation, wrote to the authorities of the cantons, and
requested that some person furnished with necessary
credentials should be sent to co-operate, with the
power of the secular arm, in the work of reform.

The authorities were much gratified by the deference
paid them by the Cardinal, and sent envoys[1] from

[1] These were Buntineri, Rolli and Zambruni.

each canton to accompany him in his visitation, armed with due powers, and fully acquainted with the mind of those who accredited them.

Lamentable, indeed, was the state of confusion and disorder that they found. Notoriously was this the case among the clergy who, having obtained their benefices, in many instances it was to be feared, by simony, lived in the commission of many flagrant and scandalous excesses. Those who did not go to so great lengths gave themselves up to worldly business and traffic, while their churches and all that concerned divine worship were in a condition of neglect than which nothing could be worse. The most Blessed Eucharist was reserved in a way that showed they had lost all reverence for It,[1] while the other Sacraments were treated with shocking carelessness. The churches received so little attention as hardly to have any sign of the sacred purposes they ought to serve. Many sins and enormities were rife amongst the flocks of these negligent pastors. As the good shepherd went on his way discovering with his own eyes fresh proofs of these miseries, tears started from his eyes. It was some consolation to him to know that the people of these districts were extremely simple, their sins arising more from ignorance than from malice, whence he had great hope with the help of God of bringing them

---

[1] See the saint's words in Oltrocchi from a letter of his to Mgr. Ormaneto, dated 5 November, 1567. "Præterquam quod Sanctissimum Christi Corpus in pulverulentis vasibus occurrit, sordidisque theois semestri et amplius spatio ibidem neglectum, in templo quodam ad manus venit Ejusdem fragmentum carie exesum, et calice attrito partim inhærens partim linteolo, quo viso totus cohorrui."

to a better state. The overwhelming amount of work
to be done only spurred him on to greater exertions,
as he yielded to no difficulty and shrunk from no
fatigue in penetrating to every spot, however wild
and unapproachable, travelling sometimes on foot
over mountains and valleys and almost inaccessible
tracks. Even the natives were struck with astonishment at the hardships he cheerfully underwent and
the austere life he led, sleeping upon hard boards and
living upon their own coarse food, from all of which
he might have been dispensed in so arduous an undertaking.

Great however was the reward of his labour. He
gradually brought back the clergy to a better way,
and worked a marked reform in the lives of the people,
confirming them in the profession of the faith in which
many had begun to waver. The decorum of public
worship was restored, and the spiritual authority of
the Archbishop was acknowledged throughout the valleys, with the full consent of the temporal lords, who
were completely won by his fatherly counsels. On
one occasion when these envoys remarked that they
left everything in his hands as a tribute to his goodness and sanctity, he bade them remember it was not
to himself they should make the offering, but to God
and His Church. A good impression was made upon
all by the liberality with which he bore all the expenses
of the journey, including those of the envoys and their
attendants.

On the completion of the visitation, the Cardinal
assembled the clergy of the district he had traversed,

and impressed upon them both in his own words and those of others, the obligation they were under of living holily, and guiding their flocks in the true way of eternal life, calling upon them with great earnestness to turn over a new leaf, and obey the laws of the Church.

It would be impossible to speak adequately of the light and life infused into all who took part in these meetings.   Greater weight, moreover, was given to the words of the Cardinal, by one of the Swiss envoys, who, in the name of the government, said that they were quite sensible that they had been to blame in suffering the secular power to exercise authority over ecclesiastics; he submitted, however, that they had been forced to this in a measure by the bad lives of the priests, and by the neglect of former Archbishops to correct such flagrant scandals, or to look after the poor people of these distant valleys.   That this would no longer be the case he was assured, for not only had the sacred Council of Trent been held, but its decrees had been received, and ought to be observed by all. They were therefore resolved to submit themselves entirely to the Cardinal, their Archbishop, who was their only rightful pastor and ruler.

To crown all his labours, the clergy were called upon publicly to receive the Tridentine' Decrees, as well as those of his provincial and diocesan synod, each making his profession of faith accordingly.

When taking leave of the people, the Archbishop gratefully thanked the envoys for the attention they had rendered him throughout the journey.   In separate letters to each of the authorities of the cantons, he expressed the same sentiments, pointing out also that they were not to interfere with the people in matters of faith. The friendship thus begun was continued and strengthened throughout succeeding years. The rulers for their part, lent their whole authority to his measures for the propagation of the faith, and the salvation of souls. With the consent of the Sovereign Pontiff, he admitted six youths from these districts into his seminary, in order to strengthen this good-will, and on his return to Milan, sent them several good priests, who by preaching the Word of God, and the due administration of the Sacraments, gave the assistance that was so much needed by these poor sheep of the flock.

CHAPTER XIV.

REFORM OF THE FRATI UMILIATI AND OF THE CONVENTUALS AND OBSERVANTINES OF THE ORDER OF ST. FRANCIS.

1567.

As we have already mentioned, St. Charles was the Protector of the community of the Frati Umiliati, or Brethren of Humility, and as such he carefully watched over them, and others committed to his charge by the Holy See.

The Umiliati had in many particulars departed from the regulations of their institute, and were especially neglectful of the rule of community life.

The Order was originally founded by some Milanese gentlemen in thanksgiving for their release from a long captivity under the Emperor Conrad, or according to others, Frederic Barbarossa. They resolved to have all things in common, and adopted the rule of St. Benedict.

For a long time they lived in exact observance of community life, and regular discipline flourished among them, their numbers and wealth increasing in the course of time.

But after a while discipline began to be relaxed, the practice of having private property crept in, and increased by little and little, until at last the superiors of monasteries, who had the title of Provosts, made themselves masters of the whole temporalities of the community, becoming mere titled dignitaries.   Considering themselves to be proprietors instead of stewards and administrators of the revenues, they left for the maintenance of the brethren a modicum which was barely sufficient for this purpose.   They renounced the office at will, as if it had been a mere titular benefice, in favour of their own nominees.   Hence arose a multitude of abuses.   The superior was loth to diminish his gains, and consequently opposed the increase of the number of the brethren.   Worse than this, persons addicted to vice were admitted into the Order who were quite unfit for it, and the superiors squandered the ample means at their disposal in licentious living, like men of the world, many of them devoting themselves to the pleasures of the chase and to profane pastimes, to the great scandal of the people. Thus, perforce, they shut their eyes to the infraction of the rule among the brethren, just as if exact observance had altogether died out.

Filled with grief at the sight of these poor souls thus blindly wandering along the road that leads to perdition, St. Charles resolved to lose no time in restoring them to their primitive observance.   To this object he had directed the attention of Monsignor Ormaneto, when he sent him to Milan during the pontificate of Pius IV., directing him to hold a Chapter of the Order and to impose certain regulations for the correction of abuses. A stronger hand, however, was needed in order to eradicate the evil. The Cardinal, therefore, begged for the assistance of the Holy See. His intention was to commence the reform by depriving the heads of the Order of all claim to the possession of private property, by putting an end to the practice of making their position of superior a titular dignity to be held in perpetuity. The next step was the foundation of a novitiate for the training of postulants in the true spirit of the institute and the observance of exact discipline. These two points he considered as the basis in all reforms of religious orders.

St. Charles obtained from his Holiness two Briefs, the first of which empowered him to apply the tithes of the revenues of all superiors of houses to the purpose of founding a novitiate ; and the second conferred on him the authority of Apostolic Delegate, enabling him to make any provision he deemed necessary for the well-being of the various houses he wished to reform. The Archbishop foresaw only too plainly that he would meet with opposition in the course of these measures.

At a Chapter of the Fathers held at Cremona, St. Charles published this second Brief, of which no intimation had as yet been given. So much prudence directed his measures at this Chapter, that by the grace of God a good reform was effected. The right of private property was forbidden to the superiors of the different houses of the Order, and it was decreed that henceforward the revenues should be held in common amongst all the brethren. The superiors were to be elected by the suffrages of the community, and the office to be held for three years only at a time. The practice of electing superiors for life was abolished. At the same time St. Charles confirmed a Superior-General of the Order, who was to hold his office only for a certain term of years, and made other rules in order to renew the ancient fervour of the brethren. These constitutions gave great satisfaction to the majority, who seemed at first disposed to adopt them. But some superiors, led by self-interest and unmindful of the grace they would have gained by obedience, opposed St. Charles step by step with the determination of regaining their former position. They petitioned the Holy Father, and endeavoured to induce influential persons to recognise the abuse that had, they averred, been committed in thus depriving them of their property.

St. Charles met all this clamour with unalterable firmness. He overcame their opposition according as it arose in various ways; and he resolutely enforced observance of his decrees. The heads of houses were thus reduced to silence, though not to submission. The devil, with his accustomed malice, took occasion of their evil dispositions to excite them to the commission of the outrage which we shall have occasion to relate.

St. Charles was also Protector of the Franciscan Order. It received no small share of his attention and solicitude, so widely spread and beneficial as it was to the Church at large. The different reforms which had been effected from time to time in various places had divided this Order into Conventuals and Observantines. In some of the principal houses of the Conventuals the custom of private property had been introduced, and had almost banished holy poverty, the mainstay and anchor of the Order. This abuse prevailed to such an extent that some of the religious, arrogating to themselves a certain authority or superiority over the others, lived apart from them in houses of their own, fitted up with every comfort and luxury. St. Charles lost no time in bringing them back to their ancient observance, and was assisted in his labours by Cardinal Alessandro Crivelli, whom he made Vice-Protector of the Order in Rome. The latter appointed certain of the most exemplary and zealous among the Fathers to visit all their houses, and reform them according as they found need. None are indeed so well able to conduct a reform as those who, having lived under the rule, are necessarily the best informed as to its need of correction, and the proper way of effecting it.

The Cardinal found that amongst certain brethren of the Observantines a spirit of private property had made considerable way. Its consequence was that in this way they made parties and influenced the elections to offices.

Being thus surrounded by their own creatures, disunion and jealousy began to be rife among the members of the community. It would often happen that superiors were elected to please a faction, without any regard to merit or fitness, and thus quite unsuitable for their work, and incapable of maintaining order and obedience, their only object being to promote the interests of their own favourites and adherents.   As a natural consequence relaxation of discipline followed, and the community began to decay.   Laying the pruning-knife to the root of the evil, St. Charles forbade all private property, and removed the most factious and influential heads of houses to remote and insignificant communities, thus putting an end to party spirit.

It had happened some time previously that a good religious of the Order, a native of Lisbon named Amadeo, lamenting the too evident relaxation of fervour, had begun a reform.   Not finding himself equal to the task of bringing the whole body back to a strict observance of the rule, he withdrew from them with several others of his own way of thinking, and formed a separate community, which took the name of Amedei,[1] owning, however, obedience to the same superiors as the others.   For a little while these brethren went on well, but as human nature is ever prone to evil, needing a resolute grasp to keep it continually in check, before very long their fervour waned, and they became only distinguished from the rest by an abnormal separation from the body of which they had been members.   This disunion, utterly contrary to the spirit of religious brethren, very naturally brought forth a multitude of scandals.

[1] The Amedei were a branch of the Franciscans established in Italy, calling themselves, after their founder, "lovers of God." St. Pius V. in 1566 united twenty-eight of their monasteries to the general body of the Order, but some houses by permission adopted the Cistercian rule.

Another breach in the Order had been made by some brethren who called themselves Chiareni.[1]

St. Charles took counsel with the Holy Father, and obtained a Brief empowering him to unite these two branches with the body. He convoked a congregation for the purpose at Milan, in the Monastery of Our Lady of Peace, one of their chief houses, and explained to them the purport of the Brief, and the measures he intended to adopt in the exercise of his faculties. The brethren, however, were most strenuously opposed to the union, and as if excited by an evil spirit, set themselves clamorously against him. The bells were rung, as a sort of declaration of war; many, indeed, were quite prepared to lay hands upon the Cardinal, had he taken definite action. Perceiving their distress, the saint withdrew, and with his usual patience postponed carrying out his reforms until such time as they had recovered from their excitement, his resolution to do what behoved him as a just and faithful protector of the Order remaining unchanged; viz., to reunite the scattered members to the parent stock, and to abolish the divisions of Amedei and Chiareni. Nor was his intention modified in the least by the interposition of princes and other persons of influence.

When it was a question of punishing the authors of the tumult, though their want of respect for the authority of the Sovereign Pontiff in his own person, as their

[1] The Chiareni, so called from Chiarena, a stream of the March of Ancona, where Brother Angelo founded a Franciscan community, subject to the Bishop of the diocese, in 1302. Some houses in 1472 joined the Observantines, and in 1510 and 1566 the rest were united to the same branch of the Order.

Protector had been open and inexcusable, the saint, with characteristic mildness, so far from chastising them according to their deserts, interceded for them with the Holy Father, and obtained a free pardon for them.

Note on p. 181.—The Frati Umiliati.

The brethren of this Order, who were at this time only about a hundred and sixty in number all told, were in possession of upwards of ninety-four houses, each of which could accommodate a hundred brethren, but often two would occupy a whole house.

P. 183.—A Chapter of the Fathers.

This Chapter was held in May 1567, and at the suggestion of the saint, the Father Luigi Bascapè was chosen General.

CHAPTER XV.

1568.

DURING the first years of the pontificate of Pius V.,
a great scandal arose in consequence of the heretical
doctrines of a certain preacher at Mantua. When the
Father Inquisitor proceeded, in accordance with the
duties of his office, to take steps against the offender,
the miserable man incited the people to active resistance, in the course of which two Dominican religious
were killed.

The Holy Father was deeply grieved at this lamentable occurrence, not only on account of the insult
offered to the Holy Office, and the apostolic authority,
but also for the loss of so many souls. Fearful lest
the fire of heresy would spread far and wide, and
involve Italy in a conflagration, he saw that prompt
measures alone would stop it, and that Cardinal Borromeo was of all men the one most fitted for the task.
As he had seen proofs of the judgment and prudence
of St. Charles, joined to zeal and capacity for the

successful conduct of affairs, when he carried on the
government of the Church under Pius IV.; his Holiness lost no time in conferring ample powers upon
the saint to enable him to overcome this attack of
the evil one.   Overwhelmed as he was with press of
business, St. Charles accepted the new burden without
hesitation, in a spirit of ready compliance with the wishes
of the Pontiff.   Notwithstanding the urgency of the case,
he thought it necessary solemnly to commend the matter
to God in the Forty Hours' prayer before the Blessed
Sacrament, after the example of the primitive Church.
In February 1568, he reached Mantua, and by his
wisdom and prudence entirely convinced the accused
of their errors, so that without further controversy they
abjured their heresy, with the vindication of the authority of the Holy Office and punishment of the offenders.
The citizens returned thanks to God for having sent them
an angel to deliver them from the peril with which
they had been menaced; while the Holy Father and
Sacred College could not refrain from testifying their
appreciation of the Cardinal's prudence.

So highly did the Pope value the capacity shown by
St. Charles in this emergency that he entrusted him
with another mission.   A certain religious house had
become infected with heretical tenets.   Several of the
community who had been previously leading careless
lives, devoid of the spirit of their institute, had not
only themselves fallen a prey to the infection, but had
carried it into other parts of Italy.   As the contagion
was spreading from day to day, St. Charles, armed
with full powers, set himself vigorously to suppress the

evil. Obtaining information of the secret haunts of heresy, he imprisoned its chief abettors in order to give them an opportunity of acknowledging their folly, and to prevent them bringing others to similar destruction. Within a short space of time the danger was averted without any disturbance.

Thus did the servant of God deliver Italy, under Divine Providence, from the destructive ravages of heresy that threatened to blight the harvest of the Faith.

Note on p. 189.—A certain preacher.

This was one Francesco Callaria of Lacchiarella, in the diocese of Milan. By order of St. Pius V. he was taken to Rome, where he was tried and condemned. See Catena's life of St. Pius V.

P. 190.—A certain religious house.

Peter Martyr Vermiglio, of the Regular Lateran Canons, was here the stumbling-block on which fell his brethren Celso Martinengo of Brescia and Girolamo Zanchi of Bergamo, and others.

CHAPTER XVI.

1568.

THE intervals of leisure between the important matters which took him away from the diocese were employed by St. Charles in the spiritual concerns of his soul. He went through the spiritual exercises according to his annual custom, and he also made a general confession of the sins of his whole life to Alessandro Sauli,[1] one of the Regular Clerks of St. Paul, provost of St. Barnabas in Milan. St. Charles held this priest in the highest esteem, and set great store by his counsels, to which he often had recourse. He afterwards spoke of this retreat as the beginning of his spiritual life, counting as nothing all that he had hitherto done.

The great success of all the undertakings of the Saint gave much pleasure to the Holy Father, and he spoke of his merit to the Sacred College of Cardinals. In a letter addressed to Cardinal Giovanni Battista

[1] Afterwards made Bishop of Aleria, then of Pavia; beatified by Benedict XIV.

Cigala, the Pope says of him that he knew no Prelate so diligent in all things concerning the honour and service of God, nor so resolute in maintaining the liberties of the Church and the authority of the Apostolic See. The Pope frequently expressed a wish that the Church had half-a-dozen such Cardinals, and used to propose him as a model to the other members of the Sacred College. When he desired to stir them up to any great work, or to draw their attention to any defect, the Holy Father would say, " Only copy Cardinal Borromeo." Although the Cardinal was under thirty years of age, such was the confidence of the Pope in his wisdom, that he entrusted him with matters of the first importance.

But four months had elapsed since he left his diocese, and yet the heart of the good pastor yearned to return to his flock. He petitioned the Sovereign Pontiff to release him from further engagements, urging the need of his presence at home, more especially because it was necessary to hold another diocesan Synod. He added that his absence was doing harm, inasmuch as evil-minded persons misinterpreted the continual business which kept him away to be but a pretext for not returning at all. This tended to chill the earnestness of the good, and to harden sinners in their licentious courses.

The Holy Father, respecting his scruples, granted the permission he sought, so that he returned to Milan in June, 1568, and was received with joy by his delighted people. Without any loss of time, he at once began to prepare for holding his diocesan synod, which he fixed for the fourth day of August. One of his chief reasons for summoning it was his wish to repair the shortcomings which his late visitation had made manifest.

As this was the first diocesan synod held by him since the celebration of his first provincial council, he ordered its decrees to be read, as binding the clergy. Many other measures were also enacted for the reform of the diocese, all of which are comprised in the " Acts of the Church of Milan."

As the saint was always careful to perform every action pertaining to the service of God with scrupulous punctuality and order, so was he wont to bestow more than ordinary care upon the celebration of his synods, and affirmed that they were most powerful means of restoring discipline and divine worship, and preserving the purity of Faith unscathed. In order to make his pastoral solicitude better understood, we will take this opportunity of explaining his method of holding these synods.

Before opening them he was careful to have information of all irregularities and want of proper order, by means of the visitations he had made in person and by his deputies, especially the congregation of the sixty rural deans of the diocese and the six prefects of the city, held every year. This meeting was always held early in January, and the priests attending it were required to have visited their districts and deaneries previously, and to have noted down all defects and shortcomings. The session of this congregation lasted many days, and served as a preparation for the synod which was to follow. A detailed account of all that had been reported was then made out, after which they proceeded maturely to consider the various measures proposed. It was the constant wish of the Cardinal that each person should be free to make any suggestion he thought proper; and when all had spoken, he selected what he deemed the best counsel, and committed it to writing. To facilitate this arrangement, each person was furnished with a desk and writing materials, so that they might note down the various difficulties that were brought forward, and the remedies suggested. On these occasions the rural deans lived in the Archbishop's house at his expense, the congregation never breaking up under a fortnight or three weeks, or at least until effectual measures had been taken for the furtherance of Christian life and the reform of abuses.

Two other important benefits resulted from these congregations. The points so minutely discussed served not only as matter for the decrees to be made, but also elicited from him pastoral letters and counsel most beneficial to the souls under his care. The discourses and opinions enunciated at these meetings were of the utmost value to the various priests who assisted thereat, forming them in discipline, and giving them useful suggestions for the management of their parishes. They received illumination also by the wisdom of the Cardinal and his faithful attention to the guidance of the Holy Ghost, which enabled him to solve perplexing difficulties which were beyond the scope of ordinary understandings.

One of his clergy declared that he had learnt more at one of these congregations than from many years' study.

This was his first preparation for the Council. As the time drew near, he called upon the clergy and people throughout the diocese to make instant prayer and frequent processions to implore the assistance of the Holy Spirit. The saint had the most entire trust in the power of prayer to draw down the Divine blessing, and hence he exhorted all to go to Confession and Communion with this intention. His own indefatigable labours in his humility he considered as nothing beside the prayers of fervent priests in the holy sacrifice of the Mass.

Just before the Council, two congregations were held in his presence of all the urban and diocesan visitors. In these meetings the form and order to be observed in the sessions of the Council was settled, and the officers elected. The clergy were informed where they were to lodge, as they were forbidden to stay at inns. The Cardinal made provision in his own house for those who came from a distance, and for all poor priests. A certain number of ecclesiastics were deputed to keep order and watch over the due observance of the prescribed regulations. In short, every possible provision for all cases was made at this congregation, so that there was not the smallest matter which was not done according to rule. The result was that the synods were always conducted with decorum and gave great edification to all.

On the day fixed for the Council, the clergy went in

procession to the church of St. Ambrose. All knew their own place, for each member of the Chapter and each head of a parish had the image of the holy Patron of his church placed over the seat he was to occupy. Tables of directions were posted about in different places, enjoining silence and gravity whilst falling into order. The Cardinal then sang the pontifical Mass which opened the session of the Council, and watched continually over all, for their edification and spiritual advantage. Not content with attending to the ordinary objects of a synod, making enactments and passing decrees, he was earnestly solicitous for the advancement of his clergy in piety and devotion, and directed all his efforts to increasing in them the love of God and zeal for the salvation of souls, knowing from experience that the spiritual well-being of the flock depends on the holiness of the clergy. The session of the Council was looked upon by him as a harvest-time wherein he laboured to gather fruit by his counsels and admonitions. His burning zeal gave life and warmth to all. Sometimes he would give private advice according to the circumstances of each; and at other times, would instruct them from the pulpit with the authority of a pastor. His discourses were full of the unction of the Holy Spirit and models of sound doctrine. He spoke so fervently and pierced the hearts of his hearers that they were completely carried out of themselves, and rapt, as it were, into heaven. I myself can bear witness to these workings of the Spirit in my heart and in my brethren at these meetings. His discourses touched with compunction and quickened all in the desire of well-doing. On each of the three days of the synod he preached two sermons, one after the Mass, with a gospel appropriate to the synod; the second at the opening of the session after dinner.

The laity were always rigorously excluded, in order that he might confer with his clergy more freely upon their failings. He desired each priest to say Mass every day, but when this was not possible through lack of time or of altars, he exhorted them at least to go to communion at his Mass, that each might be rendered more fit for the indwelling of the Spirit of God and receive the abundance of His grace. Though the fervent prayers and the public ceremonies fostered a great spirit of devotion among all, yet it was the presence and personal influence of the saintly Cardinal himself which filled up all that was wanting. Always composed, placid, and full of fervour, his union with God never for one moment interrupted, he was seen among his clergy like a burning light illuminating and kindling all with heavenly radiance.

The attention of the Cardinal was by no means confined to interior matters. He made a careful scrutiny during the session of the synod into all particulars of the condition, office, and obligations of each member. The prefects of the clergy were charged to examine even into their dress, to take particular notice of the bearing and demeanour of each, so that there should be nothing, however trivial, contravening the decrees or unbecoming to their clerical character, according to the holy Council of Trent.

The clergy habited in cassocks, closely shaven, and of grave deportment, presented the appearance of an assembly of religious brethren; so that the people conceived much veneration for the ecclesiastical state from which they had formerly shrunk, on account of the corruption and depravity that had abounded.

At the close of the synod copies of certain prayers, recommending to God the various necessities of the Church, were distributed among the clergy to be used in their churches on all festivals. Before the final dispersion, all who desired it were admitted to an audience of the Cardinal, who devoted several days to giving spiritual counsel and advice to each individual, according to his needs.

No wonder was it that each of these favoured priests went to his home refreshed and invigorated in interior spirit, and filled with the determination to lead a holy life entirely devoted to his flock. No account henceforward was taken of any difficulty in the path of duty, and no obstacle was suffered to interfere with the execution of his decrees.

Such were the fruits of his synods, the most efficacious means employed by the saint in the reform of his diocese.

Note on p. 195.—Lived in the Archbishop's house.

Possevino in his life of the saint tells us that he was accustomed to entertain at bed and board more than two hundred of his priests at these times.

CHAPTER XVII.

1568.

DURING this year St. Charles brought to completion a work commenced at Milan twelve months previously. A number of fallen women had been gathered together by a charitable Spanish lady, Isabella di Aragona, some time before this. She received those who had no other shelter into a hired house under her management. On her death St. Charles took up the work, and to give it greater stability and order, committed the charge of it to a company of religious women, twelve in number, of the third Order of St. Francis, and gave them the church and presbytery of St. Benedict in which to carry it on, and bought the next house to it for their own abode. As the parish of St. Benedict was but a small one, he suppressed it, and united it to the adjacent parish of St. Peter.

These two houses afforded ample accommodation for the new institute, and enabled him to establish a regular enclosure. He gave it the name of " House of Succour," because it was intended for the succour of unhappy women who, having fallen into sin, had no place whither they could flee for protection.

This work caused him a considerable outlay, not only in adapting the building, but also in providing the inmates with necessary maintenance. For their permanent support he assigned a regular monthly alms chargeable upon his own income, besides occasional donations as needed, and a certain fixed sum which he had set aside from the first for this purpose. Ever intent on the welfare of his flock, this house and its inmates were not forgotten by the Cardinal, even when he was absent on the business committed to him by the Holy Father. It was indeed at that time that he drew up a rule for the government of the community, which he sent to the committee of its temporal administration, together with a letter dated 10th May, 1568, recommending this foundation to them in terms of most paternal charity.

After his return to Milan and completion of the business of the second diocesan synod, he gave this rule to the religious in charge of the institute, and wrote them a letter on the observance of it, dated the 24th September following. This rule directed that the persons to be admitted into the House of Succour were to be, first, women who had fallen into sin; secondly, those who, having contracted unsuitable marriages, could not live with their husbands; and thirdly, those who were destitute of suitable protection, and in danger of losing their honour or their livelihood. It was provided that those who composed the first class should be admonished by their confessor,

and by the nuns, in all charity, to sincere repentance
for the past, in order that they might ultimately enter
some convent of penitents, or lead virtuous lives according to their station in the world. Those of the
second class were to be received till such time as they
should be reconciled with their husbands, and the
spiritual directors and others were exhorted to use
their best endeavours to bring about this end. Those
of the third class were not to be suffered to depart
until some permanent provision had been made for
their future security. This good work has continued
to this time, and has rescued many souls from peril
and ruin. There are seldom less than eighty women
at a time in the House, all of whom are governed
according to the rule laid down by the Cardinal.

His chief care after the close of the Council was to
continue the visitation of the diocese, especially in the
remote parts and the borders, where heresy abounded.
In several of these localities he found the people so
neglected that they were little better than savages, and
he had to undergo a vast amount of labour in striving
to imbue them with his spirit, and bring them back to
the way of salvation from which they had grievously
strayed. The priests in these parts gave great scandal
by their lives. Many who had the cure of souls could
not say the words of absolution in the sacrament of
penance, and were not acquainted with the cases in
which absolution was reserved to the Pope or the
Bishop. Some even never went to confession themselves, and used to give themselves up without remorse

to every kind of vice. Their people again were so ignorant that some hardly knew how to make the sign of the cross.

The heart of the pastor was wounded at the misery he was called upon to witness, but far from despairing, he set to work like a diligent husbandman to eradicate vice and to sow the seed of a sound knowledge of the things of God. Regardless of trouble and peril, as he travelled from place to place, on one occasion he met with the following accident. Coming to the Introzzo mountain on the borders of the Valtellina, he was stopped by a torrent, much swollen and rendered almost impassable by the late heavy rains. A sturdy mountaineer, Domenico Vallinello by name, offered to carry him across on his back. On reaching the middle of the stream, however, the courage of this man forsook him, and dropping his burden he took to his heels with all speed from fear of punishment. It was thought that nothing less than a miracle could have rescued the Cardinal from the midst of the rushing waters, encumbered as he was by his long cassock. He got to the other side, however, in safety, having to walk a quarter of a mile in his wet clothes before reaching an inn. There he had the runaway brought before him, when instead of a punishment, he thanked him and gave him a crown piece. The memory of this incident is still preserved by the name of " Valle del Cardinale " given to the place where it occurred.

During this visitation he came across several con-

vents of nuns in which discipline had become greatly
relaxed, causing much scandal. He made several attempts to restore strict observance, but without effect.
There remained no alternative but to suppress these
communities and distribute the nuns among better-
regulated convents.

There were some cases of misconduct that called
for especial correction, impertinent and opprobrious
language being addressed to the Cardinal by some
unhappy women, to whose insults he turned a deaf
ear in his solicitude for the honour of God and the
salvation of their souls. His corrective discipline was
not confined to the nuns alone, but was exercised
also upon ill-conditioned persons who were in the
habit of visiting these convents, to the scandal of the
people. The blessing of God rested upon these
labours, and they bore fruit in the rescue of those
poor nuns who had been running blindly along the
broad road to perdition.

An incident must here be mentioned which occurred
at Monza, in the visitation of a convent of nuns at
that place. An evil spirit had for some time past
annoyed the inmates of the convent of St. Catharine,[1]
molesting them in all their occupations, disturbing
them in the dormitory at night, following them by day
into their work-room, and snatching their materials
from their hands. The continuance of this annoyance
became very wearying, the more so that there seemed
no way of escape from it. At this visitation he was

---

[1] United by the saint to the convent of St. Martin.

made acquainted with full details of their distress, and they begged him to give his blessing to the house, as they judged that his sanctity would be sufficient to drive away the evil spirit. The saint readily complied with their petition, whereupon the annoyance ceased.

CHAPTER XVIII.

April 1569.

ONE of the provisions of the Council of Trent was that
Metropolitans should hold a Council of the Bishops in
their province every three years.   At the expiration of
this period, St. Charles convened his second Provincial
Council, held on the 24th April, 1569, and delayed
till after Easter with the permission of the Sovereign
Pontiff.   All the Bishops who had assisted at the first
Council were convened on this occasion, and its decrees
are preserved in the printed collection of the " Acts of
the Church of Milan."

It may not be out of place here to give a brief
account of the method and order he was wont to
observe in the celebration of these Councils, especially in his latter years, as additional evidence of his
unwearying and tender care for his flock.   No sooner
had he closed the session of one Council than he commenced preparing the matter of the next.   This he
did by examining the note-books kept for this purpose,
recording all the wants of his province and each bishopric

in it. More than this, in his paternal solicitude he
was at pains to procure information concerning the
life and administration of the Bishops, of which he
made use when the time came for holding the Council. He likewise recommended each Bishop to depute
two prelates to visit their respective dioceses, and make
a report of abuses and irregularities. These were to be
referred to the deliberation of the Bishops to whom they
were to make their report.

Through all these channels St. Charles learnt many
facts, which enabled him to form a tolerably correct
opinion of the condition and needs of each diocese.
These formed the groundwork of the decrees proposed.
Thus by these means, and by the light with which he
was favoured by God, he was enabled to discern the
remedies for disorders, and to put an end to numbers
of abuses. In difficult cases also, he used to make
trial in his own diocese of the remedy that occurred
to him, and if he found it to work successfully, he
prevailed on the Bishops to make use of the same
throughout the province by a conciliar decree.

It was his custom to spend several days in retirement to prepare for the work of the Council when the
year came round. In this retreat he was joined by
men of experience in such affairs, with whom he
conferred upon the matters to be discussed, and drew
up decrees in proper form and order. Two months
before the time for the Council, he gave notice to the
Bishops and all who who were to take part in it,
including the synodal visitors, and two Canons from
each cathedral Chapter. For this purpose he sent

round an ecclesiastical notary, so that all might be at
Milan by the appointed day.   Most exact himself, the
Archbishop required the punctual attendance at his
Council of all his suffragans, even though they were
Cardinals, unless really prevented by some legitimate
impediment.   His single-mindedness in this respect
was strikingly shown in the following occurrence :—

A Cardinal [1] of high position, Bishop of a see in the
province of St. Charles, happened to be at Milan at the
time of a provincial Council.   A notice to attend was
sent to him, as to the other Bishops.   He sought, however, to excuse himself on the plea that he was about to
repair to Rome.   St. Charles, knowing that the journey
could very well be deferred, reminded him of the express
direction of the Council of Trent requiring his attendance at the Council.   His representations having no
effect upon the Cardinal, who continued his preparations for departure, St. Charles sent Monsignor Caesar
Speciano, his vicar-general, to remind him that he was
bound by order of the Holy See to take part in the
deliberations of the Council.   The Cardinal was thus
obliged to submit, to his great mortification.   Had
St. Charles been inclined to truckle to the laxity of
great men, he might have found abundant reasons for
winking at the absence of this Cardinal, besides that
immediately suggested by his dignity.   But it was not
so.   His mind was firmly set on promoting the glory
of God, and the welfare of Holy Church, and he would
not excuse himself from the requirements of duty
with any unworthy pretext.

[1] The Cardinal of St. George, Bp. of Novara, Giov. Ant°. Serbelloni.

Another Prelate of his province wished to absent himself from the Council, alleging that he was bound to attend to the affairs of a certain prince, being indeed at that moment engaged as an ambassador on his behalf. St. Charles, who objected to the practice of Bishops taking part in secular matters without an express permission from the Sovereign Pontiff, would not receive this excuse, but took the opinions of the assembled Bishops upon the mode of treating the defaulter. The result was that he was cited to appear at the Council, in obedience to the Tridentine decrees. The Prelate was unable to resist this formal summons, and accordingly repaired in haste to Milan. The Cardinal received him with open arms, and explained to him in the most affectionate terms the necessity under which he lay of doing his duty by the Apostolic See, and his Metropolitan Church. In this manner the saint so completely won him over that he gave up all participation in secular affairs, and resided at his see, at least during the remainder of the episcopate of St. Charles.

On the occasion of holding a Council, he used to invite three Bishops of his province to deliver a sermon, assigning a separate day and subject to each. At the same time he addressed a pastoral letter to all the Bishops, to be read to their people, in order to stir them up to make preparation on their part for the Council by prayer, processions, good works, and the reception of the Holy Sacraments of Confession and Communion, as he wished all to take part in invoking the help of God on the work. In his own church he was still more zealous. It was his practice to make a retreat of several days before the day fixed for the Council. This time was spent in devout communing with God, in spiritual exercises, prayer and contemplation, accompanied by fasts, disciplines and vigils. It was his custom to allow himself about four hours' repose at night, but on these occasions he retrenched even from this, and spent nearly the whole night in prayer. It was his wish that all should receive Holy Communion for his intention on the Sunday before the appointed day. A plenary indulgence having been obtained was granted to all who, having confessed and communicated, should visit the Metropolitan church, and pray for the success of the Council. The day of this general Communion was also set apart for the devotion of the Forty Hours in the same church, as capable of containing a larger number, in order that their prayers might be offered with greater fervour. All the chapters of the city clergy attended as distinct bodies, and the different religious orders and parochial clergy had hours assigned to each. Every hour there was a sermon from the pulpit, to enkindle devotion and fervour in their petitions. To ensure the hour of prayer being kept up during the whole time the Session lasted, he prescribed the time at which it should be taken up by each church. Besides all this, a continual succession of visits was kept up at the seven privileged churches, and for this purpose on each day the Council sat, a particular hour was assigned to each of the parishes of the city, in order that the faithful of the same might go thither in procession with their clergy and banners. All superiors, chapters, and rectors of the churches throughout the city and diocese were also to institute a procession on the Sunday to invoke the assistance of the saints, and all priests had to say the Mass of the Holy Ghost, or at least the Collect belonging to it, every Thursday for this intention.

Before the arrival of the Bishops, the Cardinal was wont to hold one or more congregations of the clergy, at which he arranged all necessary matters concerning the celebration of the Council. Among these matters was the mode of receiving the Bishops and others who attended. Apartments in the Archbishop's palace were allotted to them and to their retinue; and each was provided for in accordance with his rank and position at the expense of the Cardinal. All was done with such order and propriety that, notwithstanding due economy was observed, all bore witness that they were as well cared for as when at home.

When they drew near the city, he sent his Vicar-general and others to meet them at the distance of about three miles from the walls with mules laden with everything necessary for their solemn entry. This they did by his desire, giving their blessing to the people who thronged the roads as they passed. They were then conducted to the cathedral, where they were met by the Canons, who preceded them to the High Altar. Here they spent a short time in prayer before the Blessed Sacrament, returning, accompanied in the same manner, by the door at which they had entered.

When all the Bishops had arrived, four congregations of Theologians, Canonists, Ecclesiastical rites
and ceremonies, and of conventual discipline were
formed.   The Cardinal was surrounded in this way
by the most eminent men in the province, for he
had requested each Bishop to bring with him the two
ecclesiastics of his diocese most skilled in theology
and discipline.   Two or three Bishops were deputed
to preside over each congregation : they were to be
present at the deliberations held every day upon the
different matters before the Synod.   When each
subject had been maturely discussed and put to the
vote, St. Charles proposed it to a secret congregation of Bishops who held two sessions in the day.
After they had again sifted and passed them by
common consent, the decrees were drawn up and read
before the public congregations held the day before
the synodal session.   When these decrees had received
the assent of all the Bishops they were reckoned to
have passed, and were promulgated on the following
day by receiving once more the consent and approba-
tion of the Bishops in the session held in the metropolitan church.   If it happened that any of the
matters proposed by the Cardinal were not agreeable to
the Bishops, he would put them by for another time, as
conscious by interior light that such measures, though
misjudged now, would one day be properly appreciated.
In subsequent councils they were again brought forward, and were always ultimately accepted.   As time
went on, the Bishops recognised more clearly the necessity for his reforms and were consequently more ready

to adopt them. Their experience of his wisdom deepened year by year, and this, added to their own increased regularity of conduct, made them ready to further all his measures for the good of the province. In his latter years indeed, they were content to submit entirely to his judgment.

The deliberations of the Council were interspersed with sermons and addresses in Latin, delivered by the Cardinal himself or by one of the Bishops, on the importance and fruit of the work in hand. The Bishops and their households were enjoined to fast on the day preceding the opening of the Council that they might be the better fitted to receive the grace of God.

While these solemn exercises were taking place in the Council, in the cathedral three sermons a week by able preachers drew a large concourse of people. Twice a day there were lectures in the Archbishop's chapel, in the morning on ecclesiastical discipline, in the afternoon on the Psalms. These services were for the benefit of the clergy and others who came with the Bishops, as a preservative against idleness or unprofitable intercourse with seculars in the city. Every evening prayers were said in common in the same chapel, with music, and the points of the meditation for the next morning were read, all the Bishops attending together with the Cardinal. St. Charles also made a practice of seeing each Bishop in private, and made the most minute inquiries concerning the conduct of his affairs, private, domestic and diocesan. He inquired more particularly as to the acceptance in

their several sees of the decrees of the Council of
Trent and of such provincial councils as had already
been held. One of the synodal decrees ruled that
each Bishop should render an account to the Council
of the revenues and emoluments of his diocese. This
provision the Cardinal was very particular to have
duly carried out. Certain ecclesiastics were appointed
at each Council to investigate the administration of
the revenue of each see, and make a report thereon
to the congregation of the Bishops. This measure
had a most beneficial effect, not only in procuring the
equitable distribution of the revenues of which it took
cognisance, to the great advantage of the poor; but
also by the example it set to clergy and people for
the regulation of their affairs.

St. Charles never missed the opportunity afforded
him on these occasions of administering fatherly
correction and advice to his suffragans. In cases
where his admonitions did not appear to bear fruit
he had recourse to the Holy Father, that by his
supreme authority the Prelate might be brought back
to a better mind. The care of the Bishops of his
province was considered by St. Charles to be among
the most important of his duties, for he knew that upon
the Bishops depended the well-being of their flocks.

He was much grieved, on one occasion, to hear that
one of the Bishops [1] had said that he had not enough
to do. He was a man of considerable influence, both
on account of his wealth, and the importance of his

---

[1] Cardinal Giovanni Delfino, Bishop of Brescia, who died in 1584. He
had been employed as Nuncio in France and Germany.

see, wherein, however, he had shown little anxiety to promote the measures of reform advocated by St. Charles. The holy Archbishop, ardently desiring the salvation of his soul, sent Monsignor Antonio Seneca a distance of sixty miles to point out to the listless Bishop the various functions and obligations of his vocation. He was to impress upon him that his consecration had been no mere outward ceremonial, but the pledge of labours to be undergone for the salvation of the souls of his flock. Monsignor Seneca fulfilled his mission with ready zeal, but unhappily the dispositions of the Bishop were not favourable, as he received the envoy in a very bad spirit, and alleged that the Cardinal was going beyond his duty. St. Charles felt keenly the imminent spiritual danger of his suffragan, and wrote him a letter urging forcibly upon him the importance of the office to which he had been called, and dwelling in detail upon the needs of his diocese, with all of which he had an intimate acquaintance. He was somewhat severe in his strictures upon his conduct, and added by way of reproof at the close of each subject: "After this, can a Bishop say he has nothing to do?" Neither would he receive any explanations from him, but earnestly begged him to confess his mistake.

Some little time after this the Cardinal went to Rome, to give an account to Gregory XIII. of a mission with which he had been entrusted. He took advantage of this opportunity to submit to the Pope a copy of the letters he had addressed to the Prelate, begging his Holiness to second them by a word from himself.

As the Bishop in question enjoyed the particular favour of His Holiness, the Holy Father was not slow to accede to this request, and by his apostolic warning the Prelate was moved to acknowledge his shortcomings, and, in a letter to Monsignor Seneca, he expressed his contrition for not having received the paternal admonitions of the Archbishop in a proper spirit.   The assiduous care of St. Charles in watching over the conduct of his suffra-gan Bishops was, by God's blessing, of inestimable advantage to the province.   In his time they were true shepherds of souls, punctual in fulfilling all the duties of their calling, and their lives shone forth as bright examples, and many of them died in the odour of sanctity.

During the time of the Council, St. Charles liked to make personal acquaintance with each Bishop.   He treated them with the greatest courtesy, and won their regard and affection.   He always joined them at the morning repast, which all took in common, and which, while moderate and frugal, was suitable and sufficient. Whilst their bodies were refreshed by food, their souls were strengthened by the reading of a spiritual book, or by a discourse from one of the clerics of the seminary.

Many of the Bishops were in the habit of coming to Milan several days before the opening of the Council, and of remaining after its close, in order that they might enjoy the benefit of familiar intercourse with the Car-dinal.   He on his side, did not suffer them to be idle, but gave to each some function or occupation in the service of the Church, in accordance with their several capacities and inclinations.   He used indeed to defer a number of episcopal functions in his cathedral to the time of this meeting of Bishops, such as the clothing or profession of nuns, the administration of the Sacrament of Confirmation, and the consecration of altars. He begged their assistance also in preaching, holding spiritual conferences, and in giving lectures on spiritual subjects in his colleges and seminaries. One special function was always reserved for these occasions, viz., the translation of the relics of the saints, with a view to the increase of devotion in the Bishops themselves towards holy relics, as well as to honour the latter by the greater solemnity given by such an array of the pastors of the Church. These good Prelates returned to their homes filled with a share of the burning zeal and fervour of their metropolitan.

At the conclusion of the Council, which usually lasted about three weeks, St. Charles sent copies of the decrees to Rome by the hands of a Prelate for the inspection of the Supreme Pontiff. On the occasion of this second Council, he made choice of Monsignor Francesco Bonomo,[1] of Cremona, Abbot of Nonantola. This despatch was accompanied by a letter in the name of all the Bishops who had assisted at the Council, formally submitting all their decrees to the judgment of His Holiness, to be corrected and amended by him according as he should deem expedient. On receiving the confirmation of the Pope, they were printed, copies being sent to all the Bishops that they might put them in force in their several dioceses.

[1] Afterwards Bishop of Vercelli, and Nuncio to Switzerland and Germany.

During the nineteen years that St. Charles presided in person over the metropolitan see of Milan, he held six provincial councils according to the Tridentine decrees, that they should be held every three years.

A Cardinal [1] of high standing, afterwards called to the chair of St. Peter, gave it as his opinion that the multiplication of Councils might at last prove burdensome. On hearing this, St. Charles made reply, that as it was the order of the Council of Trent that the ancient discipline should be restored, he considered himself under the obligation of continuing to hold Councils till his province should be brought back to that model. He added : " I am not only holding these Councils for the sake of the present time, but for the benefit of my successors for many years to come." We have seen his words fulfilled to the letter, for seven-and-twenty years elapsed before the next Council was held by his illustrious successor, Cardinal Frederic Borromeo, his cousin, in 1609.

Truly it is surprising that with all the burden of other affairs, the saint yet could do so much in this way, and we can only account for it by the zeal and the Divine Spirit by which he was animated.

The measures proposed and perfected in his councils have served as the model of reforms throughout the sees of Christendom, the means of guiding countless souls in the way of salvation, and more than anything else, have given effect to the decrees of the holy Council of Trent, and have thus been of incalculable service to Holy Church.

[1] Nicolò Sfrondrato, Bishop of Cremona, afterwards Gregory XIV.

CHAPTER XIX.

1570.

DURING his residence in Rome in the time of his uncle Pius IV., St. Charles had many opportunities of making acquaintance with the Order of Regular Clerks called Theatines. He had often gone to their house at San Silvestro, on the Esquiline, for the purpose of spiritual refreshment, and in this way had formed a high opinion of their merits. He had become acquainted there with Guglielmo Sirletto,[1] a learned man who was made a Cardinal by Pius IV., at the recommendation of the saint. The zeal of these Fathers for the salvation of souls, and their labours in the pulpit and confessional, made him desirous of having them in his diocese. Through his negotiations with the superiors of the Order, fourteen religious were sent to Milan. The Cardinal assigned to them

---

[1] Born at Guardavalle in Calabria in 1514, was Librarian of the Vatican, assisted in the reform of the Roman Missal and Breviary, and in the preparation of the Vulgate version of the Bible and of the Catechism of the Council of Trent, dying in the year 1585 at the age of 71.

in the first instance the Church of Santa Maria near
San Calimero in Porta Romana, with the house
attached to it. They were precluded by their rule
from possessing anything either in particular or in
common, and depended on the alms of the faithful
without going out to beg. When they arrived in
Milan in 1570, the saint furnished the house for
them, and gave them requisites for the service of
their Church, till the charity of the people came to
their assistance. The church and living of St. Anthony,
then held by Monsignor Marsilio Landriano,[1] was
afterwards given to them, with greater advantage both
to themselves and to the people. The Cardinal was
greatly consoled at their success, and the citizens
welcomed the arrival of the priests, labourers so fervent
in working for the salvation of souls. St. Charles
always held them in high esteem as cherished fellow-
labourers.[2]

He likewise introduced into Milan the Fathers of
the Society of Jesus, to whom he gave the church
of St. Fidelis. These Fathers had accomplished so
much good among the people by means of their
sermons and labours in the confessional that the building could no longer contain the concourse of people
who gathered around them, and the need of providing a
new church was recognised. The Cardinal resolved to

---

[1] Afterwards Bishop of Vigevano.

[2] St. Andrew Avellino appears to have accompanied these Fathers to
Milan on this occasion. This saint was born in 1520 at Castro Nuovo,
in the kingdom of Naples, entered the community of Regular Clerks or
Theatines in 1556, and after persevering in the same for fifty-two years,
died at the age of 88 in 1608. He was canonised by Pope Clement XI,
circ. 1710.

Lays the Foundation of San Fedele. 221

rebuild the edifice from its foundation, and instructed the architect Peregrino to prepare a design. On the 5th July 1569, he blessed the foundation-stone, going in solemn procession from the Cathedral, accompanied by the Governor and Senate and a large assemblage, where he sung Mass and preached on the glory of erecting a sanctuary to God.

The following inscription was graven on the stone :—

D.O.M.

CAROLUS BORROMAEUS S.R.E. PRESBYTER CARDINALIS
ARCHIEPISCOPUS MEDIOLANENSIS
IN HAC DIVI FIDELIS MARTYRIS AEDE RESTITUENDA
LAPIDEM HUNC A SE RITIBUS ECCLESIAE BENEDICTUM
PRIMO POSUIT
III NON. JULII M.D.LXIX.[1]

St. Charles contributed generously to the building fund, and stirred up the people by his example to similar liberality. It was by alms alone that it became as we now see it, one of the most considerable churches of the country, and a lasting memorial of the generosity of the saint.

[1] Charles Borromeo, Cardinal Priest of the Holy Roman Church, Archbishop of Milan, dedicated to God this first stone at the rebuilding of the church of St. Fidelis the Martyr, on the 5th day of July, 1569.

CHAPTER XX.

1569.

ALTHOUGH the dispute concerning jurisdiction had been suffered to sleep for awhile, doubtless by the permission of God that His servant might have time to work, yet the enemy of mankind was still on the alert to stir up plots against the saint. On this occasion his instruments were certain persons who had taken umbrage at the Governor of Milan because he lived in terms of friendship with the Cardinal, and had suffered the officers of his Court to exercise their functions without impediment. Under cover of zeal for the royal prerogative, they took advantage of his good-will to accuse him of lukewarmness in the service of his royal master, and of suffering those privileges to be infringed which it was his duty to maintain in their integrity. The satanic cunning of this intrigue was soon apparent. If there was one part of his duty on which the Governor more especially prided himself, it was the exact performance of the obligations of his

office. Disturbed by the dread of being found wanting
in anything that concerned the honour of the King,
he imagined that some public act was necessary on
his part in order to assert the royal jurisdiction.   Under
the advice of these crafty plotters he published an
edict on the penalties incurred by all who in any
way infringed the aforesaid jurisdiction.   At first sight
it might not have seemed that the edict was directed
against the liberties of the Church, but experience
soon proved the contrary.   Notaries and other laymen,
imperfectly acquainted with the limits of the jurisdiction of the Church courts, began to be very chary
of prosecuting any suit at all in them lest they
should unwittingly incur the threatened penalties.
The Archbishop's courts were thus indirectly circum-
scribed in their rights, and the saint was in consequence much troubled.   Not only was the course of
business disturbed, but a settled purpose, however
glossed over, was evinced of interfering with the
liberties of the Church.   His sorrow reached its
climax when a rumour was spread abroad to the effect
that he had himself given occasion for the promulgation of this edict.   It was said that he had affronted
the Governor on St. Bartholomew's Day by closing
against him the church dedicated to that saint.
Nothing could be more perverse than this statement.
St. Charles had indeed closed the church on that day,
but the order was dictated solely by his zeal for the
honour of God; for the people instead of keeping
the festival properly made it the occasion of a public
fair, with much that was unseemly and unbecoming.

The Cardinal could not overlook these scandals, or neglect to provide against them. Far from taking offence, the Governor was heard, on the contrary, to commend his zeal.

St. Charles was perfectly aware of the storm that would fall upon his head if he offered any opposition to the new edict. He was aware also of the influence of the power arrayed against him. With this full consciousness, therefore, of what he had to expect he set himself to assert boldly the independence of the ecclesiastical power. In his heart he preferred to lay down his life rather than surrender the trust which God had committed to his charge.

While the saint was preparing himself by prayer for the approaching contest, the devil planned a new assault by means of certain ecclesiastics whom the saint had occasion to reform. There was a collegiate church and chapter at Milan under the title of Santa Maria della Scala, which had been founded by Beatrice della Scala, wife of Bernabò Visconti, lord of Milan, and was called after her name.[1] The dukes of Milan had the right of presentation to the canonries. The dukedom being now in abeyance, the patronage consequently was in the hands of the King of Spain. The chapter had been considerably enriched by the benefactions of Francesco II., Sforza, duke of Milan, who procured several privileges from the Apostolic See in the year 1531. Among these was a bull exempting it from the jurisdiction of the Archbishop, provided, however,

---

[1] The celebrated Theatre of La Scala was built on the site of this Church in 1777.

that he should give his consent, as clearly appears from the following clause ; "*Si venerabilis fratris nostri moderni archiepiscopi Mediolani expressus ad id accesserit assensus.*" [1] As neither the Archbishop at that time nor his successor had given the required assent, this permission remained a dead letter.

When St. Charles came with his clergy to visit this church in its turn, the Canons immediately began to make opposition. There were some indeed who would willingly have submitted, but the majority denied his authority over them by virtue of the privilege we have cited. The Cardinal entertained a · grave suspicion of the validity of this claim, and ascertained after consulting authorities that his suspicion was well grounded, and that the Canons were clearly in the wrong. Notwithstanding this opinion in his favour, the Cardinal would not do anything without submitting it in the first instance to the judgment of the Sovereign Pontiff. He gave his Holiness all necessary information on which to found his decision, and abstained from saying a word which could bias him in any way. Having examined and weighed the claim of the Archbishop and the pretensions of the Chapter, the Pope through Monsignor Ormaneto, whom he had sometime before called to Rome on business of the Apostolic See, decided that the right of the Archbishop to visit the Church of La Scala whenever he thought proper was clear and indisputable. Still, St. Charles would do nothing that could be deemed

---

[1] "Provided that the express permission of our venerable brother. the Archbishop of Milan for the time being, shall have been obtained."

hasty, and allowed two months to pass before taking any further step. The Chapter, therefore, had ample time to reconsider their conduct, and might have submitted with good grace to the Archbishop, since they could not but acknowledge that his right was now established.

The patience of St. Charles did not produce the effect he had hoped. Far from recognising the goodwill he bore them, the Canons persisted in their obdurate resistance to his authority. About this time the Archbishop's Vicar-General had been forced to proceed against one of the ecclesiastics of this church. Still adhering to their erroneous allegation of exemption from archiepiscopal jurisdiction, the Canons determined to excommunicate him, and deputed one Giovanni Pietro Barbesta, a priest of Pavia, to carry out their intention. He was a worthy instrument for such a design, for, being ignorant of the facts and wanting in learning and judgment, he could not appreciate the merits of the case on which he was appointed to pronounce, and was capable, as will be shown, of lending himself to still greater scandals. Meanwhile he performed all that was required of him, by pronouncing excommunication against the Archbishop's Vicargeneral, and also his Attorney-general, as guilty of contempt of apostolic authority, and published the certificates of the act of excommunication in the places of public resort. The Canons had done well in making choice of this man : for no one of any discretion would have committed such a blunder. They relied also on having the support of the public officers of the King, under whose immediate jurisdiction they professed to be. They had some grounds for this expectation on account of the late edict on the royal prerogative.

Meanwhile St. Charles had been weighing the difficulties in which he was involved. All other considerations gave way before the expressed wish of the Pope that he should make his visitation of the church. He resolved to do so regardless of danger, for he was ready at all times to offer up himself in defence of the rights of God and of His Church.

In pursuance of this decision, he sent a formal notice on the morning of the 30th August, 1569, by Monsignor Lodovico Moneta, to announce his approaching visit to the Canons. On receiving this intelligence they abruptly concluded the office they were singing, barred the doors of the church, and withdrew to the churchyard, without even waiting to take off their choir-habits. The most turbulent among them was a Calabrian, Marcantonio Patanella,[1] who had been the leading spirit all throughout the opposition offered to the Archbishop. No sooner had Moneta announced his mission than this man got up and arrogantly declared that the church and the clergy were subject only to the King, and that the Archbishop had no sort of jurisdiction over it or them; adding that he would advise the Cardinal to be cautious how he comported himself in this matter, lest he should court his own destruction. He bade him also not to forget the severe edicts lately published against those who

---

[1] This man held a post in Milan as "regio economo," probably collector, or treasurer of royal dues.

infringed his Majesty's rights.   Moneta paid no attention to this harangue, but turned to the other Canons and asked their opinion, for he was aware that there were some among them of better dispositions.   The minister of Satan drowned their replies by noisy talk, and succeeded in irritating the rest against Moneta, whom they drove out with yells, without regard either for himself or his office.

Before many days the Archbishop, undaunted by their violence towards his messenger, presented himself at their gate in pursuance of his notice.   He was mounted, and vested in the pontifical habit he was wont to wear at a visitation.   But the same evil temper still prevailed.   They had, moreover, associated with them on this occasion a number of laymen, armed for the express purpose of opposing the visitation by force.   St. Charles then dismounted from his mule, and took the Cross into his own hand, in order to pronounce the sentence of excommunication, hoping that as Christians and priests they would reverence the sign of salvation and the person of their Archbishop.   But these wretched men, blinded by Satan, had cast off all fear of God and respect for His minister.   Their lay supporters rushed upon the Cardinal, brandishing their arms wildly, and shouting, " Spain ! Spain ! "   Then, with violence, they closed the door of the church against him.   The Cardinal met all this clamour like a lamb, and their outrages failed to draw one bitter word in reply.   With his eyes fixed on the crucifix, he recommended himself and these misguided men to God.   The witnesses who were examined in the process of his canonisation deposed that he was several times in great jeopardy from the shots of the Canons' supporters, and that the Cross which he held in his hand was injured. His Vicar-general, Monsignor Giovanni Battista Castello, who accompanied him, set up a public notice that the Canons had incurred the censures of the Church by their violence, and, notwithstanding his official character, they treated him with equal contumely, driving him away with blows and cries, and tearing down the notices. To crown all, they insolently set up Barbesta to declare the Cardinal himself deprived of his sacred functions for having contemned the authority of the Apostolic See, having the bells rung and notices posted in public to give greater notoriety to their act.

CHAPTER XXI.

1569.

THE conduct of the Canons of La Scala had scandalized not only the friends of St. Charles, but even those who were not warmly inclined towards his administration. All therefore were unanimous in censuring them for their insolence towards their Archbishop. The saint grieved that there should be men who had dedicated themselves to God so lost to a sense of their obligations as to rage in such guise against their pastor. He was disposed to treat with moderation the insult offered to himself, observing that it was no new thing for the servants of God to suffer affliction, and that they had ever been hated by the world, even as our Divine Lord had predicted : *non est discipulus super magistrum ; si me persecuti sunt, et vos persequentur.*[1]

But he felt bound notwithstanding, to exercise his authority in the defence of the rights of his office. Accordingly, after spending some time in prayer before the Blessed Sacrament, he confirmed the sentence of

---

[1] "The disciple is not above his master; if they have persecuted me, they will persecute you also" (St. John xv. 20).

excommunication which had already been published
by his Vicar-general, making special mention of
Patanella who had been the chief actor in the last
outrage, as well as of all those whose names were
known to him, as having incurred the penalties
mentioned in the sacred Canons, and particularly in
the Constitution of Boniface VIII., concerning offenders
against members of the Sacred College. He then
gave notice of their offence in writing to the Governor
and Senate, bidding them observe that if they had
been in any way accessory to it, they also had thereby
incurred the censure of the Church. He likewise
informed the Holy Father of what had occurred, as
a matter of great moment, demanding the special
assistance of the apostolic authority, and that the late
edict promulgated by the Governor called for some
decision on the part of the Pope, in order to clear
away embarrassments caused by late events. Monsignor Cesare Speciano, one of the Canons of the
Cathedral and a member of his household, was charged
to lay this matter at the feet of his Holiness. The
Pope was indignant at the unworthy conduct of the
Canons of La Scala, and declared all that Barbesta had
done was null and void, and cited Patanella and
others to appear at Rome. Patanella started for
Rome, bent on disputing the proceedings, but died a
miserable death on the journey. One of the laymen
who had shot at the Cross came to a like end, dying
suddenly at an inn at Lambrate, whither he had gone
a few days after his outrage.

Speciano energetically pleaded the cause of the

Archbishop. The Pope ordered that it should be thoroughly discussed. He was heard to say that when it was a question of defending or asserting the rights of Cardinal Borromeo, he was bound not to spare even his own life; speaking of the Cardinal as single-minded in the service of God and His Church, whose zeal always proceeded from a pure source, and was kindled by his keen perception of the obligation under which he lay of labouring in the service of His Divine Master. He also embodied these sentiments in two letters addressed to the Governor of Milan on the subject of La Scala, as will be seen in the next chapter. His Holiness was inclined to leave the affair in some measure to the action of time, that powerful healer of differences. St. Charles knew well that he could rely upon the good-will of the Holy Father and that the rights of his see were safe, but at the same time did not omit to take such measures as prudence suggested for the furtherance of the cause. He wrote to all among his friends, who were in a position to render assistance, in a spirit of moderation and wholly free from any murmur at the tardiness of the proceedings. Neither did he recriminate upon his opponents, but on the contrary, excused them whenever possible, drawing attention to the fact that many of the King's ministers were not to be confounded with the offenders, as upright and sincere in their intentions and prevented from acting upon their con-viction by circumstances beyond their control.

Yet there were times when the servant of God was disturbed in mind because of these contentions. He would consider within himself whether the obstructions he daily met with, and the disputes that arose were not owing to some fault of his own, and the words of the prophet Jonas rose to his lips: *Tollite me, et mittite in mare, et cessabit mare a vobis.*[1] Not only was he ready to make any personal sacrifice for the good of his see, but his natural disposition inclined him to prefer the tranquillity of private life to the cares of the pastoral office, had not the desire of conforming himself to the good pleasure of God kept him stedfast in his work. He saw it was a question of the maintenance of his episcopal authority, which evil-doers and others wished to restrain, and determined to stand or fall by his prerogatives, and rather to die than suffer loss to the souls he loved. All this time, efforts were being made to force or cajole his friends and counsellors to forsake him, and he was strenuously urged, even by his relatives, to yield the point.

Not for an instant did he waver in his trust in the goodness of God, and in the justice of the Holy Father. He placed much reliance also on the good dispositions which the Catholic King had always evinced towards the Church, and he took care to explain the state of the case to him, as his opponents had written to Spain to injure his credit with the King. The members of the Royal Council, in particular, were assured by these men that the Cardinal was actuated by different motives from those which he gave out to be his

[1] "Take me and cast me into the sea, and the sea shall be calm to you" (Jonas i. 12).

guiding principles; and that it would be impossible to maintain the royal jurisdiction in Milan, or indeed to govern the province at all, if he should be allowed to stay there. Those and similar insinuations were so industriously spread abroad, that the saint at last found it necessary to contradict them, lest the King should really be deceived by these devices, and be led to give some decision adverse to the rights and interests of the Church.

The saint was intimately acquainted with the Archbishop of Rossano, Giovanni Battista Castagna,[1] who was the Apostolic nuncio in Spain. To him St. Charles addressed himself to explain the singleness of his intention and his devotion to his Majesty, and begging his good offices with the latter against calumny and prejudice. The Archbishop laid the facts before the King, showing that the trouble at Milan had been in no way caused by any fault of the Cardinal, and that the affection of the latter for his Majesty, made him ready to prove in every way his sense of the favours bestowed on his father, and on his brother. He had indeed given proof of his gratitude whenever occasion had offered during his stay in Rome. He urged that there was not the slightest foundation in fact for the accusation of double-dealing which had been brought against Cardinal Borromeo, alleging that he was incapable of entering into such schemes, and that it was proved by his disinterestedness in renouncing so many honourable posts, in order that he might be free to attend to the service of God. Before acting

---

[1] Afterwards Urban VII., 1590.

he had taken counsel of prudent advisers, and could not be accused of lightly formed judgment. Still less could he be held to have been indifferent to being in unity and peace with the royal functionaries, for it was manifest that he had sought concord by every reasonable means. He urged that the edict of the Governor was published in contravention of the rights of the clergy, and gave a complete narrative of the affair of La Scala, showing that the right of visiting claimed by the Archbishop clashed in no way with the royal jurisdiction ; that the powers he desired to exercise concerning the chapter were purely spiritual ; and that as he only had in view the good of souls, his measures of reform could not but advance the royal authority, since government never was more secure than when the people lived in the observance of discipline and in the fear of God. The King, after listening graciously and giving the matter deliberate consideration, decided in favour of the Cardinal.

CHAPTER XXII.

1569.

THE Canons of La Scala, perceiving that matters were not going so smoothly as they had anticipated, once more addressed themselves to the officers of the King, and begged them to assert the royal right of patronage over the foundation. Those among them who were the most opposed to the Cardinal entered readily into the proposal, and contrived so effectually to work upon the mind of the Governor, that he at last believed it part of his duty to accede to their request, for the defence of the royal prerogative. They also contrived to undermine his good opinion of St. Charles, persuading him that the saint was an ambitious and turbulent prelate whom it was necessary to check lest the whole of Milan should fall into his grasp.

The Governor became the tool of these malicious men, and wrote to the Pope, repeating all the false charges they had made against the Cardinal, complaining that by unreasonable innovations he was setting all Milan by the ears; adding that unless the Pope would check him, he should be compelled to banish the Cardinal for the sake of the peace of the State. To this he added a petition that his Holiness would allow the case of the Canons of La Scala to be argued before some judge in Milan instead of at Rome, alleging a Bull of Leo X. in favour of this exemption.

The Holy Father was not slow to recognise in these charges new machinations of Satan against the Cardinal. Actuated by the independence which has ever characterised the Pontiffs in matters concerning their pastoral office, he did not shrink from administering the rebuke he deemed necessary, and addressed the two following letters to him :—

First Brief of Pius V., of holy memory, to the Governor of Milan.

"Beloved Son, health, and apostolic benediction. The misunderstanding which has arisen between Our well-beloved son, Charles Cardinal Borromeo, and the Canons of Santa Maria della Scala, to which your Excellency refers in your letter of the first of September, has for many reasons filled Us with deep concern.

" First, We are grieved to see the dignity of the Cardinalate, so near to Us and to Our apostolic See, treated with so little consideration, and especially that those who have been guilty of this unseemly conduct are ecclesiastics, who were bound to defend and hold it in honour, had it been impugned by others.

" Next, We grieve because there are many unworthy men who take advantage of occasions such as these in order to push their aggressive designs. Nothing serves their purpose better than a dispute between members

of the hierarchy, particularly when they can induce
men high in secular authority to give them their
countenance and support.   It need hardly be said
that a pastor of the Church cannot be offended without that offence being felt by Her supreme Head.   If
the Canons had any valid claims to maintain against
the Cardinal, they should have proceeded in the
courts of law, and not by violence and force of
arms.   But as We understand the case, it would seem
that the right of visitation really appertained to the
Cardinal, and that they have suffered themselves to
be led astray by the devil, who is ever plotting to mar
the good understanding which is wont to reign among
the ministers of the Church.   They have so greatly
exceeded their powers and prejudiced the Cardinal,
that We are bound to use the authority committed to
Us by God in restraint of the sinfulness of man, and
to award them the chastisement they appear to have
merited.   In which matter We count upon the co-
operation of your Excellency, as we cannot think that
you would lend your aid to screen them from the correction they have deserved.

" With regard to the differences which have arisen
between you and the Cardinal, We will shortly send
you a Nuncio who will make known to you more fully
all Our sentiments upon the subject.   He will also
acquaint you with certain considerations affecting the
government of the province, as well as the rights and
liberties of the Church.

" Touching the allegation of your Excellency, that the
Cardinal has been precipitate and injudicious in his

administration, though We should desire to give all due weight to your opinion, We cannot but form Our own estimate of him, upon his counsels and action during the pontificate of our predecessor, Pius IV., of happy memory. His conduct then was far from conveying this idea of his character, nor have We ever heard that any held such an opinion of him. Were it indeed so, it would be scarcely credible that he should not have been betrayed into some exhibition of it during the time he has governed his diocese. To Us it seems indeed a hard case. It has pleased Almighty God to bestow upon your city of Milan a pastor, whose every desire is devoted to the souls committed to his charge, and whose only aim is to reform the evil customs that have obtained among them. Now, the very persons who are more especially bound to reverence and support him, turn against him, and reproach him with charges which have not so much as a shadow of foundation. This is in conformity with the Word of Truth itself by the mouth of the Apostle that: ' All who will live godly in Christ Jesus shall suffer persecution.' There remains for them this consolation that the fruit thereof is sweet, and its end glorious if they accept it willingly for the sake of His holy name.

"Given at Rome, at the Palace of St. Peter, this tenth day of September, 1569, in the fourth year of Our Pontificate."

Second Brief.

" Beloved Son,—In answering your two letters of the 28th September, We will strive to bear in mind the dignity of Our office, and the admonition of the Apostle, both of which alike warn Us to lay aside vain disputations, and to treat only of those things which are necessary. There would appear to be much in these letters which it will be better to excuse with the affection of a father rather than require an explanation. For, seeing We have a sincere affection for your Excellency, We desire that you should receive Our word, even as it is written, and give it due weight. For We have had in view the benefit of your soul as well as the defence of truth and justice, and We pray Our divine Lord that He will dispose your heart to receive it in the spirit of fatherly charity in which We write.

" To begin with that part of your letter in which you have said so much on the conduct and capacity of the Cardinal, We assure you from Our heart that had We not by other testimony a perfect acquaintance with his life and character, as well as with the matter to which you refer, We should have been led by the statements you have made to entertain grievous and unjust misgivings concerning his integrity.

" As We know him well, We can come to no other conclusion than that the affair is the work of the enemy of mankind, whose perpetual object it is to foment strife and disunion where concord and harmony have prevailed, and to mar that which is fair and upright. He has not been slow to perceive the happiness that would have arisen had your Excellency and the Cardinal continued of one mind, and united in will and deed ; with inveterate malice he has set himself to undermine the fair structure by his lying deceits ; the greater the fervour with which the servant of God pursues his labours, so much the craftier are his machinations against him. We cannot be blind to his arts who have seen them reproduced from age to age. It was thus he stirred up the envy of the Jews to compass the death of our Redeemer; it was thus that, by a multitude of false accusations, he tormented the soldiers of the Cross. But the eternal wisdom of the counsels of God has ever confounded his wiles, and foiled him with his own weapons. For which cause it is Our duty to warn you not to be led astray by craftiness, and We bid you take heed lest that which you deem you have undertaken in good faith in support of the royal authority should, by a hidden judgment of God's justice, turn to its overthrow.

" As to the request you urge so constantly, that We should permit the cause of the Canons of La Scala to be argued before a Milanese court, We regret that it is impossible for us to comply with it. For it has always been the custom of the Apostolic See to take cognisance of the more important causes, and what cause can be more important than one involving a Cardinal of the Holy Roman Church, the nearest dignity to Us and to the Holy See. Concerning the apostolic letters from Our beloved son, his Catholic Majesty, in which it is shown that Our predecessor, Leo X., ordered that the affairs of the province of Milan should always be heard before the courts of, that province, We observe, that even were it so, it appertains to Us to modify the concessions of Our predecessors according to the exigencies of the times, and that it would hence be nothing new or unjust did We make the present case an exception from the general rule, if we judged that times and persons rendered that course advisable. But there is no need for this, for these very letters apostolic expressly exempt from their provision not only all cases affecting Cardinals, but also those relating to ecclesiastical benefices.

"As to the threats in which your Excellency indulges of expelling the Cardinal from the city and state of Milan on account of your zeal for the jurisdiction of the King, We might indeed call you to account for this on the ground of equity and justice; but We will only admonish you in fatherly affection to take heed to your ways, lest you wilfully plunge yourself in straits whence you may hardly find a way of escape. Beware then lest this pretext of defending the royal jurisdiction prove not a snare in which you may be taken as so many before you, for it is not many years since a governor of Milan incurred the censures of the Church by a similar error. The same being afterwards sent as ambassador to our predecessor, Paul III., was stopped on his journey by an order forbidding him to enter Rome under penalty of imprisonment. His peace was made with the Pope by the intervention of one of the Cardinals, but before the news reached him, and he could be absolved, he was suddenly called to his account. This was permitted by God that others might learn from this example that He would suffer no man to thrust himself sacrilegiously into the affairs of His holy service. Bear in mind, moreover, that while imperilling your own soul, great glory would accrue to the Cardinal were he permitted to suffer exile in defence of the prerogatives and the liberties of the Church; and should he even shed his blood in the cause, he would rejoice that God had so honoured him. But for yourself eternal disgrace would be your reward for the share you had taken therein.

" We have judged it well to write thus to you, both out of the fatherly affection We bear you and also in the exercise of the pastoral office laid upon Us by God. We trust that in this, as well as in all other matters which touch the freedom and dignity of the Church, your Excellency will do that which shall bear witness to your piety and zeal for the Catholic faith.

"Given in Rome at St. Peter's, the 8th day of October, 1569, in the fourth year of Our Pontificate."

CHAPTER XXIII.

October 26th, 1569.

WE have already had occasion to mention the various efforts made by some in authority among the Umiliati to abolish the reforms set on foot by St. Charles, and to return to their former condition. Perceiving at last that they would never succeed in turning him from his purpose by ordinary means, they listened to the suggestions of Satan, and determined if possible to take away his life.

The conspirators were three in number: Girolamo Legnano, rector of the Church of St. Christopher at Vercelli; Lorenzo Campagna, rector of Caravaggio; and Clemente Mirisio, rector of St. Bartholomew in Verona. Its execution was committed to a certain priest [1] of the same order, Girolamo Donato, surnamed Farina. He was but too willing to undertake the office, like a Judas, on consideration of a bribe of forty crowns. The only difficulty was to procure the money; for this there were but two ways open to them, both

---

[1] The legal records of the court call him Deacon only.—O.

involving the commission of a crime: either to steal
the silver vessels and ornaments of the Church of
Brera, the principal establishment of the Order in
Milan, or to rob the treasury appointed by the new
constitutions for the common funds of the brotherhood.
The votes were in the first instance, given in favour
of the second plan, and for this purpose an attempt
was made to burst open the door where the money
was kept. In this they failed, and then resolved to
strangle the treasurer and take the keys. Brother
Fabio Simoneta, the treasurer, was a pious man and
good religious; and when they tried to execute their
evil intentions upon him, they found him at prayer in
the Church. Whilst they disputed among themselves
as to who should put the rope round his neck, our
Lord in compassion for His faithful servant confounded their plans, so that they could not agree,
and they came away baffled. At last Farina
himself found means to make away with some
of the sacred vessels of the Church of Brera
which he sold; he then disguised himself in a
secular dress, and travelled from place to place,
spending the proceeds of his sacrilege in licentious
living. When it was all spent, he stole a weapon
wherewith to effect the murder. This was about the
time of the dispute with the officers of the Crown,
who, Farina hoped, would be suspected of the homicide.
He therefore hailed this as a favourable opportunity,
and after some deliberation resolved to shoot the
Cardinal as he was going to the Church of St.
Barnabas to say Mass. This attempt failing, the

Oratory of the Archbishop's Palace was chosen for the attempt.

We have already mentioned the practice of the Cardinal of spending an hour in prayer with his household in the community room, after the Angelus. This room is now the chief apartment of the Bishop, but it was at that time fitted up as a chapel because the Oratory was in course of construction. Other devout persons of the city were admitted to these gatherings, and on a certain Wednesday evening, the 26th of October, 1569, the miserable Farina obtained entrance among the household. It was the custom on these occasions for an anthem to be sung, and on the night in question about 8 o'clock the choir were singing one arranged by Orlando Lasso, beginning: *Tempus est, ut revertar ad eum, qui me misit.*[1] They had just uttered the words, *Non turbetur cor vestrum ; neque formidet,*[2] when the assassin, who had taken his stand dressed as a layman close to the door, four or five yards from the saint, fired his piece loaded with ball. The charge struck the Cardinal, who was on his knees before the altar. The sudden report of fire-arms produced a panic in the assembly, every one rose in confusion and the singing ceased; the saint quietly motioned all to keep their places, and finish their prayers. Thus Farina had ample opportunity to escape without being recognised or even observed. The Cardinal thought he had been shot through the body, and putting his hand immediately to the place,

[1] "It is time for me to return to him who sent me " (Tobias xii. 20).
[2] "Let not your heart be troubled, nor let it be afraid" (St. John xiv. 27).

reckoned he had received a mortal wound. Raising his eyes and hands to Heaven, he commended himself to God, giving thanks that he had been counted worthy to suffer death for justice sake. But when the prayers were ended and he had risen from his knees, it was found that the ball which had struck him about the middle of the spine had not even pierced his clothes, but leaving a mark upon his rochet, had fallen harmlessly at his feet. Some of the shot had penetrated to the skin, but without making the least abrasion, or daring to spill the blood of the holy prelate.

No wonder that the ball as well as the rochet and cassock worn by the saint were eagerly sought after and preserved by pious persons. They still remain to bear testimony to his merciful preservation. The ball was long preserved by Giulio Petruccio, the almoner of the Cardinal, and is now in possession of the Oblates in the Church of the Holy Sepulchre. The rochet was sent to Rome, and after some time, came into the hands of the Cardinal Paolo Sfrondato of the title of St. Cecilia. He gave it to the French Cardinal de Sourdis, Archbishop of Bordeaux, who deposited it in the Church of the Carthusians in that place. The cassock is in the care of Monsignor Lanfranco Regna, Provost of St. Ambrose the Great at Milan.

When the saint had withdrawn to his apartment, he found that though there was no wound, the ball had occasioned a slight swelling of the part. This always remained in token of his miraculous escape, and was seen by many after his soul had passed to its reward. We could have no clearer proof of the Divine Power which intervened for his preservation, for whilst the bullet had touched him so gently, some of the remaining shot penetrated a table of solid wood standing near, and made a hole in the opposite wall.

As God permitted the devil to torment Job that he might be an example of patience to posterity, so may we say that He permitted this occurrence to serve as an instance of the sincerity and strength of mind of the saint. Neither the sudden alarm nor the actual danger with which he was menaced, betrayed him into any expression of annoyance. With calmness he continued his prayer, and restored composure to all present. Nor would he suffer any search to be made for the assassin, thus forgiving the injury on the spot.

A great commotion was excited throughout the city by the tidings of this event. The palace was besieged by inquirers, all of whom were loud in denouncing the malice that had been displayed, as well as in celebrating the deliverance as miraculous. Among the rest came the Duke of Albuquerque, the Governor, who met the Cardinal with every expression of esteem and sympathy, promising his assistance in searching for the assassin, and asking to see the place where the crime was attempted, as well as the ball, rochet, and cassock. He resolved to bring the offender to justice in a manner that should mark his sense of the crime, and serve as an effectual example to others. For this purpose he

was going to examine some members of the household
to obtain all possible information, but St. Charles would
not however allow it, though the Governor remained
with him till ten o'clock at night, and induced others
to unite their persuasions with his. But they could
not prevail on the saint to alter his resolution. He
had forgiven the offender from his heart, and would
not take part in any proceedings against him. At the
same time he thanked the Governor, but endeavoured
to impress upon him that it was altogether a personal
offence, and a matter to which he attached no importance whatever, further than that it served as a new
motive of gratitude to God, who had so graciously
interposed in his favour. He added that he should
esteem it a real service if his Excellency would
instead employ his zeal in defending the rights of the
Church against the aggressions which grieved him
from day to day, as in the case of La Scala, and that
to pass over such attacks against his archiepiscopal
authority was to encourage the plots of ungodly men.

To this the Governor replied that in matters involving questions of law his hands were tied, as he
could not act without the concurrence of the Privy
Council and Senate, who thought that he ought not to interpose. It was otherwise he said in the present case,
and he assured the Cardinal that his life and person were
as dear to him as his own, and that he felt honoured
in being able to constitute himself his champion. He
did not belie these professions: that same night he issued
a proclamation containing full particulars of the occurrence, declaring that the Cardinal had by the grace of

God been miraculously preserved unscathed, and called upon every one who had any knowledge of the culprit to come forward and declare the same immediately, or at furthest within the space of two days, under pain of death and confiscation of property. On the other hand rewards were promised to all who should be instrumental in bringing the offender to justice. These proclamations were published the following morning, and renewed on several occasions. The gates of the city were kept closed for three days, so that no one could pass out without being subjected to scrutiny. Several persons were arrested, who were thought likely to have knowledge of the author of the crime, or of his confederates, no precaution being neglected that prudence could suggest.

The Governor offered to provide the Cardinal with a bodyguard; this the saint refused. Ten halberdiers, however, were sent to guard the palace every night, during the time of the evening prayers. The Governor visited the Cardinal frequently, and on the second day remained to dine with him, dismissing his suite in order to testify more plainly the good understanding there was between them.

The Senate in a body visited the Cardinal on the following day, each one testifying his anxiety like the Governor. He satisfied them in the same terms, and had similar expressions of good-will from the magistrates, the colleges of advocates, and other gentlemen of the city.

In acknowledgment of the signal mercy of God, St. Charles called together the clergy of the city, and in a solemn procession gave thanks for the miraculous preservation of his life.

Shortly after this the saint withdrew to the Carthusian monastery of Garignano, where he spent some time in retreat and meditation on the spiritual advantage that he ought to derive from his miraculous escape. Considering that God had thus wonderfully granted him a new term of life, he resolved to devote himself more thoroughly to His service. Accordingly he determined to lead from that time forth a higher and better life, reckoning his past as of no consideration. He wrote the following letter to the Pope, to whom a detailed account of the matter had already been given.

Letter from St. Charles to Pope Pius V.

" Your Holiness will have been informed by Monsignor Ormaneto of what has happened three days ago. It will be a cause of sorrow no doubt to your Holiness, although it bears testimony to the mercy of God in vouchsafing to preserve me in a manner so unusual. He has done this, not out of regard for me, who am indeed most unworthy of so great a favour, but on account of the office to which He has called me, and to give me more time to do penance, of which my great need is known to Him, or for other reasons into which it is not fitting to inquire curiously. Your Holiness may, therefore, be glad rather than sorry. For my part, I shall never cease to give thanks to God for my escape, and hope it may be to His honour and glory."

As soon as the Holy Father received this letter, he wrote in his own hand to the following effect:— That the persecution of the just was no new thing, as since the days of Abel men had done the like, but the more they strove to do wrong, the more signally were they covered with confusion in the end. He had been particularly grieved by the blindness of those who, not choosing to walk in the fear of God, were in danger of falling into snares whence they would find there was no way of escape. He gave great thanks to God for preserving the life of such a man as the Cardinal, and thus confounding the plots of the Evil One.

Whilst he commended the unbounded reliance of the Cardinal in the goodness of God, he besought him for the future to take more care of a life so precious to the Church. He entertained no doubt that Almighty God would in His own time punish the authors of the crime. He counselled him to pray and ask the prayers of others that it would please our Divine Lord to enlighten the darkness of their minds.

We have given thus briefly the chief points in the reply of the Holy Father, which was expressed in terms of paternal affection. He afterwards held a consultation with the Sacred College of Cardinals, in which he took occasion to express his grief at the commission of such a crime, and pointed out the mischief which ensued when those who are at the head of the State show hatred of their Bishop, or suffer it to be perceived that there is any want of agreement between them, since this serves to encourage the designs of evil men. He exhorted all to unite in giving thanks to God for His mercy in preserving the life of the servant of God in so signal a manner. He also desired his nuncio in Spain to narrate to the King all that had occurred, and to improve the occasion by urging the proof it afforded of the justice of the Cardinal's cause, so that his Majesty might direct his ministers in Milan to act accordingly.

The news of the miracle soon spread throughout Rome, and thence into distant countries. Everywhere the impression produced was the same. Letters of congratulation poured in upon the Cardinal from princes and nobles in all parts, expressing their horror at the crime, and their joy that it had been hindered. Some enlarged upon the malice of the assassin, and the degeneracy of the times; others dwelt upon the goodness of God thus signally manifested by the exercise of His power, even in these latter days, and on the patience and endurance of the servant of God. Among these was the Cardinal Marcantonio Amulio, who was wont to say that he scarcely knew which was the greater miracle, the preservation of the saint from harm, or his perfect self-possession at such a moment. There were some who looked upon it as an example which ought to encourage the pastors of the Church to exercise the duties of their vocation with courage and constancy, since here was a manifestation of the constant watchfulness of the good Providence of God. A few there were who took a loftier view; they would not rest content with merely rejoicing over it as a piece of good fortune; they saw in it a testimony from God of the merit of this Defender of the liberties of the Church by awarding to him the palm of martyrdom at the same time that He preserved the martyr in a marvellous manner in His service.

We must not here omit to mention a saying to which this remarkable incident gave rise. It was said that the rochet of Cardinal Borromeo was harder than any coat of mail.

While various persons were thus drawing edifying lessons from the occasion Satan was not idle, for there were not wanting those who unblushingly called the whole affair an artifice of the Cardinal, in order to increase his reputation with the people.

But gentlemen from far and near were prompt to offer their assistance in defending him, though the saint courteously excused himself from accepting their offers.

Gratitude and sympathy were everywhere shown, in thanksgiving to God, and in supplication for a continuance of His mercy to the Cardinal. Many of his friends, fearing lest his life should be menaced by other plots, urged him earnestly to take more care of himself, to which he always replied that he would have no arms of the flesh, but would trust only to the spiritual weapons of his pastoral office, lest otherwise his church should suffer loss, which he could not bear. He often said that he had found great advantage from the prayers of pious persons on his behalf, and that the night prayers which he continued to offer in his house as before, were much better attended than they had been before. This he held to be the best possible precaution he could take, at the same time that it was of great benefit to the souls of others.

Origin of the Frati Umiliati.

It is said that the Emperor St. Henry II. in 1014 banished into Germany some of the principal inhabitants of Milan, Pavia, Lodi, Cremona, and other places, as prisoners of war. They there formed themselves into a society assuming the name of Umiliati, or Humbled, in reference to their unfortunate condition. They applied themselves especially to the manufacture of woollen cloth, and on their return to Italy in 1019 they worked together as a corporate body. They are with certainty traced up to the year 1134, when certain gentlemen of Milan, under the direction of St. Bernard, with the consent of their wives, made religious vows, adopting the rule of St. Benedict, with certain particular constitutions, and building the monastery of Brera. Their order was approved by Innocent III. in 1200, and increased so much that in the Milanese province alone they soon had two hundred and twenty houses. About 1550 they had fallen into such relaxation that in ninety-seven houses they had only a hundred and sixty-two brethren, with an annual revenue of 60,000 crowns. —*Tiraboschi, Vetera Humiliatorum monumenta. Milan,* 1766.

CHAPTER XXIV.

OF THE CONSOLATION GIVEN BY GOD TO THE SAINT
IN THE IMPROVED CONDITION OF HIS DIOCESE.

ALTHOUGH our Lord is accustomed to suffer His servants to be afflicted in this life, so that they may be
refined like gold in the furnace, and may be kept
humble lest the continual outpouring of His blessing
should fill them with any spirit of self-complacency, as
the Apostle says of himself: *datus est mihi stimulus
carnis; ne magnitudo revelationum extollat me;*[1] yet
at the same time He is wont also from time to time
to let them taste of His consolations that they be not
borne down by the weight of His Cross, for thus it is
He brings them to perfection.   It was no less so
with the saint.   If at one time God suffered him to
endure great contradictions, the season of consolation
was not far off when He gladdened him again by the
success of his labours for souls, and the increase of
graces with which He adorned the soul of His servant.
He now gave him consolation after the struggles he
had gone through in maintaining the authority of his
office.   Since his deliverance he found the veneration

[1] "There was given me a sting of my flesh, lest the greatness of the
revelations should exalt me" (2 Cor. xii. 7).

for him increased, the rancour of enemies changed in many cases into good-will, while the Catholic King sent him assurance of his cordial support, thus contributing greatly to his peace of mind.

The apostolic nuncio, as we have related, in his audience of the King had the happiest influence upon him, for when informed of the attempt on the Cardinal's life he was much grieved, and wrote to the Duke of Albuquerque denouncing the edict against the archiepiscopal jurisdiction, and requiring its suspension as wrongful to the Church. Further than this, he ordered him to take immediate steps to bring the conspirators in the affair of La Scala to justice, and intimated that so far from desiring that this chapter should be exempted from the jurisdiction of the Archbishop, he, on the contrary, begged him to undertake its visitation and reformation. Although the saint had besought him to exercise his royal authority rather against the impugners of ecclesiastical jurisdiction than against those who had conspired against his person, he would not himself by any means suffer so flagrant a crime to go unpunished. In conclusion, he charged the Governor to show greater alacrity in future in defending the Cardinal and furthering his wishes.

From the spirit of this letter it may be gathered that the King gave other orders which were not made public. The upright dispositions of the prince were highly applauded in the letters of the apostolic nuncio, and of the most reverend Father Vincenzo Giustiniani,[1] sent to Spain by the Pope concerning the affairs of

---

[1] General of the Dominican Order, and afterwards Cardinal.

Milan. Both these prelates dwell on the good-will shown by his Majesty towards St. Charles.

On receipt of the King's letter, the Governor lost no time in withdrawing the obnoxious edict, as he had also received a pastoral admonition from the Sovereign Pontiff that he had incurred the censures against those who violate the freedom of the Church.

But when it was found that the abrogation of the edict did not remove all the disabilities in the way of the due exercise of the Archbishop's rights, which was a source of no small anxiety to the Sovereign Pontiff, the Duke, who was most anxious to give satisfaction to the Vicar of Christ, as well as to set his own scruples at rest, applied to St. Charles, with whom he was now on good terms, to assure his Holiness that he had done all that in him lay to withdraw the edict ; so that it was not his fault that the desired effect had not been attained. He accordingly received a brief from the Pope with a faculty to his confessor to absolve him from all censures, so as to take part in the coming festival of Christmas, as became a Catholic prince. The brief, however, contained the clause that if by the end of the octave of the Epiphany he had not reinstated the Church in the full and free exercise of all the rights which it enjoyed before the edict was issued, he would again subject himself to the sentence from which he was now set free. The Governor desired to obey in all respects the wishes of the Sovereign Pontiff, and also to deliver himself from the censures of the Church. He therefore directed the President of the Senate to allow all the functionaries of the archiepiscopal Courts, in his own name and in faith of his princely word hereby pledged to them, to exercise their various duties and faculties, and to act with all freedom, as they were wont before the publication of the edict. The same orders were sent to the civil governors of the other districts of the state, requiring them also to place the ecclesiastical courts on their old footing.

All this was done before the end of the time fixed by his Holiness. The church Courts were again opened, and their business carried on as usual. Some of the former evil counsellors of the Duke endeavoured indeed to turn him from his purpose, but he would not again listen to them, knowing that he was carrying out the just intentions of his royal master, and acting in a way worthy of his own dignity. Nor did his fidelity to the Church pass without acknowledgment. Besides the satisfaction of his conscience, his firmness in this matter won him the applause of the people, and the cordial approval of the saint.

Meanwhile, the cause of the persons excommunicated for their treatment of the officer of the Archbishop's Court was heard at Rome. The course of the action was stayed by a petition presented by the defendants on the part of the Cardinal himself, praying for their absolution, which was granted on condition that they made satisfaction to the Church for their offence. Still, a report obtained that as they professed themselves penitent for what had taken place, no farther notice would be taken of the matter, and that such was the royal pleasure. St. Charles on

hearing this report saw that such a course was quite
unworthy of so right-minded a prince, and wrote to
Spain to ascertain the fact. As the answer bore out
the expectation of the Cardinal that the King was of
the opposite opinion, they had only to make a fitting
submission to their pastor and humbly ask him for
absolution. St. Charles, desiring nothing more than
their restoration to the communion of the Church, in
order to invest the act with solemnity and in pursuance of the ordinance of the Apostolic See, erected a
platform before the great door of the cathedral where,
on the vigil of Christmas 1569, the King's Attorney-
General and the notary who shared his sentence of
excommunication, presented themselves on their knees,
and prayed for penance and absolution. Then having
rescinded the sentence of exile against the Bargello or
officer of the Archbishop, and formally restored to him
his arms, they took a solemn oath at the hands of the
Cardinal never again to molest the Church or infringe
her jurisdiction. This promise having been further
secured by a public document, the Cardinal raised the
censure of the Church which lay upon them, and took
advantage of the occasion to explain the censure of the
Church as a warning to the bad and encouragement of
the good. The captain of justice, who had been
made a senator of Milan, was also one of the excommunicated, and behindhand in asking for absolution,
but had applied to the Cardinal for leave to attend
the wedding of a relative at Alessandria della
Paglia, and on receiving a refusal went in defiance of the sentence of excommunication. He was

taken ill on the following night, and died in a few days.

This visitation of the hand of God was regarded by all as a punishment for the outrage offered to the Church, and a warning against despising her censures. A similar end awaited another, who had been summoned to Rome to answer for himself. A most inveterate enemy of St. Charles, he found himself struck down by sickness, with great distress of mind and conviction that he was tormented by evil spirits. Though exorcised, he could obtain no relief in mind or body, and wasted away miserably in a short time. Nor did these signal chastisements end here, for others, who had engaged in these sad transactions met with divers calamities, in a manner which extended even to their children.

CHAPTER XXV.

THE CANONS OF LA SCALA BEG FOR PARDON AND ABSOLUTION.

1570.

THE provost of La Scala, Bernardino Bianchi, who had not taken part in the outrage, at this time besought the Cardinal to remove the excommunication from him. The saint, who in passing the sentence had chiefly desired to bring the offenders to a sense of the crime they had committed, gave him absolution in public before the door of the church of San Fedele. He, on his part, recognised the Archbishop for his rightful superior, and promised him fidelity and obedience. The others, with the Calabrian at their head, held out a while longer, in contempt of the excommunication, adding sin to sin, and, as a special defiance to the Cardinal, celebrating their religious offices with greater solemnity than usual. But when they heard the miserable death of their ringleader, and that the Pope was going to inflict upon them the chastisement they merited, they began to yield and repent of their past transgressions. Pius V. in his zeal for the liberty of the Church had, on account of their obstinacy, intended to subject them to the penalties of the constitution of Boniface VIII., the least severe of which is that such persons should be considered *ipso facto* degraded and deprived of their benefices.   But the saint had no desire that the personal offence to himself should be visited severely on the Canons.   All that he wished was that the rights of the Church should be vindicated.   He accordingly entreated the Holy Father very earnestly to act with clemency in the matter.   Yielding to his solicitation, the Pope ultimately left the decision of the matter to his judgment.   Believing them repentant, and seeing that they were ready to amend their conduct and obey him in the future, he absolved them with solemn ceremonies on Sunday, 5th February, 1570, in public, before the great door of the cathedral, after he had received their public confession and had imposed on them a salutary penance.   Entering the church, they were made to kneel before the high altar, and there declare that they owed subjection to the Archbishop of Milan, and took an oath of obedience at the hands of the Cardinal, beseeching him humbly to remove the interdict from their church.   After preaching a sermon on the occasion, the saint walked in procession to the church of La Scala, amid general rejoicings.   He reconsecrated the churchyard, the scene of the outrages, and then took possession of the church.   One of the penances which St. Charles imposed on the Canons was, that for the ten following years all the clergy of the Church should repair in a

body to the Cathedral on each anniversary of the
Nativity of our Lady, and there, humbly kneeling at
the feet of the Archbishop before the high altar, should
renew their prayer for his forgiveness, and acknowledge
his jurisdiction over them. This was punctually fulfilled, and was considered a slight penalty as compared
to what they had rendered themselves liable under the
sacred Canons, a punishment which but for the intercession of the saint with Pius V. would most certainly
have been brought home to them. It was the desire
of the Pope, however, that there should be a reserva-
tion in the pardon thus accorded of the right of further
prosecution against those who had conspired together
to take arms and do violence to the person of the
Cardinal. In pursuance of this they were imprisoned, as a matter of form, for a short period ; but
while deprivation of their benefices was under discussion, the good pastor interceded again for them with
the Holy Father so effectually that the decision in this
case was again left to him. No sooner was this done
than, with the tenderness of a father, he restored them
to liberty, and the only restriction he made in restoring
their benefices was that they should give alms of a
certain amount towards the building of the cupola of
the great church of St. Ambrose.

Meantime Barbesta, in expectation of a punishment
in proportion to his offence, was kept in durance by
command of the Pope. When abandoned by all, the
Cardinal gave him a declaration in writing that it was
his wish that some advocate should undertake his de-

fence. As none came forward, the saint requested Monsignor Ormaneto to crave the mercy of the Holy Father, who sentenced him merely to banishment, and even this penalty was afterwards remitted through the intercession of St. Charles.

CHAPTER XXVI.

DISCOVERY AND EXECUTION OF THE CRIMINALS NOT-
WITHSTANDING THE MEDIATION OF THE SAINT.
SECOND VISIT TO THE SWISS VALLEYS AND
SWITZERLAND ITSELF.

1570.

INDEPENDENTLY of the royal ordinance to that effect, the Holy Father desired that every effort should be made to find the perpetrator of the attempt against the Cardinal's life. In the first instance he called upon St. Charles to publish the names of any on whom suspicion fell. But the saint had already forgiven the injury, and had never suspected any one for a moment. He answered therefore in all sincerity, that while conscious of his duty and obedience in the matter, there was no one whom he could suspect of a murderous intention. His labours for the reformation of the souls committed to his care had turned many of those who were lax against him, but he could not fix upon anyone as likely to have intended to kill him. This, however, he would say, that many persons whom he deemed innocent had been accused. Soon after this he was informed that an apostolic delegate was coming to accelerate the investigation. This intelligence pained him, for he was ex-

tremely desirous that no one should suffer on his
account. Accordingly he immediately wrote to arrest
further proceedings, protesting that nothing could be
more opposed to his wishes than that it should be pro-
secuted on his account. But the Pope, considering the
offence that had been committed against God and His
Church, would not yield to his entreaties, but desired
that justice should take its course. In pursuance of this
determination he sent Monsignor Antonio Scarampa,
Bishop of Lodi, with a mandate, to publish the penalties against those who, having knowledge of the delin-
quent, should not come forward and give information
of the same. Whilst engaged in carrying out these
orders, one of the three conspirators and another privy
throughout to the plot, presented themselves and
declared the particulars of the affair, though not so
completely as they had previously done to the Cardinal. In the course of their examination, however,
the account they gave was so confused and contradic-
tory that they excited grave suspicions about themselves; indeed it was hardly possible they could
conceal the fact of their being seriously involved.
They were accordingly imprisoned, to the sorrow of
the Cardinal, who felt great compassion for them and
wrote to Monsignor Ormaneto praying him earnestly
to move the Holy Father to have mercy on them.
But it was not easy to overcome the determination of
the Supreme Pontiff to execute justice. Moreover,
soon after the prisoners confessed the whole truth, both
as to themselves and their accomplices. By this means
the part which Farina had taken was brought to light,

and he was found disguised as a soldier in the service
of the Duke of Savoy, who at once gave him up on the
request of the Pope.   Farina confessed his guilt in
prison, and all four were sentenced to death.   On the
28th July, 1570, they were handed over to the civil
power, and were condemned to the gallows by the
secular judge.   The provosts of Vercelli and Caravaggio were beheaded, as being of noble descent.
Farina showed every sign of true compunction, and,
during the ceremony of his degradation, said that he
had put on the sacred vestments unworthily, and it
was most fitting he should now be stripped of them.
In his last moments he besought the people who
surrounded the gallows to pray for him, and forgive
his crime of seeking to take away a life so precious to
the world.   Such confidence had the charity of St.
Charles inspired, that one of those who were executed
felt no hesitation in recommending to his care a niece
who would be left destitute at his death.   The saint
promised to provide for her, and kept his word.   The
fourth prisoner was sentenced to the galleys, as there
were some grounds for deeming him less guilty than
the others.   The saint did not fail to take advantage of
this circumstance to apply for his pardon, intending to
place him in a monastery.   But his Holiness met the
application with the words of the Prophet: *Potestne
æthiops mutare pellem suam ?* [1]   The saint nothing
daunted renewed his petition, and at last obtained a
remission of the sentence to confinement for a certain
time in a monastery.

[1] "Can the Ethiopian change his skin?" (Jeremias xiii. 23.)

Whilst the people were gazing on the sad spectacle
of the execution of these criminals, St. Charles was so
much moved by his compassion for their fate, that he
was desirous to leave the city for a time. Accordingly
he took a journey into Switzerland to visit the three
valleys of his diocese, which he traversed with his
usual exertions and fatigue, defraying as before all
expenses out of his own means, and bestowing abundant alms on the poor, and for the maintenance of
churches. He then crossed the mountains to the
German side, ostensibly to visit his sister, the Countess
Hortensia, at her castle of Altaemps ; but his real object
was rather zeal for souls, as he deemed it a good
opportunity to treat with the secular power in those
parts on matters most important to the Catholic
religion. After this he passed through all the
Catholic cantons one by one, accomplishing many reforms with great tact, but not without difficulty, for
there were many bad examples to be found among the
clergy of these remote parts, and more than one
monastery where religious observance had fallen so
far into decay the brethren thought it no scandal to
be waited on by women-servants, even in their cells.
In others hospitality was so freely exercised that the
license of a tavern reigned within the walls. It was
the care of St. Charles to put an end to these disorders,
and he knew so well how to win the co-operation of
both clergy and laity that they gladly submitted in
everything to his authority, as to a father. His
labours were attended with a great blessing, more
especially the measures he concerted with the authori-

ties of the cantons for the repression of heresies which
at that time were making havoc among the flock.

The principal places visited by him on this occasion were Altorf, Unterwalden,[1] Lucerne, the chief
town of the Catholic cantons and their principal
seat of government, St. Gall, Zurich, and Altaemps,
where he paid a short visit to his cousin, Count An-
nibale Sittich.   But he did not make any long stay
here, but hastened on to the labours awaiting him in
other places.   On his homeward way he visited at
Schwytz the image of the Madonna di Guado, where
he was seen to shed many tears.   All along the way
the people came out to meet him, and accompanied
him from place to place with great joy and every
mark of honour.   The very heretics joined in his
praise, and often exclaimed that he was indeed a good
man and one whom they could trust, because he set
a good example.   The Catholics who flocked around
him, vied with each other in obtaining beads and
rosaries and the like which he had blessed.   So great
was the devotion of the people towards him in some
villages that they fell on their knees before him in
tears, and cried that God had sent light into their
distant dwellings.

During this journey he had to pass through a part
of the country which was occupied entirely by heretics.
On entering one of the villages to take a meal, he
was entertained by one of the great men of the neighbourhood in the name of the rest, who brought him

----

[1] Where he visited the relics of the blessed Nicholas Flue, celebrated
Mass and gave communion to a great number of people.

also presents of wine and provisions, as was the custom with persons of note. Notwithstanding their heresy they held him in great veneration. The same was the case at St. Gall, where not he alone, but all his company were entertained by the heretics. As he passed through their town, all the people, men and women, gathered round him, though at other times they could not bear the sight of priests; so greatly did the odour of his sanctity soften and vanquish all prejudices.

Note on p. 270.—The Madonna di Guado.

Our Lady of Einsiedeln, where, as the saint says in a letter to Cardinal Altaemps of September 10, 1870, he was much edified by the piety and devotion of the people.

CHAPTER XXVII.

THE difficulties in the way of reforming the Umiliati seeming to baffle even the efforts of their protector, at length determined his Holiness Pius V. to suppress the Order.

After the conspiracy against the life of St. Charles, he found he could in justice no longer spare a community which had so little regard for one who was their protector and Cardinal. To do so, would, he felt, be a dishonour to God and a scandal to the people. Fearing to err, however, in a matter of such importance, he consulted the members of the Sacred College, who strongly supported him in his purpose.

When the news was reported at Milan it made a great impression both on the people and the community, the counsel and intercession of St. Charles being eagerly sought by all. With his sanction it was determined that the congregation should send their superior-general, Father Luigi Bascapé, to the Holy Father, to promise in the name of the Order to adopt any reform that he might see fit to make, that the city should send its petition in writing to the same effect, and that the Cardinal should support it by a letter from himself, urging the reasons likely to move his Holiness, and assuring him that he entertained hopes that the fathers would accept his decrees of reformation.

The superior-general accordingly repaired to Rome, and throwing himself at the feet of the Pontiff, humbly begged mercy for his family, at the same time presenting the letter entrusted to him by the Cardinal. Neither the one nor the other changed in any measure the mind of the Pope, who was too indignant at the crime, and too incredulous of their amendment not to feel that the measure of their iniquity was full.

His Holiness did not fail to commend the charity of the Cardinal, and his faithfulness to the evangelic counsels : *diligite inimicos vestros, et benefacite his, qui oderunt vos.*[1] But as the Vicar of Christ he saw that nothing less was required than the abolition of the Order, which accordingly by his Apostolic authority he solemnly suppressed.

Perhaps there is no clearer evidence of the crying abuses existing in this community than the fact that, although it possessed ninety-four convents, the whole number of religious did not amount to more than one hundred and seventy-four, many of the houses being without inmates while the superiors appropriated all the revenue. The Pope afterwards published the Bull of their suppression, in which he set forth the evil lives of the religious, and the crime

[1] "Love your enemies, do good to them that hate you " (St. Matt. v. 44).

from which the Cardinal had been preserved, by the
special interposition of Divine Providence. To each
of the brethren he assigned a befitting pension for his
support during the remainder of his life, reserving to
himself the right of presentation to the benefices after
their death. When St. Charles heard of this disposition of the temporalities of the Order, he sent Monsignor Speciano to Rome, to beg that some share of
these might be apportioned to his colleges, and other
pious works. To this the Pope graciously assented,
giving him for this purpose the church and house of
Brera, where he founded the College of Jesuit Fathers,
with their public schools. He also gave him San
Giovanni at the East gate, whither he removed his
great seminary; La Canonica at the New gate, which
he made a seminary for moral theology; St. Mary's,
where he erected his college for the young nobility; San
Spirito, which he gave to the Swiss College, but which
is now used as a convent, as the Swiss College was
subsequently removed to a more convenient site; also
the convent of the nuns of Santa Sophia, at the Roman
gate near San Calimero; and others, the income of
which he used for the maintenance of the cathedral.
All those places which had been served by bad
religious, were now really devoted by the saint to the
salvation of souls.

Note on p. 273.—"Ninety-four convents," &c.

These numbers differ slightly from those of Tiraboschi, p. 255. The
discrepancy may be explained by the fact that the latter writes of the
Order in the year 1550. Probably two or three houses were suppressed
in the interval, and the number of the brethren thereby increased.

CHAPTER XXVIII.

DEARTH IN MILAN—EXERTIONS OF THE SAINT IN AID OF THE PEOPLE—FURTHER REFORMS.

1570.

THE deficient harvest of the year 1569 had resulted in a period of great privation, which was much felt in the Milanese district. The poor were threatened with starvation, as they were unable to purchase bread or other kind of food at any price within their means. They flocked into the city from the poor districts, to beg succour from the citizens. Our saint could not bear the sight of their misery, but in his fatherly love took their needs upon himself, and directed his almoner to open his hands wide and help all who were in need, especially poor religious, who had much to suffer.

Besides this he made large provision of bread, rice, and vegetables in his own house, and distributed daily to all who applied, caldrons full of soup in the portico, so that access was easy to all.

By these means he relieved as many as three thousand persons daily for several months, during the whole time the dearth lasted. All this entailed a very great

outlay, and obliged him to beg of the nobles and rich
men of the city, to whom he addressed moving exhortations to be liberal towards the poor in their great
necessity. His example bore fruit, and many vied
with him in the abundance of their alms-deeds.   Particularly was this the case with the Governor, the Duke
of Albuquerque, who gave a penny every day to all who
begged an alms at his gate. Many others sent large
amounts to the saint to be distributed by him.   In
this way he often received considerable sums without
even knowing from whom they came. So great was
his care of the poor, that it has been established that
during this season of scarcity not one person died of
want.   Nor were his labours confined to Milan.   His
precautions and earnest applications to those who had
means went far towards alleviating the prevailing distress throughout the diocese.   With this intention in
view, he did not spare himself the fatigue of travelling
from place to place to stir up the charity of all.

This same year was remarkable for a prodigious fall
of snow in this part of Lombardy. So heavy was it that
the roofs of many houses were broken in. Moreover
when the masses of snow froze in the streets, they
became so completely blocked that it became necessary to hew out ways to make a passage from one
street to another. Even so they were still quite
impracticable for horses and carriages, and foot pas-
sengers were obliged to have sharp points of iron fas-
tened to the soles of their shoes to avoid falling on the
slippery surface. In the country the snow had fallen
in some parts to a depth of nine feet, the heaviest fall

ever known in those parts. But this was nothing to
what they looked for in spring time, when the melting
of the ice would bring a flood to wash away the growing crops, and the foundations of the houses.

St. Charles foresaw the calamity, and gave himself
up to prayer and fasting, in order to move Almighty
God to spare His people, and called upon all to join
him in the work. His supplications were answered
in a wonderful way, for instead of the deluge which
was expected, the snow melted away by insensible
degrees without inconvenience. Everybody looked
upon this as miraculous, as the great body of water
was disposed of in a way so much out of the common.
The veneration of the people for the saint was thereby
much increased, as also when it was found that the
prospect of the harvest was more abundant than any
previous year within the memory of living man.

Intelligence was received about this time that the
Grand Turk, the relentless enemy of Christians, was
preparing a great armament, and that he had already
declared war against Venice by landing a force of
cavalry and infantry in the island of Cyprus. All
the zeal of Pius V. was stirred up at the news of this
threatened invasion. He immediately adopted methods
to defeat it. Besides providing subsidies for carrying on the war, he set on foot a League among the great
powers of Europe against the barbarians; but placed his
chief reliance on the grace of God, by calling on the
whole city of Rome to join in earnest prayer, in public
and in private, and forbidding masques, theatrical performances, and the banquets that usually take place

between Christmas and Lent. In an apostolic letter of the year 1571, granting many indulgences, he invited all Christendom to unite in supplicating Almighty God not to judge them according to their iniquities, but look down with mercy upon the calamities and perils that threatened His people ; and defend them from the hosts pouring in upon them ; disposing the hearts of all Christian princes to sink all animosities, and present a united front to the enemy of religion.

The victory of Lepanto on 7th October, 1571, was the answer to these prayers, and to the intercession of Pope Pius V., of blessed memory.

St. Charles did not lose this occasion of benefiting his flock. At the first sound of alarm, he addressed a pastoral letter to the city and diocese on the gravity of the danger, and the necessity of deprecating the wrath of God by prayer and penance. At the same time he dwelt upon the follies to which thoughtless and pleasure-seeking men were apt to give themselves up during the time of the Carnival. He pointed out how they are a fruitful source of sin and evil, crying to Heaven for judgment, and most surely calling down the scourges of Divine justice. He concluded with a moving exhortation to the people to live as Christians in the practice of good works, to shed around them the lustre of a blameless and holy life, and by a true and worthy spirit of penance to gain the help of God in the hour of need.

Solemn processions of clergy and people showed the spirit of devotion that animated the hearts of all. Prayers were said and the Blessed Sacrament exposed in the Churches, particularly those served by Regulars, for many days in succession, with every facility for the people at all hours. These exercises of devotion took place during the three weeks immediately before Lent,—a time when, through a bad habit, men were wont to think themselves entitled to greater license than at other seasons,—and thus proved an antidote to many disorders. Nor was his zeal yet satisfied. Knowing that the people readily accepted spiritual food when provided for them, he ordered that on all the principal festivals, the offices of the Church should be sung with greater solemnity than was customary. Besides all this, he set on foot so many other exercises of piety that there was no time left vacant for frivolous worldly amusements. By these means the face of the city was quite changed, and the streets no longer resounded as of old with the shouts of idle masqueraders and trumpets calling the people to profane diversions, but instead there were heard hymns of praise and prayer. Processions threaded their way through the city, asking the blessing of Heaven, accompanied by pilgrims who scourged themselves publicly in token of their spirit of penance.

A long-standing abuse was at this time put down by the saint. On the first Sunday of Lent the people were accustomed to eat meat, and to indulge in all manner of revels, as if it had been the closing day of the Carnival; an occasion of many sins. To prevent these disorders, St. Charles invited all the people to come to Holy Communion at the cathedral on that day, and, that they might do so with greater devotion and more abundant fruit, he recommended them, besides the ordinary necessary preparation, to join in special fasts and prayers. The people obeyed his wishes cheerfully, and the week before the first Sunday of Lent was spent in devotion and every sign of penance. When the Sunday arrived the concourse of people was so great, that though the Archbishop began to give Communion at break of day he had not concluded by the hour of Vespers.

By all these pious exercises his flock was restrained from much sin, and kindled to devotion and fervour: this happy change, no doubt, moved our Divine Lord to look down mercifully on His people, and grant the victory with which He was pleased to bless the Christian arms.

CHAPTER XXIX.

1571.

THE rulers of the Swiss cantons had always held St. Charles in great honour on account of the fame of his holy life which had spread throughout Christendom. Their veneration for him was greatly increased since he had been among them and they had themselves been witnesses of his saintliness and his success in reclaiming souls. They found by experience that the truth of the matter far exceeded the report that had gone abroad, and their admiration for him grew in proportion as they became better acquainted with his life and actions. His heart in turn was filled with an ardent desire to strengthen their faith, and help them in the way of salvation. This good feeling was of the greatest benefit to the people at large, and especially on the following occasion. Two school-masters had established themselves in the diocese of Como, who, under pretence of giving a liberal education to youths under their charge, sowed among them

the seeds of the heresy of Calvin. Others also of
the same sect had, under various pretexts, introduced
themselves with similar intentions into different parts
of the diocese. The watchful eye of the pastor soon
perceived the threatened danger. He had not failed
to take warning from similar attempts in other places,
and he knew well that harm would come to his flock
if measures of precaution were not speedily taken. It
was with great anxiety that he saw the practice pre-
valent among the Swiss of sending their children to
be educated in the heretical cantons, in order to learn
the German language, to the great detriment of the
country; for by their means the erroneous principles
they had imbibed were spread far and wide on their
return. Still the evil was as yet in its infancy, and
might readily be crushed by a vigorous hand. The
year before, when he was on his journey beyond the
Alps, he had made some remonstrance against this
pernicious practice. The answer he then received
was that it was a question to be referred to the
National Assembly or Diet, which was attended by
the principal men of all the cantons, both Catholics
and Protestants; because these new teachers had taken
care to settle in towns which were under the jurisdiction of all the cantons.

When the Cardinal heard that the Diet was about
to be held, he sent Ambrogio Fornero,[1] a native of
Switzerland and the Swiss representative at Milan,
to attend it. He was furnished with all necessary
credentials in order to visit the authorities of the

---

[1] At the time a member of the Cardinal's household.

Catholic cantons before the opening of the Diet, and dispose them to further the settlement of the question at issue. The saint recommended him at the same time to be liberal in presents, and to give state banquets according to the custom of the country, to show the respect and affection which he entertained for the authorities. Fornero presented himself at the first meeting of the Diet, and stated the requests of the Cardinal under three heads. First, that the obnoxious teachers should be withdrawn and that no heretical teachers should be permitted in the Catholic cantons. Second, that none of the inhabitants of the cantons should be permitted to send their children into the heretical cantons, either to learn German or to be instructed in any trade. Third, that no Protestant official or functionary entrusted with any public office should be suffered to interfere in any matter concerning the Catholic religion, but that there should be a Catholic officer appointed, whose business it should be to inquire into cases of apostasy and to bring offenders to justice; since the heretics would not allow the establishment of the Holy Inquisition in the hands of priests or religious. The Catholic cantons readily accepted these propositions, and they were considered in the Diet in spite of the difficulty of punishing the teachers of false doctrines. But still the respect in which the very name of the saint was held prevailed over these obstacles, and a decree was passed that these teachers should be banished from the Catholic cantons under heavy penalties; also that none of the subjects of the territory, south of the Alps, of whatever station in life, should henceforth send their children to heretical countries for education.   There was appointed, in conformity with the desire of the Cardinal, a new officer, the Chancellor of Locarno, one of the principal towns of the territory, with jurisdiction over all matters pertaining to religion, and instructions to prohibit all heretics from interfering with the faith in future.   These instructions were carried out, and Fornero himself conducted the heretical teachers beyond the mountains, and so freed this part of Italy from heresy.

All were struck with astonishment at the expedition with which his measures were undertaken, and the way in which he won the consent of those among the authorities who were already tainted with heretical tenets.   This was indeed one more striking proof of the universal esteem felt for him.   But for his vigilance and energy, the country might have been devoured by heresy, as had but lately been the case in the neighbouring valleys of Chiavenna and Valtellina.

While these matters were proceeding, St. Charles was again busied in the work of his diocese, and his reforms.   His health began, however, to suffer from the fatigues and austerities with which he afflicted his body.   A malady occasioning much suffering about this time was endured by him with patience, and accepted with joy as coming from the hand of his Heavenly Father.

Scarcely, however, had the treatment of the physicians begun to relieve him, than in his zeal he renewed his labours, so that, little by little, he fell back into his former weak state. This was a source of great anxiety to his friends, who took the opportunity to urge him to be more careful of his health, if not for his own sake, for that of his diocese, to which his life was so important. They pointed out to him that if he was taken away, the work of reform would be stayed and his labour rendered in vain.

The saint received these admonitions with a recognition of the affection that prompted them, but replied that, while his friends were so mindful of his bodily health, he must beg of them not to forget the consideration of the health of his soul ; he reminded them that spiritual and ecclesiastical matters were not to be measured by the life of one individual, but by the providence of God. He was, moreover, convinced that whatever depended on the life of any poor mortal must come to a speedy overthrow, for the Lord himself had said by the prophet Isaias that to trust in man was to rest upon a broken reed.[1] These sentiments shew the absence in our saint of all solicitude for his bodily health. He had abandoned life itself to the keeping of God and the service of His Church. Moreover he blamed himself if he in any way faltered, but at the same time gave the glory to God for all the good he had effected, esteeming himself only as a frail and unworthy instrument in His hands.

Having partly recovered from the dangerous consequences of this illness which overtook him in the

[1] Isaias xxxvi. 6.

month of June, he set out on his usual visitation of his diocese in August.   When at some distance from Milan he heard that the Governor, the Duke of Albuquerque, was fast sinking under a serious illness, and that his life was despaired of.   Much grieved at the intelligence, for the saint bore a lively recollection of his good-will towards himself, he hastened back to Milan, but only arrived in time to console the Duchess for the loss of her husband.   The sympathy and counsels of the saint proved no small alleviation of her sorrow.

In this same year, 1571, the Franciscan brethren had restored their church dedicated to Saints Nabor and Felix, whose relics were preserved there.   On the occasion of reopening it, on 4th September, 1571, St. Charles verified and placed them beneath the high altar, together with relics of St. Barnabas, and of two Archbishops of Milan, Saints Caius and Maternus, the bodies of St. Fortunatus and St. Felix, martyrs, and of St. Savina, matron, replacing them with fitting honour in their resting-places.

CHAPTER XXX.

1572.

THE illness of St. Charles did not yield to the treatment of his physicians, and he at last met with a dangerous relapse, accompanied by low fever and catarrh. It was feared that consumption would set in, and carry him to the grave. From medicine he obtained no relief, and the malady continued unabated till the following summer. During this illness his evenness of temper and union with the will of God were no less remarkable than his spirit of thanksgiving to Him for having been pleased to visit him in this way. He regretted nothing but his inability to labour as heretofore in his diocese, though he did not even now neglect to watch over his flock. It is wonderful to trace out the ways in which God continually tried the endurance of His servant, who stood firm against every onslaught, strengthened in the love of God to meet still fiercer attacks. Though suffering from illness, he occupied himself in preparing the matter for his third diocesan synod, which he had fixed for the 15th April. But this proved to be more than he was able to do, as his strength of body was unequal to the strain.

The Cardinal was still in a suffering condition when news reached him of the serious illness of his Holiness Pius V. Soon the worst apprehensions were fulfilled, and whilst the saint was calling upon his flock to unite with him in prayer for the restoration of this great Father and Pastor, he heard of his death on 1st May, 1572. The Church lost in him a saintly Pontiff, whose single aim it had been, by spreading the Faith and reforming the flock, to promote the glory of God.

St. Charles's physician had at this time begun a new course of treatment, and had prescribed that he should be kept perfectly quiet. He would, however, allow nothing to hinder him from celebrating the obsequies of the Pontiff, and stirring up the people to pray to God for a worthy successor. Abandoning the care of his health to His good providence, he set out on his journey to Rome to assist at the forthcoming election. His doctor remonstrated with him in vain. Humanly speaking, it would seem that a long and difficult journey suddenly undertaken and rapidly pursued, after so many months' illness, would give a shock to the system, and entirely check any treatment on which the physicians trusted for his recovery.

But the saint was not to be restrained by these considerations. He knew that he had influence with the Cardinals, and he would not forego this opportunity of exercising it for the glory of God in a matter of such importance. At the same time, he submitted patiently to the treatment prescribed, and stored the medicines in his baggage. Every provision was made for his diocese during the time of his absence, and, after public prayer, he set out on the day after the tidings came of the Pontiff's death. He used a litter,[1] with frequent relays of mules, and thus was enabled to continue his journey without interruption, and with such expedition by day and night that he reached Rome at the same time as two Cardinals who had travelled post from an equal distance. Thus he was early enough to enter the Conclave at the same time as the rest of the Sacred College. Two noteworthy occurrences happened during the journey. One was that the mule which bore the drugs with which the doctor had provided him fell into a river at a short distance from Bologna: the various bottles and cases were overturned and carried down the stream, and were never recovered. When the saint heard of it, he observed with a smile, that it boded well for his health, as it was a sign he had no further need for these appliances. Contrary to the opinion of the faculty he grew notably better each day of his journey, an improvement which he referred to the good pleasure of God to make use of him in the election of His Vicar upon earth. The other circumstance was that he was perfectly able to say Mass every day, notwithstanding the speed of his journey and its fatigues. Yet before leaving Milan he had been obliged for

---

[1] In 1564 Pius IV. begged the Cardinals not to make use of carriages, but afterwards they were in such general use in Rome that St. Charles used to say : "Omnia vanitas praeter currum in urbe—All is vanity except a carriage in Rome."

many days to omit saying Mass on account of his malady. It was on the 12th May, 1572, that the Cardinals assembled in Conclave to elect a successor to Pius V. On the following day they unanimously elected Ugo Buoncompagni of Bologna, Cardinal of the title of San Sisto, who took the name of Gregory XIII.; the second Pontiff whose election may be said to be owing to St. Charles. He had been made Cardinal by Pius IV., and enjoyed the intimate friendship of St. Charles, when the affairs of the Church were in his hands during that pontificate, and had assisted him in bringing the Council of Trent to a conclusion. The saint was thus well acquainted with his merits, so that together with all those who were guided by his opinion, he cheerfully concurred in the nomination, and felt much satisfaction at seeing the Chair of St. Peter filled by one who was so well able to carry out the constitutions of the Council of Trent in the extirpation of heresy, and promotion of the faith. The charity and zeal of this Pontiff were abundantly proved by the numerous colleges he founded, by which the Church of God has been much benefited. Gregory XIII. was not slow to prove his high appreciation of the Cardinal, for he would not give him permission to leave Rome till the end of October, in order to avail himself of his advice and assistance both in the administration of the city and of the universal Church. The saint also left his mark upon the pontifical household, considering it most important that the Head of the Church should rule it well, in order to give good example and show mankind how to live according to the precepts of the Gospel.

Besides the counsels which he thus offered to the Holy Father in all humility, he left with him a priest of his own household, Bernardo Carniglia by name, as a spiritual man, who was also well acquainted with matters of ecclesiastical discipline, and qualified to assist in measures of reform.

The Cardinal presented the Pontiff with several works of the Fathers and saints, addressed to those who have held the Apostolic office: such as the book of St. Gregory on the Pastoral Office, and that by St. Bernard, entitled " De Consideratione," sent to Pope Eugenius; as an expression of his fervent desire to kindle in the Pontiff a fire of zeal for the benefit of the Church of God. With the Cardinals and prelates also, he exercised his influence by urging upon them the exalted duties of their office, and their special obligations to live holy lives, and to set an example of virtue to all.

Whilst thus occupied with these matters the Cardinal did not forget his duty to himself and to his own diocese. His health not being perfectly restored, he still continued some of the remedies prescribed for him. But when the doctors disagreed, those of Rome strenuously urging him to try the baths of Lucca, and the faculty at Milan as strenuously opposing this course, St. Charles solved the question by giving up doctors and medicine altogether, according to the advice of prudent friends. He now followed only the rule of life he had formerly drawn up, and this plan succeeded, for he had no sooner returned to the use of ordinary food than he grew gradually better, and before long he was once more as well as he had ever been. He felt now as if he had emancipated himself from a state of bondage, and begun to return to his practices of austerity. Indeed he increased his mortifications, and by this means made rapid strides in the path of virtue and perfection, becoming a shining example, leading many to live spiritual lives.

He had several times applied to Pius V. to accept his resignation of the office of Grand Penitentiary, that of Protector of many religious Orders, and of Arch-priest of Sta. Maria Maggiore. His Holiness would never relieve him of these burdens, though he dispensed him from the necessity of residing habitually in Rome, or from performing any part of the duties that might interfere with the administration of his diocese. The saint now renewed his application to the new Pontiff, deeming that the time devoted to these offices was so much stolen from more immediate duties. Gregory XIII., however, was just as unwilling as his predecessor to release him from obligations which he fulfilled so well. Upon the continued application of the saint he did, however, so far consent on the condition that St. Charles should select his successors in the offices. This caused a further delay, as the saint was desirous of weighing his decision well. In the meantime he turned his attention once more to Milanese affairs, and, in the first place, gave directions that the diocesan synod should be held in his absence according to the arrangements he had made. He now entrusted the matter to his Vicar-General, Monsignor Castello, and wrote to his clergy to explain his detention at Rome by important affairs, in obedience to the commands of the Sovereign Pontiff. When about to return he asked for spiritual treasures for his beloved Church, and obtained from the Sovereign Pontiff many privileges and abundant faculties for its government. Among other concessions he obtained divers indulgences for the practice of daily devotions, which he had recommended throughout the diocese; for the schools of Christian doctrine, the societies of penitents, and for the indulgence of the seven churches in Rome, for the same number of churches in Milan. Furnished with these treasures he started homewards, stopping on his way to visit the Holy House of Loretto, whither he arrived on the vigil of All Saints, and gave great edification to the pilgrims by passing the whole night in prayer in the Chapel of Our Lady, in imitation of the holy fathers.

Book III.

CHAPTER I.

ST. CHARLES RESIGNS THE OFFICE OF GRAND PENI-
TENTIARY AND OTHER DIGNITIES; FOUNDATION
OF THE COLLEGE OF BRERA; THIRD PROVINCIAL
COUNCIL.

1572.

UPON his return to Milan, St. Charles, after he had
duly weighed the arguments of the Sovereign Pontiff
respecting his resignation of the offices before mentioned, determined to give them up, as intimated in
the following letter, which he despatched after his
arrival at home, in order to free his mind from
scruples about the nomination of fit successors. For
the office of Grand Penitentiary, as it was one of great
importance, he had suggested to the Holy Father the
name of Cardinal John Aldobrandini,[1] whom he judged
fit by his learning, prudence, and integrity to fill it
worthily.

[1] Brother of Pope Clement VIII., 1592–1605.

Letter of St. Charles to Gregory XIII.

" Most holy Father,—After my return to the church committed to my care, I have deemed it right no longer to delay coming to a decision concerning the office of Grand Penitentiary, and to resign it . as my conscience has constantly and urgently demanded of me. For it is manifest that it is a great disadvantage to the pastoral care of the see of Milan that I should be absent from my proper sphere of labour in order to fulfil the requirements of that office. I have, therefore, resolved to give it up altogether. Since it has pleased our Divine Lord to commit to the hands of your Holiness the government of His whole Church, and in particular the power of conferring all the offices and dignities for His greater glory and the salvation of His flock, and has further promised the special and unfailing assistance of the Holy Ghost in all these matters, it would seem that I cannot more effectually set my conscience at rest than by leaving the matter entirely to your Holiness. I, therefore, hereby, of my own free will resign the office of Grand Penitentiary into the hands of your Holiness as into the hands of Christ, whose Vicar you are on earth, praying His Divine Majesty to grant you abundant light and grace, that you may be guided to a fitting choice of one who, not being bound to residence or other duties as I am, may be free to employ his zeal in the service of God for the welfare of souls. For the same reason I further resign, of my own free will, the office of Arch-priest of St. Mary Major, as well as the Protectorate and Censorship of the Franciscan and Carmelite Orders, of the convent of St. Martha in Rome, and of all the other congregations of Regulars of which I have charge.

"In conclusion I humbly kiss the feet of your Holiness, and commend myself and this Church of Milan to your paternal care and tenderness in the bowels of Christ.[1]

"MILAN, 19*th November* 1572."

The Pope was graciously pleased, on receiving this letter, to relieve him of the various offices, which he conferred on other Cardinals, assigning to Cardinal John Aldobrandini the post of Grand Penitentiary as St. Charles had advised.

Up to this time he had continued to hold his first ecclesiastical appointment, viz., the benefice of Arona; not, however, on account of any particular attachment to it, for he had long been detached from all affection for things of this world, but because he was not yet able to make up his mind exactly what use to make of it. At first, it had been his intention to make a collegiate church of it, in which daily residence should

---

[1] St. Charles writes to Bernardo Carniglia, his agent at Rome, on November 19, 1572: "Before my return from Rome I made known to the Pope my desire of being relieved from the burden of so many responsibilities. He urged me to name some Prelates for these offices. As I was silent he dismissed me, telling me to delay my purpose till I should be at Milan, and could think about the matter calmly. I am still of the same mind, as may be seen from the accompanying letter to his Holiness. Should he again ask me to name my successor in the office of Penitentiary, leave everything to his judgment, only telling him that I thought it my duty, while I filled the office, to put up no post for sale, and beg him to press on the work of its reform which I have begun."

be obligatory, or to give it to some reformed congregation of Regulars, who should undertake the spiritual
care of the neighbourhood, which stood in need of
religious ministrations. But the first plan did not
altogether satisfy him, and the second failed to obtain
the approval of the Holy Father. Both schemes
remained consequently in abeyance for a time. Meanwhile he spent the whole of the revenues in alms
and in maintaining upon the spot a number of
efficient priests, as the monks had given up the
charge.

It then occurred to him to devote the revenues
to an important work which he had been meditating
for some time, in order to supply a pressing need both
of the diocese and of the whole province. He had
seen from the first that his clergy were deficient in
their knowledge of theology, and had already taken
some steps towards a remedy by inviting the Jesuit
Fathers to establish themselves provisionally and give
public lectures at the house of St. Fidelis until a
college should be erected. Whilst in Rome he
brought the matter under the notice of his Holiness,
and obtained from him permission to resign the
benefice of Arona in favour of this college. He then
entered into a negotiation with Cardinal John Paul
Chiesa, who at that time held *in commendam* the
provostship of Brera which had belonged to the Frati
Umiliati, and obtained from him the houses of
residence, which were large and commodious, with
spacious grounds. He also obtained a portion of the
revenues to provide for the maintenance of the Fathers

who were to serve the Church. This he gave to the
Jesuit Fathers on the 4th October of the same year
(1572), acting under apostolic authority. Such was
the beginning of his celebrated college for teaching
grammar, the classics, and theology, according to the
provisions of their institute. This foundation was a
proof of the love he bore his native city, enabling
the good Fathers to serve God, and to confer great
benefits on students, among whom were found many
men of ability who, but for this provision, might have
passed their lives in obscurity. He made over to the
Fathers the abbey of Arona, where they established
their novitiate, as it was especially adapted for this
purpose, on account of the beauty and salubrity of
its site. Nor did the saint in his zeal overlook the
needs of the surrounding population, for he made it
also the residence of several priests who were to
attend to their spiritual wants, so that he had every
reason to be satisfied with this distribution of the
property, as it amply provided the means of grace to
numbers, and conferred a lasting benefit on the
diocese.

Others, however, took a very different view of the
matter, his relations among them; who complained of
the alienation of the patronage of a benefice which
had long been in the family, and thought, if he did
not want to hold it himself, he might at least have
resigned in favour of some one of them. But the
saint, whose sole aim was the honour and glory of
God, saw no reason to change his determination, as he

could not but rejoice over the advantages likely to accrue from its foundation.

It has proved indeed one of the greatest of the benefits he conferred, for not only has it been the means of instructing his clergy in theology, but it has also provided the diocese with men of erudition, according to the intention of the Council of Trent. It has sent out also a succession of men well fitted for the duties of the pastoral office, and this not alone for the diocese of Milan, but likewise for distant provinces, as numbers of clergy as well as laity were attracted thither to finish their studies, just as in Rome students flocked to the colleges founded by Gregory XIII.

Having satisfactorily arranged this undertaking, he found himself free to devote the rest of the winter to the care of his diocese. He was employed at this time chiefly in carrying out the reforms he had begun, more especially in various communities of nuns, according to the powers which he had obtained for this purpose from the Holy See. He was also much occupied with the preparations for his third provincial council, which was held on the 24th April, 1573. Among the prelates assembled we find Cardinal Paul da Rezzo,[1] Bishop of Piacenza, of the Congregation of Clerks

[1] Paul Burali da Rezzo or d'Arezzo was born at Itri, near Gaëta, in 1511. He entered the congregation of the Theatines in 1557, and was made Bishop of Piacenza in 1568, and Cardinal of the title of St. Pudenziana in 1570. Like his predecessor in the see, Bernardino Scotto, called the Cardinal of Trani, he came to the Provincial Council here mentioned, after entering a protest against being held to be subject to Milan as metropolitan. In 1576 he was translated to Naples by Gregory XIII., where he died in 1578 at the age of sixty-seven. The cause of his canonisation was introduced in 1624, and he was declared *Blessed* by Clement XIV. in 1771.

Regular. He was a man of holy life, learned, and a firm friend of our Cardinal. A number of decrees were made on this occasion, touching divine worship and ecclesiastical discipline, and the better observance of festivals throughout the province. St. Charles then forwarded the decrees, as he always did, to the Sovereign Pontiff for confirmation, by the hands of Monsignor Castello, his Vicar-General, whom he also commissioned to lay before his Holiness certain reforms proposed, not only for his own diocese, but also for the whole Church, a special point being that synods should be regularly held in each province, a matter which had hitherto been neglected.

CHAPTER II.

1573.

WHILE St. Charles was busied in his ordinary pastoral occupations, a fresh storm was raised up against him on the old question of jurisdiction, which had not as yet been decided, in consequence of the death of Pius V.

As we have already mentioned, the Governor of Milan, the Duke of Albuquerque, had passed to a better life some time before these events, and the military commandant now held the office provisionally. On occasion of the Carnival this year he gave orders for the representation of a hunt of wild animals for the diversion of the crowd, to be held in the piazza in front of the cathedral. As soon as the Cardinal heard this, his zeal for the honour of the House of God led him at once to prohibit its being held in that place under pain of excommunication. The commandant obeyed without hesitation, and transferred the scene of the games to the castle square. He was, however, considerably nettled at this interference with his authority, and soon began to show signs of resenting it, being urged thereto by certain individuals who had no good intentions towards the Church, and who suggested that very little respect had been shown him by the action of the Cardinal.

Before very long another occasion presented itself of creating animosity against him.

Some persons, who had profaned the Festivals of the Church, having been punished by the ecclesiastical courts, brought the matter before the Deputy Governor, urging him to restrain the ecclesiastical functionaries from taking cognisance of such cases. Being thus irritated in various ways, he tried by different means to induce people to give entertainments and public balls and dances on feasts and holidays, knowing that he could not displease the Cardinal more than by such acts of profanation. However, he failed in his design through the piety and good feeling of the people. Nor was he permitted to attempt any other innovation, for, within a very short time after these occurrences, he fell ill and died.

We have already had occasion to mention that Pius V. had sent Father Vincenzo Giustiniano, a Dominican, into Spain to treat with his Catholic Majesty respecting the matter of ecclesiastical jurisdiction in Milan, and that his labours had resulted in the King's sending instructions to the Governor to spare no pains in settling the dispute by a fair adjudication, after which matters went on smoothly for some time, the piety and good-will of the president of the senate, Giovanni Battista Rainoldo, tending in no small degree to promote this understanding, and for the moment the Ecclesiastical Courts exercised, without let or hindrance, authority even in lay causes which fell under their jurisdiction. But on the death of the Governor the aspect of affairs changed. His temporary successor, Alvaro de Sande, seems not to have been acquainted with the mind of his Catholic Majesty with respect to religion, and lent himself to the malicious designs of the disaffected. We have already given some account of their intrigues, but worse remains to be told.

The new Governor, Don Luigi di Requesens, had been the king's ambassador at Rome during the pontificate of Pius V., and during his residence there had formed a close friendship with St. Charles, and was well acquainted with his upright character, and his loyalty to the Spanish monarch. Nothing, therefore, seemed to hold out a fairer prospect of continued peace and cordiality between the ecclesiastical and civil authorities; the event, however, proved widely different from these expectations. The ill-disposed persons who had before menaced the tranquillity of the Archbishop, being men of bad lives, were once more led on by the enemy of souls to array themselves against him.

The new Governor was known to them to be a man of considerable sagacity and ability, and to be fully alive to the importance of ingratiating himself into popular favour, while not less anxious to preserve his fidelity to his royal master free from all taint of suspicion. Consequently, on his accession to office, the persons whom we have described surrounded him,

and represented to him that he could do no greater
service to the King than by defending his prerogatives
against the alleged aggressions of Cardinal Borromeo,
whose object, according to them, was gradually to
usurp the royal authority; and they hinted that his
predecessor had held the reins too loosely, and that he
could not make himself more popular with the people
than by throwing off the yoke of the Church.   .

Nothing could be more specious or better calculated to serve their purpose.   For what magistrate
who aimed at establishing a character for zeal and
devotion to his prince would not have hailed such an
opportunity of giving proof of his assiduity?   Thus
the saint was involved in great difficulties.   The
Governor, all this time, imagined that he was doing
good service to his royal master, and, in reality, was
acting with an upright intention, for it does not seem
to have occurred to him that he was being deceived
by evil counsellors.   It was not long before two very
favourable occasions presented themselves for the exercise of his supposed loyalty ; and for this, additional
facility was given by the absence of St. Charles, who
was at the time occupied in the visitation of his
diocese.   A gentleman having obtained a Brief from
the Apostolic See for the furtherance of a lawsuit in
which he was engaged, the Governor fancying he discerned a slight here offered to the royal prerogative, forbade it to be heard by the Judge, alleging that to have
recourse to such briefs without obtaining the permission
of the Crown was illegal.

The Sovereign Pontiff was much displeased at

this occurrence, and intimated to the Governor that he had incurred the censures of the Church, from which he urged him, in terms of paternal affection, to clear himself. These remonstrances produced the desired effect, and the Governor begged for absolution, which was given him by Cardinal Chiesa, who was at the time in Milan. St. Charles himself absolved the judge at the door of his archiepiscopal chapel.

The other occasion was of graver import, and produced more perplexing results, and opened up again the old controversy with the Senate of Milan, and caused greater scandal. It happened that two years before certain letters had been received from the King of Spain containing much that was contrary to the rights of the Church. The evil counsellors surrounding the Governor now persuaded him to produce them. But before taking any active steps he gave the Cardinal, as if in joke, some intimation of what he had in reserve. St. Charles, without hesitation, warned him with his habitual gentleness, but at the same time seriously, to desist from such proceedings, as he would never suffer an infringement on the rights of the Church.

Notwithstanding this reply, no sooner was St. Charles absent from Milan than the Governor informed his Vicar-General of the letters he had in his possession. The holy Cardinal heard with deep regret of the hindrances thus thrown once more in his way. He grieved, too, no less over the outrage offered to the honour of God, and the thoughtlessness of one whom he esteemed, and of others associated with him,

in exposing themselves to ecclesiastical censures. Without loss of time he retraced his steps to Milan, and
with great forbearance endeavoured to make the Governor sensible of the real state of the case, that he
might see the injustice of the course he was following,
and abandon it. For. this purpose he asked for the
assistance of Cardinal Chiesa, who had considerable
influence with the royal authorities, both on account
of his position as a Senator of Milan, and of his personal character which commanded general respect. He
thought that the representations of such a man, added
to his own, would give sufficient evidence of the
threatened mischief. But the malicious influence
which was persistently applied on the other side
counteracted their united endeavours, and the Governor would not recede from the offensive position he
had taken up. The Cardinal might now justly have
pronounced sentence of excommunication against him,
but he was willing to show every consideration for
his office, and, moreover, his natural tenderness had
made him shrink from having recourse to measures
of severity. Again he sought the intervention of
those whose position enabled them to do so with effect,
and by their means he brought forward arguments to
prove not only that he was invading the liberty of
the Church, but was acting in direct opposition to the
mind and intention of the King, as his own letter sufficiently proved. These remonstrances were backed by
some reference to the duty, which must, in the event
of protracted hostility, devolve upon him, of asserting
the honour of God, and publicly declaring that the

censures of the Church had been incurred. But these and other friendly overtures failing to soften him, the saint found himself at last obliged to allow justice to take its course. The reluctance with which he yielded to this painful expedient is sufficiently shown by the fact that he sent the Governor a special notice of his determination, although in no wise bound to do so, seeing that the scandal had been so notorious. His anxiety for the honour of God and the defence of His Church in this matter are well depicted in his own words : " Should we be obliged to publish this excommunication, which may God forbid is our continual prayer to Him, the Father of mercies, then your excellency, and all by whose fault or act it will be brought about, must be well aware that in the day of wrath you will have to render an account thereof to Christ, our Lord and Judge, and to His Church."

Other testimony to the grief here expressed is found in the deposition of Giovanni Fontana, Bishop of Ferrara, in the process of the canonization of the Saint. He says that, when St. Charles summoned the Congregation to deliberate upon the case, it was noticed by all that he had been shedding tears.

However, when all his charitable overtures had been refused, St. Charles found the time was come when he must nerve himself to an act of severity, which could no longer be deferred. That no precaution might be omitted, he had first sent to inform the Sovereign Pontiff of his determination, after having himself investigated the law of the Church on the subject.

When this resolution became known to his family and friends, he was immediately assailed by them on all sides with entreaties that he would reconsider the step. They represented to him the danger to which he was exposing himself and them by provoking the royal displeasure in the event of the King espousing, as might well be expected, the cause of his representative. Their forebodings of ruin to their house could not fail, they thought, to move his compassion. It required all his courage to tell them that while his affection for them remained undiminished, and though it would grieve him very sensibly that they should have to suffer on his account, yet that, at the same time, he was bound to prefer his duty to the love of relatives, and could not suffer any human affection to interfere with what he owed to God and His Church, for whose defence he would, if need were, lay down his life. He continued, that should he entertain any other views he could never hope to be a good Bishop, or even a good Christian. At the same time, he besought them to bear with him, although he could not yield to their entreaties, for it became his sacred calling to strip himself of every earthly attachment for the honour of God. He bade them put their trust in the Divine protection, which could never fail either himself or them, as the cause in which he was engaged was most just, and one which concerned the interests of Almighty God. He begged them to recommend the matter to God in their prayers, trusting implicitly in His Divine assistance, and assured them that his own should not be wanting.

His resolution became in a very short time known all over Milan. As it was a matter of public importance, every one felt an interest in it, and all awaited the issue with fear and apprehension.

The municipal authorities of the city, after long and earnest deliberation, decided to send Count Tazio Mandello, with other members of the council, to implore the Cardinal, in the name of the city, to stay the proceedings. They urged their plea with great earnestness, pointing out the consequences that might be expected, and the possibility of a rising of the people. They urged also that the good works which his zeal and devotion had set on foot might suddenly be ruined. They begged him to remember that he was himself by birth a son of their city, and now, by his office and dignity, had become its Father. In these terms they besought him not to visit the sin of others upon them, his loving children and fellow-citizens. St. Charles received their representations with his wonted urbanity, but told them decidedly that, while they were not wrong in appealing to his sense of what was due to his native city, or to the respect and affection he owed them, he could not alter his determination. He added that nothing could have induced him to such a step but the sense of justice and the demands of conscience. He prayed them to let this consideration be his justification in their eyes, since nothing could release him from the obligation of having a greater regard to God than to the world, as he was bound to place the Divine

honour and glory above any other consideration what-
soever.

The delegates could say nothing in reply to this
unanswerable argument, and returned to the council.[1]

---

[1] Notwithstanding all this opposition of the Governor, in a letter to
the king of Spain he told him "that he had found at Milan a second
Ambrose."—O.

CHAPTER III.

1573.

THERE is no doubt that the meek and humble spirit of St. Charles would have been greatly relieved could he have found any just pretext for withdrawing from this excommunication of the Governor. But it was no longer possible to delay the measure, severe as it might seem, as there was no other way of maintaining the authority of the Church, which was his only aim.

He was so firmly persuaded that these reasons left him no alternative, that, setting aside every other consideration, even regard for his personal safety, in the true spirit of a Bishop he publicly pronounced the sentence of excommunication against the Governor, the Grand Chancellor, and some who were their associates, in conformity with the resolution he had previously submitted to the Holy Father.

Printed notices of the act were posted up in the public places throughout the city, and a copy was sent to Rome by a special messenger, with further explanations of the reasons for his resolution, to be laid before the Holy Father.

The Governor was enraged beyond measure by the excommunication launched against him. He considered that a grievous injury had been done him, and his creatures were ready enough to kindle his indignation, and to persuade him that the sentence was unjust, and, consequently, the sentence was null and void.   They persuaded him to publish a manifesto in every town of the province, justifying his own conduct, and throwing the blame on the Cardinal. This was once more the occasion for disseminating all manner of slanderous reports, and he was maliciously accused of harbouring a secret design of exciting the people to revolt, and subverting the royal authority. But two measures which they induced the Governor to adopt were more grievous to St. Charles than all the personal calumnies which were heaped upon him.

There existed in Milan at that time, as at the present day, several societies of penitents and other confraternities, who used frequently to meet in their public oratories for devotional exercises.   These the Governor now forbade, publicly, under heavy penalties, to hold their meetings, except in the presence of a person deputed by him to attend in the name of his Catholic Majesty, that they might not be made the occasion of treacherous designs.   He further ordered that when they went in procession clothed in sackcloth, as was their custom, they should no longer conceal their faces, but to prevent suspicion they should allow themselves to be seen and recognised by all.

The persons composing these confraternities were for the most part artisans and mechanics, who being employed in their various trades on working days, met in their chapels on festivals with the single object of joining in acts of devotion for the good of their souls. They were, of all people, the last who ought to have been suspected of harbouring seditious sentiments, being among the best conducted and most loyal of the King's subjects.

But even though they might have submitted to the interference, it was generally impossible to obtain the attendance of the required officer. Thus their religious gatherings were effectually interrupted to the no small grief of the Cardinal.[1]

The other vexatious measure of the Governor was to deprive St. Charles of the castle of Arona, in which, as it was a border fortress of the Milanese province on the Swiss side, a garrison was usually kept. He accordingly sent Count Giovanni Angosciola, governor of Como, with a body of soldiers to take possession of it in the name of his Catholic Majesty, pretending that as from its position it was a key to that side of the province, it ought not to be left in the hands of those whose allegiance was doubtful. There happened to have been left in charge of the castle one Giulio Beolco, a man of military experience, and faithful to his liege lord, St. Charles. He at once refused them admission, but despatched a messenger to

---

[1] St. Charles writes to Ormaneto, "that now no instruction in Christian doctrine was given in the afternoon, and that the confraternities did not meet in the churches for the divine office in the morning."

St. Charles, to know what were his orders. Without hesitation the saint desired him to deliver the fortress into the hands of the Governor of Milan, and to remove all doubts, sent him his countersign, a half-crown piece of Lucca. He also begged his uncle Count Francesco Borromeo to explain to the Governor that if he had given him the slightest intimation of his desire to garrison the fortress he should have complied most gladly; so that there would have been no need of dispatching soldiers, as if he had been an enemy who was resisting his just demands instead of one of the family of Borromeo which had never failed in fidelity to their lawful prince. He added that not only the castle of Arona, but all he possessed was at the King's disposal, and nothing could give him greater pleasure than to be able in anything to serve his Majesty; for he was most devotedly attached to his person, and was ready to comply with his wishes in everything, while duty did not interfere. But, he continued, he could not overlook the injury done to the Church, and was prepared to sacrifice his life in its defence.

This occurrence distressed the Cardinal very much; not that he cared for the castle of Arona,[1] but he feared that it might make an unfavourable impression on the King and induce him to alter his friendly policy towards the Church. It was precisely this that his enemies attempted to compass; but the

---

[1] His words to Castello then at Rome on this subject were: "If this is to be the end of the discussion that I am merely to lose the castle of Arona, then I refuse not the condition, provided that the peace of the diocese is gained at the price."—O.

King's good sense did not suffer him to listen to these malicious interpretations, and his appreciation of the Cardinal's right intentions in all his reforms was not to be so easily destroyed.

Nicolò Ormaneto, lately made Bishop of Padua, was at this time the Papal Nuncio in Spain, and his intimate acquaintance with St. Charles' plans of reform enabled him to confirm and increase the King's esteem of him. He reminded the King of his services to the State during the war against the Turks, and the disturbances in Flanders; of his solicitude for the welfare of Milan especially, into which he had infused such a religious spirit, that among all his Majesty's subjects, there were none of whose loyalty and obedience he was more sure. The King was so pleased with this account of the Cardinal that he desired to have it in writing, and that his regulations should be followed throughout the whole of his dominions; particularly the practice of the Forty Hours' Prayer, which he desired to be observed in the same manner as at Milan.

The friends and relations of St. Charles, together with the greater part of the citizens, were filled with consternation at the arbitrary and unwarrantable proceedings of the Governor. Rumours were afloat of yet more mischievous designs on his part. It was said that the Cardinal was to be taken prisoner to the castle; and again, that bodies of cavalry had already surrounded the archiepiscopal palace; and outside the city, it was publicly announced that a rising of the people had actually taken place. These reports, by,

the time they had reached Rome, increased so much
that it was said that the Archbishop's house had been
burnt to the ground.

Amid all these rumours, St. Charles preserved the
unruffled attitude which a good conscience and trust
in God inspire. His friends were urgent with him
to avoid danger by shutting himself up in the palace,
but he refused, telling them he had nothing to fear
as he had undertaken nothing without good reason;
that his only motive throughout had been to promote
the glory of God, and defend the liberties of his
Church. Therefore, he was persuaded that, if need
were, God would interpose to preserve him. Besides,
he was prepared not only to suffer, but to shed his
blood in the cause. The habit which the Cardinal
wore was by its colour a constant reminder to him
that he might be called upon to suffer death for
Christ's sake.

In this spirit he continued as usual to exercise all
his pastoral functions, and to attend to the business
of his diocese, without regard to the armed force with
which, during four days, the Governor surrounded his
palace, with the avowed intention of making him
prisoner. Though he could not but perceive that
his whole household were so terrified that it was with
difficulty he could find any one to bear the cross before
him, nevertheless he continued to go in and out as
if nothing had happened, and this even more frequently
than was his wont. This he did not merely for the
sake of showing himself, but with the object of
visiting the churches and relics of the saints, and

recommending himself to their intercession after the example of his predecessor St. Ambrose, who acted in a similar way amid the trials and persecutions to which he was subjected. Among others he visited the church dedicated to this saint, where his relics are preserved, together with those of SS. Gervasius and Protasius, whom he had specially chosen as his patrons and advocates in Heaven.

As on the direct way to these shrines it was necessary to pass the ducal palace where the Governor resided, the saint did not choose another route, but as usual passed under the Governor's windows, in opposition to the wishes of his friends, for the express purpose of showing that he had nothing to fear from him. All his trust was in God, and the event proved that He watched over his safety, for not only was he preserved from all harm, but even the soldiers who surrounded his palace would, when they saw him coming, dismount and throw themselves on their knees to beg his benediction—so great was the veneration inspired by his sanctity.

While externally so calm, the saint felt inwardly the greatest anxiety as to the evil likely to result to the souls he so dearly loved. He prayed earnestly and without ceasing, accompanying his prayer with frequent fasts and penitential exercises, that God would avert all harm from his flock.

Immediately upon the publication of the excommunication, the Governor had written to Rome, with the intention of proving its injustice and having it annulled. In order to ensure success, and obtain a favourable decision respecting the question of jurisdiction, he sent his despatch by the hands of a senator, whom he empowered to act on his behalf. This man had, however, scarcely arrived within sight of Rome, when he received a kick from a horse which laid him up for some time. On his recovery he went on his mission to the Holy Father, but at the very outset of his address he was seized with a fainting-fit, and was carried back to his hotel in a state of insensibility, and died soon afterwards, without having accomplished his business. His untimely end did not have the effect of deterring others from taking up the cause of the Governor, and constituting themselves his advocates with the Pope. The form of their petition gave additional evidence of the assurance which dictated the proceedings, for they prayed for his absolution *in case* he had incurred the censures of the Church, and alleged among other reasons, that he was on the eve of setting out on a journey into Flanders, by order of his Catholic Majesty, for the express purpose of upholding the Faith there, and putting down heretics by force of arms, and that he would probably have started before they could return.

Upon this false statement the Holy Father granted him permission to receive absolution from the sentence at the hands of any priest, thinking he was already too far from Milan to apply to the Cardinal. The Governor not having left Milan, as soon as he received the permission, obtained absolution clandestinely from a regular priest, who had not a proper understanding of the case, and did this without sending the Cardinal any notice or satisfying his requirements as in duty bound. The Sovereign Pontiff was greatly displeased when he heard how his favour had been abused, and required peremptorily that satisfaction should be made to the Cardinal, an order which the Governor was at last compelled to obey.

After this he set out for Flanders, but misfortune seemed to attend him everywhere, and before two years were over he was seized with an illness which brought him to an untimely end. Before he died, however, he sent to the Cardinal to beg for his blessing as a holy man, although he had opposed him and lent himself to the designs of evil advisers.

The news of his death was communicated to the saint by a brother of the deceased, who was then ambassador in Rome. This brother begged him to make a *memento* for him in the Holy Sacrifice. St. Charles replied that he had not forgotten him, and that he would recommend him assiduously to the mercy of God, with many other expressions of charity for his soul.

The Chancellor, who also had fallen under the excommunication, having from the first shown himself quite regardless of the censure, was seized with a deep melancholy, so that he could get no rest night or day, and was soon reduced to a very alarming condition. When the physicians could afford him no relief he became aware of the real cause of the malady, and adopted the only remedy of which the case admitted, viz., to humble himself before his saintly pastor, and to beg pardon for the offence he had committed against him. No sooner had he done so than he began to get better, and was, after a while, completely restored. Having, however, received the absolution when thought to be dying, as a case of necessity, he applied, on his restoration to health, for the regular pontifical absolution. This St. Charles, with the utmost kindness, granted, both for himself and for another who had incurred the same penalty.

Some time afterwards, having fallen ill and knowing his end to be near, he sent to beg the Cardinal to come and visit him, and give him the absolution once more, to make sure. St. Charles cheerfully assented, consoling him with paternal admonitions, and preparing him for a good death, and remained with him in his agony till he breathed his last.[1]

---

[1] St. Charles, writing of his last moments to Cesare Speciano on April 16, 1579, says: "To-day the Chancellor, who has but little hope of recovery, received the Holy Eucharist from my hands. By my advice he then made his will, and confided to me his last wishes on the administration of his private affairs."—O.

CHAPTER IV.

1573.

THE zeal of the saint for the salvation of souls constantly urged him to seek out new ways of putting every class of persons in the way of salvation. His attention was directed to the dangers to which the sons of the nobility were exposed, through the tendency of such persons to pamper and indulge their children, instead of bringing them up in proper discipline. Another consideration was the paramount importance of providing a remedy for these evils, on the ground that the good order of a state depends much on the good or bad example set by those who are in high places. Having had this always before his mind, he thought the most efficient remedy would be to found a college for the young nobility, where they might be brought up in the fear of God, out of the way of the corrupt influence and seductions of the world. He commenced this undertaking on the 4th June, 1573, by hiring a house for the purpose as a temporary arrangement. In the following year he removed the establishment to the house and church of St. John the Evangelist, formerly belonging to the Humiliati brethren, in Porta Nuova, a beautiful situation; the house being very commodious, with grounds attached, and not far from the College of Brera, whither the students went for lectures.

He called it St. Mary's College, putting it under the protection of Our Lady, and entrusted the direction of it, in the beginning, to the Jesuit Fathers, though he afterwards transferred it to the Oblates of St. Ambrose, as he did · in the case of other colleges and seminaries he founded. He also formed a committee of noblemen, laymen as well as ecclesiastics, to attend to the temporal part of its administration. In this, as in his other foundations, he displayed his munificence by expending a large sum in constructing new buildings, and in fitting up and furnishing the college. He gave them a rule appropriate to their circumstances, to train them in habits of Christian virtue, providing for their due attendance at exercises of devotion and the frequentation of the Sacraments. As he opened it to all nationalities, he had, in a short time, the happiness of seeing a great concourse of students from all parts of Italy, and even from countries north of the Alps, collected under its fostering care. The sons of princes were attracted by the great reputation of the college, not only for the excellence of the instruction imparted, but also for the virtuous training of the students, and the liberal treatment they received.

St. Charles always took the greatest interest in the welfare of this institution, and though he had taken every care to provide it with professors and directors of zeal and ability, he nevertheless kept up a special personal communication with it as a work which was very dear to him. He used to visit it several times in the course of the year, and examined the youths as to the progress they had made in spirituality and in their studies, addressing to each some words of paternal encouragement and advice. On these occasions he always gave them Holy Communion with his own hands, and regarding them as the tender plants of his Lord's garden, sought to awake in them a great desire of growing in the love and service of God. As a further mode of encouraging them, he used to take prelates and other noble persons who came to see him in Milan to visit the place, as a good opportunity for producing their compositions in prose and verse, and urging them to a virtuous emulation in their studies.

At the close of the academical year he invited a number of nobles, senators, and literary men, and held a public examination, distributing prizes with his own hands. These days gave him great pleasure, as he witnessed then the happy effects of the union of piety with the cultivation of the intellect. This work he esteemed of so great importance that he desired Silvio Antoniano,[1] who had been his secretary, to write a treatise on the best method of education. When the manuscript was submitted to him, he was not quite satisfied with the part referring to Christian piety, and

[1] Afterwards made Cardinal by Clement VIII.

therefore begged Agostino Valerio, Cardinal of Verona, to make some additions on this head. He, however, saw that it would be useful, and needed no additions from himself, and accordingly published it, with a dedication to Cardinal Borromeo.

St. Charles had long desired to restore a certain pious observance which had fallen into neglect. This was the observance of Advent, when the offices of the Church are more full than at any other time, and set before us the most beautiful mysteries of the Faith, the whole season having at one time been kept as a daily fast, with other holy exercises. St. Charles had begun some years before to observe the fast, and had made it a rule with his household to observe an abstinence from meat and milk diet during the season, and fasting on two or three days in each week. In 1573, on the approach of Advent, he determined to stir up the people to sanctify it with fasting and works of piety, conformably with the intention of Holy Church. He accordingly published a pastoral letter, in which he gave an exposition of the rites and mysteries commemorated by the Church during that season. He exhorted the people to the practice of mortification as a fitting preparation for the Feast of the Nativity, recommending them to observe the whole season as a fast, or, at least, some days in the week, and to practise works of charity and piety. He concluded with severe strictures on the recklessness of those who conformed to the corrupt custom of spending these solemn days in unseasonable and profane conviviality.

This letter is preserved entire in the seventh part of the Acts of the Church of Milan, and is well worthy of study, being full of instruction and fervour. It produced the most encouraging effect on the Milanese. They were prompt in responding to the call of their Pastor. Many fasted the whole time, whilst others observed the abstinence more or less strictly. Numbers fasted once or twice a week, and frequented the sacraments, attending the sermons and other exercises by way of preparation for the Christmas festival.

This success kindled fresh fervour in the saint, and when the carnival ushered in the Lent of 1574, he issued another pastoral in which he pointed out most clearly the great dishonour to God and the injury occasioned to souls when men gave themselves up to senseless amusements and revels unbecoming their Christian profession.

He demonstrated from Holy Scripture the importance of the Lenten season and its practices of piety; and he deplored the unhappy condition of those who thoughtlessly squandered away the days that were intended to prepare their souls for grace.

Finally, he called upon the people to show themselves now more than ever the true children of their holy Mother, and to devote themselves to certain exercises to which he particularly invited them. He exhorted them thus with the twofold intention of drawing them away from the profane diversions of the carnival, and that the anger of God might be averted from those obdurate sinners who had resisted His grace.[1] As prayer is the great means to this end, he ordered that the Blessed Sacrament should be exposed for adoration in the cathedral, and in thirty other churches, five for each district of the city. It was exposed from morning till evening, and the Deposition as well as the Exposition was accompanied by a procession. He desired the rectors of the different churches to exhort their flocks to frequent these Expositions, and to so divide the hours that there might always be some of the congregation watching before the Blessed Sacrament. He also directed the schools of Christian Doctrine to repair to one or other of the churches in procession, and in the evening after Compline, all were to assemble in the great church, where a certain space of time was to be devoted to mental prayer, or some useful spiritual exercise. This was to be proposed to them under distinct heads by a priest appointed for the purpose. As a further inducement to the people to attend these devotions, he granted certain indulgences to those who should visit the Blessed Sacrament in the churches he had appointed. Thus did he watch with pastoral solicitude over the souls of his flock, that he might draw them from the vain and sinful pleasures of the world to the rich spiritual repast that he had prepared for them.

No wonder that these exercises were greatly blessed, producing abundant fruit among the people, not only

---

[1] That he himself set his flock an example may be seen from a letter to Bonomo of February 4, 1574, in which he says: "During the next eight days I shall make a retreat and give myself to meditation, like yourself, in order to make a good confession. I have determined to pass the last days of the carnival at Milan, and to keep the people occupied in holy exercises."

in the city, but throughout the diocese, where he had also ordered their celebration. On the last Sunday before Lent, which had hitherto been the occasion of the greatest disorders of the whole year, he appointed a general Communion, which was attended by great numbers. The carnival, through the zeal of the saint, thus became a holy season like Paschal time.

He devised yet another means to counteract the influence of the carnival. This was the general Procession of the Stations on Ash Wednesday at the church of Santa Maria delle Grazie, just as in Rome they commence at the Church of Santa Sabina. He had obtained a grant from the Holy Father of the same indulgences for the churches in Milan. He drew attention to the great importance of this practice in the above-named pastoral, earnestly inviting the people to join the procession, to which thousands came, and the practice is still continued every year.

CHAPTER V.

1574.

St. Charles employed great part of this year in the
visitation of the churches of the city and diocese,
arranging for the requisite reforms, and reaping abundant fruits of his labours.

In the course of his visitation at Varese, he learnt
that the King of France, Henry III., was on his way
from Poland to take possession of the throne of France,
to which he had succeeded by the death of his brother,
Charles IX. The saint was anxious to show every
mark of respect to Henry on his arrival in his diocese.
He therefore sent a person of distinction to meet the
King at Cremona. This envoy was most favourably
received by Henry, who entrusted him with a letter
to the Cardinal, expressing his desire to make his
acquaintance. Learning that it was the King's intention to go to Monza without visiting Milan, St.
Charles left Varese for Saronno, where he expected to
receive advices from Rome as to the honours to be
paid to the King by himself as Cardinal. This, in-

deed, was a matter of perfect indifference to the saint personally, for his humility placed him far above all care for such considerations : but he was desirous of keeping up the dignity conferred upon him, which the Council of Trent had declared worthy of all honour. He had, moreover, before him the example of his holy patron and predecessor, St. Ambrose, and others, who, however humble they were themselves, always insisted upon due reverence being paid to their office, even by emperors. He did not, however, receive instructions in time, and sent therefore to Milan for prudent advisers. It was agreed that he should avoid meeting the King on his journey, because, as the latter would be in his carriage, it would not be easy to have the archiepiscopal cross borne before himself in case his Majesty should invite him into his vehicle. It was the custom of the Archbishop never to go anywhere in his own diocese without having his cross carried before him. It was therefore determined that he should visit the King at Monza, and that he should cover his head, if the king did not invite him to do so after the first salutation. These arrangements made, St. Charles sent orders to Milan to prepare a rich present for the king, as well as some articles of less value for the princes of his suite, desiring at the same time that some prelates of his household should accompany him on the occasion. When the king arrived at Monza, the Cardinal met him there on the 10th August, the feast of St. Lawrence, martyr. He took up his quarters at the house of the arch - priest, and sent Francesco Porro, a Milanese prelate, to wait upon his Majesty and inquire

at what hour it would be convenient to receive him.
The King asked the intentions of the Cardinal; to
which the prelate replied that it depended entirely on
his Majesty, to whom the Cardinal was ready at once
to pay his respects, if such was his good pleasure;
adding, that otherwise he would first say Mass, and
then wait upon his Majesty.   The King asked with
some surprise, whether the Cardinal himself would say
Mass.   On learning that it was his daily practice, he
immediately expressed a wish to assist thereat.

When St. Charles heard of the King's intention, he
gave orders to make the necessary preparations in the
church, and then went to pay his visit to the King,
desiring his cross-bearer to stand near him during the
whole interview.   On arriving at the royal apartment,
he found the antechamber occupied by musicians, who
were entertaining the King with vocal and instrumental
music.   As the Cardinal entered, they ceased, and
received his benediction on their knees.

The King received him most cordially, immediately desiring him to put on his hat, entering
into familiar conversation with him, and introducing
him to the princes who attended him, among whom
were the Dukes of Ferrara and Nevers, and a natural
brother of the King, all of whom saluted him with
great reverence.   After the interview was over, the
King walked beside the Cardinal to the church of St.
John, where they were met by the assembled prelates
and clergy, whom the Cardinal presented to his Majesty, at his request.   Then taking the aspersorium,
the Cardinal sprinkled holy water over the King and

the assembled personages: going up then to the High Altar preceded by his clergy, he celebrated Mass. At the conclusion of the Holy Sacrifice the King left the Church whilst the Cardinal was unvesting, having first saluted him with reverence. Returning to the house of the arch-priest, St. Charles sent Monsignors Porro and Moneta to present a gold crucifix to the King, and other pious gifts to the princes. His Majesty instantly gave them audience, thanked them, and ordered a thousand crowns to be given to each, but this they declined, in accordance with the Cardinal's directions. After dinner, the Cardinal again visited the King, and, whilst conversing, he took occasion to offer him suggestions as to the well-ordering of his kingdom. He exhorted him to defend and propagate the Faith in the most Christian country of France, which was at that time sadly infected with heresy. He spoke with so much grace and paternal authority that the King always retained a pleasing recollection of the interview.[1]

When the Sovereign Pontiff learnt the particulars of this interview, he commended the Cardinal greatly for having improved the occasion, and brought under the King's notice the dangers to which religion was at that time exposed in his dominions.

---

[1] Writing to Carniglia on the 11th August, St. Charles says: "I met the King at Monza, whither he had arrived the night before. This morning I paid him a visit, and took him to the church, where I said a low Mass. After dinner, I went to him again, and conversed with him until he entered his carriage. I spoke to him freely in the interests of religion and on the disturbed state of France. As far as I could tell, he was not lacking in a spirit of piety and religion, and, in a word, nothing I could wish was wanting in him."

After the King's departure, God was pleased to make the saint the instrument of a striking miracle. By giving his blessing, he cured the daughter of a nobleman at Monza of a severe illness, attributed to the agency of the devil.

After a year of great labour and fatigue in the visitation of his diocese, St. Charles, before its close, held his fourth diocesan synod. By way of preparation he formed a committee of his Vicars-General and rural deans, who sat for three consecutive weeks, and made a report on the results of his former synods, of their respective visitations, and the obstacles they had encountered in carrying out his decrees. He then drew up a statement of the abuses which remained to be corrected, and the means by which he proposed to remove them. He also set down another subject for their consideration, viz., the revision of the Ambrosian Ritual, Missal and Breviary.

By means of this congregation he possessed himself of the most minute information respecting the condition of every part of his diocese, and noted down what struck him as its present needs, with the best means of supplying them.

When he opened the synod on the 16th November in the same year, 1574, he was already furnished with all necessary information, and only had to give effect by decrees to the measures he had determined upon. Among these we may mention one relating to the observance of the feasts of the Church, and the grievous sin of violating them.

This edict was productive of much good, particularly

as it was supported by the power of his archiepiscopal tribunal. The Cardinal at the same time published another edict as to behaviour in churches and religious edifices, and the obligation of Christians to pay them due honour, and on the gravity of their profanation. At this same time he confirmed and ratified all former decrees of his synods on this subject. The document contains twenty-two articles, to two of which we here refer.

In the first he prohibited the laity from entering and occupying places in the choir during the celebration of the Divine Offices. This had also been prohibited by St. Ambrose, who would not suffer even the Emperor Theodosius to enter the choir at such times, in accordance with the canons.

The other was a revival of the Apostolic precept, that women, of whatever rank or condition, should have a covering on their heads in church, and that not transparent, but veiling the face completely. This order was so favourably received, that the Milanese women were wont to put down their veils, not only in church, but even in the streets and at the doors of their houses when the Archbishop was passing. On one occasion, as the writer walked through the streets of Milan in company with the Cardinal, a woman who passed covered her face, which drew from him the remark : "That is the right way of veiling the face, as ordered by the Church."

During this visitation of the diocese he observed that there were many collegiate foundations, which it was desirable should be transferred to other localities, on account of want of means for keeping up the celebration of Divine worship with becoming dignity. Finding that one of the quarters of the city, the Porta Comasina, was not well provided in this respect, the Cardinal resolved to transfer to it one of the above-named foundations. Accordingly, he fixed upon the collegiate church of Monate, founded in 1380 for six Canons and an Arch-priest by Bishop Besozzo of Bergamo, under the dedication of Our Lady of the Snow, the patronage being vested in the Chapter of Bergamo, in perpetuity. This he transferred, under authority of the Holy See, and by consent of the Canons, to the Church of St. Thomas in *Terra Amara*, thus changing it from a parochial into a collegiate church. Even thus, the number of Canons appeared insufficient for the needs of the locality. He accordingly added to them some canonries from Brebbia and Abbiaguazzono, with a share of their temporalities. This formed altogether a numerous staff under the direction of the Arch-priest. The arrangement gratified the Milanese, as by this means the greater offices of the Church were celebrated more worthily, and facility was given for the frequentation of the Sacraments and hearing the Word of God. A stately church was subsequently erected here.

About the same time he formed another collegiate church at Besozzo. It was a populous neighbourhood, and stood in need of a parish church, and the Cardinal deemed it therefore entitled to better spiritual provision than it possessed. It had possessed only a priory with a revenue of eight hundred crowns; while, at the neighbouring town of Brebbia, there was an ancient collegiate church of St. Peter with a Provost and eighteen Canons, besides treasurer and minor-canons, all of whom were bound to residence. As this church stood in a deserted situation amid un-healthy surroundings, and Divine worship could not be properly carried on there, St. Charles transferred six of its canonries to St. Thomas, leaving a sufficient number for the perpetual curacy of Brebbia. The revenues of the priory he assigned to the seminary of Milan, to relieve the clergy in part from the tithes they had previously been called upon to contribute.

He had thus effected four considerable improve-ments. 1. He had given the church of St. Thomas in Milan a chapter, and increased the provision for Divine worship there. 2. A Provost and twelve Canons bound to residence had been established at Besozzo in the church of St. Alexander, martyr of the Theban legion. 3. The contribution paid by the clergy to the seminary had been considerably reduced. 4. The seminary itself had been provided with a permanent fund.

CHAPTER VI.

1575.

As the year 1575 approached, when, according to custom, the Sovereign Pontiff celebrated a Jubilee, Gregory XIII. published a Bull, in which he opened the treasury of the Church, inviting the faithful to repair to Rome and gain the special indulgences by making the pilgrimage of the seven churches. This Bull, in accordance with the wishes of his Holiness, was also published at Milan by St. Charles, who desired the parochial clergy and preachers of the city to stir up the people to the proper dispositions so as to gain the fruits of the Jubilee. The Cardinal attached great importance to this occasion, looking upon it as a golden opportunity for obtaining great graces, and moving his flock to renewed holiness of life. In September, 1574, he addressed them on the Jubilee in a pastoral letter full of unction, opening with an account of the origin of this holy ordinance, the intention of the Church in its institution, the value of the spiritual treasures at this time offered to the faithful, and concluded by showing from the lives of the saints how the holy year might be well spent.

To set the example the Cardinal determined to go himself to Rome to obtain the benefit of the Jubilee, but he deferred the journey till the autumn on account of the works he had in hand. The Sovereign Pontiff could not, however, consent to this delay, and wrote to beg him to come even before the Holy Year began, as he needed his advice concerning its celebration.

St. Charles had already written to Bernardo Carniglia to beg him to submit several suggestions to his Holiness, reminding him how desirable it would be to prepare a hospital for the reception of poor pilgrims, and also to send the women of loose character out of the city, together with many other regulations of a similar kind.

On receiving this express invitation from the Holy Father, St. Charles at once set aside all other arrangements and prepared to obey it. He only requested that he might have in writing the permission of his Holiness to leave the diocese, according to the prescription of the Sacred Canons respecting the absence of Bishops. He enjoined the same on his clergy, requiring them to obtain the necessary letters before they left their cures, and when in Rome they were to present themselves to his agent there, Cesare Speciano.

St. Charles was obliged to delay his departure for some days because he had to leave instructions with his vicars-general for the regulation of the diocese in his absence. Although he used the utmost diligence, the preparation of a great mass of documents occupied many days, although he curtailed his sleep, and went almost without food, that nothing might be omitted.

At last he left Milan on the 8th December. The weather was very unfavourable for travelling. In accordance with the sacred object of his · journey, he visited all the holy places he passed, but he hastened onwards without any unnecessary delay, as he was expected in Rome before the ceremony of opening the Porta Santa, or Holy Door, which is the commencement of the Jubilee. He said mass every day before daybreak by a special faculty from the Holy See, and concluded his journey on horseback often as late as three or four hours after sunset, notwithstanding that the roads were often very bad. He was constantly leaving the high road to go and visit holy shrines, as Camaldoli, Alvernia, Vallombrosa, and Monte Oliveto. He would then spend the whole night in prayer, thus renewing, in his person, the memory of the saints who had there offered themselves a living sacrifice to God, and inciting himself afresh to imitate them.[1]

As the route lay over the mountainous parts of

[1] Lanfranco Regna, one of St. Charles's companions on this journey, thus describes it in the process of canonisation : "The Cardinal always fasted at this time on bread, chestnuts, and dried figs. It was always at a late hour that we reached our quarters, that were never arranged beforehand. On dismounting, muddy and cold as we were, often wet through and always tired, we went to his room and said office on our knees, and the litanies, and spent some time in meditation or heard a sermon or instruction from him. This took a couple of hours, and then we supped and went to bed. At an early hour the next morning we again met in his room to say office and to prepare for mass. In these devotions and in saying mass two hours were occupied, after which we mounted our horses and rode on till evening. Our resting-places were never fixed beforehand."

Tuscany, the Cardinal was often exposed to great hardships and fatigues. He spent the night at the first lodging that offered itself when he had done his day's journey; and as he would have no preparation made, it frequently happened that beds and food were found with difficulty. It was Advent, moreover, when he fasted every day as in Lent, taking nothing but vegetables and fruit or herbs (he had not yet adopted the austere practice of his later years of restricting his diet to bread and water), so that those who accompanied him on this occasion, many of whom are still living, declare that there was something marvellous about the whole of this journey.

But spiritual consolations flowed in upon the saint in proportion as he afflicted his mortal body. His very look indicated that he was constantly absorbed in God, and if he spoke it was of heavenly things. He was very desirous on this journey of furthering the spiritual interests of those who accompanied him, frequently making them earnest exhortations to kindle in their hearts more fervent love of God, and to prepare them for an abundant outpouring of Divine grace in the time of the Jubilee.

Here must be mentioned a remarkable occurrence by which God was pleased to manifest His special providence towards His servant. Their route had brought them into one of the most intricate passes of the Tuscan Apennines; the hour was late, and they had entirely lost their way in the darkness of the night. None of the party being acquainted with the road, they wandered about till past midnight in fruitless

attempts to find their way.   There was considerable
danger on account of the precipices and loneliness of
the part in which they found themselves.   The saint
recommended his little band to the care of Almighty
God to send them aid as He thought fit.   At last, to
their great surprise, they heard the crowing of a cock
at no great distance.   Following up the sound, they
came upon some peasants' huts, where they took shelter
for the night, though both beds and food were wanting.

They had, however, scarcely established themselves,
when four mules laden with provisions happened to
pass by on their way to market.   All recognised in
this a singular instance of the Providence of God.
St. Charles immediately bought what was sufficient to
supply the wants of the company; and then applied
himself to say his office, spending the whole night in
devotion, while the others snatched what rest they
could on some straw until the hour for continuing
their journey.

In this way he reached Rome on the feast of St.
Thomas the Apostle, and was received by the Sovereign
Pontiff with great joy.   The Pope at once took the
advice of St. Charles on several matters, and among
them the regulation of the Jubilee.

His business with the Holy Father concluded, the
saint withdrew to the Carthusian monastery of St.
Mary of the Angels, where he spent some days in
meditation and spiritual exercises, with fasts and
penitential works, to prepare himself to gain the
greatest possible fruit at that holy time.   He made
a general confession, and at once proceeded to visit

the churches appointed by the Sovereign Pontiff, which he did, always walking and sometimes going barefooted. He took with him his household, making them walk also, which was an edifying sight for the beholders, as they were engaged at the time either in vocal or mental prayer ; the saint, indeed, being always so united with God that nothing had power to distract his thoughts.   If they happened to pass any of the pre-lates or princes who were well known to them, he never interrupted his devotions, but merely gave them a passing recognition by taking off his hat.   This was more particularly remarkable when on one occasion the Duke of Parma, Ottavio Farnese, happened to pass ; though an intimate friend, St. Charles went on his way, the Duke being greatly edified, and declaring that the Cardinal had taught him the best way of practising the devotion of the seven churches.   But with relations and those with whom he was on terms of greater intimacy, he did not think it necessary to interrupt his devotions so far even as this.   Happen-ing one day to meet Marcantonio Colonna on the way to the church of St. Paul without the walls, that prince with his son Don Fabrizio descended from his carriage to salute the Cardinal ; the latter did not so much as give any token of noticing their presence, nor even bow to his own sister Anna, the wife of Fabrizio, who was in the carriage, but passed on as if he did not see them, wholly occupied with his meditation.   His example was looked upon with admiration, and many of the nobility even used to accompany him on his visits to the churches, following the exact method of prayer which he had prescribed to his household. Besides the churches of the Jubilee, St. Charles visited all those which were places of special devotion, or possessed any remarkable relics. Several times he visited on foot the seven churches and the nine basilicas, and nearly every day he ascended the Scala Santa on his knees. To these continual prayers he added large alms to the poor, and exercised hospitality towards the pilgrims from Milan, and indeed of all nations, lodging them in his official residence as titular of Santa Prassede, where he had taken up his abode.

All this tended to confirm his reputation for sanctity. He was held in such veneration that as he passed along every one ran out to see him, many of the people falling on their knees, all esteeming themselves happy who got near enough to him to kiss his garments. One day a woman dressed as a pilgrim, unable to restrain her devotion, threw herself at his feet and kissed them; and though he tried to free himself, he could not prevent her from publicly declaring him a saint. On another occasion a noble lady did the same, getting out of her carriage on purpose to pay him this mark of honour. Other pious persons sought eagerly to obtain any object that had belonged to him that they might keep it as a relic. Among these was Cæsar Baronius, priest of the Oratory in Rome, afterwards Cardinal, who has left a name to posterity both for piety and learning. He possessed himself of the shoes which the saint had worn on his visits to the churches, and preserved them as a precious treasure. Not many days after they came into his possession, on the occasion of a young girl, Geronima de' Pompei, being exorcised in presence of St. Philip Neri in his church of Santa Maria alla Vallicella, the shoes had no sooner touched her than the demon uttered dreadful cries as if the pains of hell were increased, till at last the remedy and the exorcisms delivered her from her tormentor.

The report of the sanctity of St. Charles spread greatly into other countries through the pilgrims, who were very numerous at this Jubilee, more particularly from Milan, as was remarked. The attention of the Sovereign Pontiff having been called to the fact that it was all owing to the pious exhortations and edifying example of the Cardinal Archbishop of Milan, he replied: "Yes! indeed. Who can hope to equal such zeal and devotedness?"

As St. Charles had come to Rome for the express purpose of gaining the benefits of the Jubilee, he devoted himself entirely to exercises of piety. From this rule he never deviated, except when the Holy Father sent for him to consult him. When he had finished his devotions, he then gave his attention to matters of business, both of his own diocese, and of the Church at large. The benefits derived from this as from all his other visits to Rome, were by no means confined to himself, but were sources of advantage to others; as is shown not only by the increase of fervour gained by residence in the holy city, which sent him back into the world possessed, if possible, of greater zeal for the service of God, but also by the spiritual counsel which, in accordance with the obligation of his office of Cardinal, he was able to give the Pontiff.   He knew his advice would be well received, and would produce fruit by stimulating his Holiness to increased solicitude in the exercise of his sublime office.   For this purpose he began with such details as the well-ordering of his court and household.   Next, he pointed out how important it was that the clergy and people of Rome should set an edifying example to so many pilgrims congregated there from all parts of the world, so that they might carry away a high opinion of the pastoral solicitude and piety prevailing in the Papal Court, to their own edification and the honour of the Holy See.   Gregory XIII. gave the best proof of his appreciation of this advice by immediately giving effect to the suggestions of the saint.   He then called the Pope's attention to the requirements of the various provinces, in order that the Tridentine reforms might be carried out, reminding the Holy Father that, as supreme Head and Pastor, he had to watch over all Bishops, and kindle in them a great love for the whole flock.

We may mention two most important suggestions of his.   The first was, that the Committee of Cardinals for matters relative to the Episcopate, now technically called the Congregation of Bishops, should be erected into a permanent Congregation, that all differences might be settled by its decisions ; but especially in order to introduce by authority of the Holy See remedies for abuses, and provisions for the better government of dioceses.   The other suggestion was that Visitors appointed by the Apostolic See should be sent into every province to receive from the Bishops reports on the state of their dioceses, to inquire into the observance of the decrees of the Council of Trent and the state of discipline among the clergy, so that notice to amend such things as were found wanting might then be sent by apostolic authority. This he took to be an excellent means of maintaining order and encouraging improvement throughout the whole Church; and also of keeping the Bishops alive to the duties and obligations of their sacred calling.

The above named Congregation was instituted in the time of Pius V., and continues to the present day to pursue its labours, being of great service to the episcopate and to ecclesiastical discipline. With regard to his plan of sending out Visitors, this had only as yet been done in the States of the Church and some other parts, and the saint now urged the Sovereign Pontiff to extend this beneficial practice to the whole Church. Accordingly they were sent out into many provinces. St. Charles, in his conscientious performance of every duty, acknowledged that, as an Archbishop, it behoved him to perform this service throughout his own province : but at the same time he begged the Sovereign Pontiff to mark that it was impossible for him to take every part of it into his account, by reason of its extent, and, therefore, he besought him to appoint Visitors for his own diocese also, though he did this principally with the view of setting a good example, and making the first experiment of the plan, in order that other Archbishops

might be more zealous in observing the ancient practice of making themselves acquainted with the whole
of their provinces by these ·visitations.   The Pope
acceded to his proposal, and appointed Girolamo
Ragazzoni, Bishop of Famagosta,[1] Visitor of the province of Milan.

Besides these matters, other measures were discussed
which had especial reference to the diocese of Milan.
The saint laid its secret needs before his Holiness,
and obtained ample faculties from him.   In particular
he obtained the Jubilee of the holy year for the city
and diocese of Milan, with power to appoint the
churches and the time and manner of fulfilling the
conditions, for the next year, 1576.   He also obtained
some privileges for the city, the Indulgences of the
Seven Churches of Rome for the same number of
churches in Milan, according to his judgment.   His
Holiness furnished him further with a number of rosaries, crucifixes, and medals, with particular indulgences
attached to them, which he might afterwards distribute
among his people for the increase of their devotion.
For himself he obtained a favour of a peculiar kind ;
namely, permission to drop his family name and arms
of Borromeo, and to adopt in the stead of the former
his cardinalitial title of Santa Prassede only, and for the
latter, figures of St. Ambrose and the martyrs Gervasius and Protasius, with the motto : *Tales ambio defen-
sores :*[2] his motives being humility and desire of imitating the saints.

---

[1] Afterwards Bishop of Bergamo.
[2] " Such are the protectors I desire."

CHAPTER VII.

1575.

GREGORY XIII., like his predecessor in the Apostolic
See, perceived great advantages to be derived from the
constant counsels of a prelate of such zeal and sagacity
as St. Charles.   He therefore urged him to remain in
Rome, that he might continue to benefit by his advice.
But St. Charles could not endure to be absent for any
length of time from his diocese, and begged the Holy
Father so earnestly to allow him to return, that the
Pope felt himself bound, however unwillingly, to give
him permission to quit Rome.   He set out, accordingly,
on his return early in February, after a stay of little
more than a month.   He returned with spiritual
treasures for his Church, filled with a new spirit to
devote himself more and more completely to the
salvation of the souls committed to his charge.

He had promised Don Cesare Gonzaga, his cousin,
and his sister Donna Camilla, that he would visit them
at Guastalla on his way home, and consecrate a church
lately erected there.   On his arrival at Bologna news
was brought him, before he had dismounted from his

horse, that Don Cesare was lying dangerously ill, and was not expected to recover. Without stopping to take any rest he immediately set out for Guastalla, whither he arrived only in time to find the prince delirious, and incapable of benefiting by his ministrations. The saint had immediate recourse to prayer, both public and private, having the Blessed Sacrament exposed in the church, where he watched all night, offering up his intercessions for his relative. Nor were his petitions poured forth in vain. Before morning the dying man recovered his senses, and God was pleased to give him such abundance of grace, that he received the last Sacraments in the best disposition, and, aided by the pious exhortations of the Cardinal, he died with great serenity and perfect conformity with the will of God, so that St. Charles afterwards was heard to say in public that he was as well prepared for death as if he had passed many years in religion. After the funeral St. Charles consecrated the church, and then returned to Milan, after having consoled his sister for her loss, and given her good counsel on the management of her family.

At Milan the people came out in crowds to welcome their beloved pastor. He immediately applied himself to prepare for the visitation of the dioceses of his province conformably with the order of the Pope. He would not, however, set out until he had given a cordial reception to the pontifical Visitor, the Bishop of Famagosta,[1] who arrived at Milan in May.

---

[1] As Bishop of Nazianzum he preached before the Council of Trent. After his translation to Famagosta in the island of Cyprus, his diocese

The Cardinal paid him every possible homage in testimony of his veneration for the holy Apostolic See, and as a lesson to his people of the reverence due to the messengers of God. He gave him all necessary information, and as a preparation, ordered prayers in public and private, together with a solemn procession, to invoke the blessing of God upon the work. Mass was then sung by Monsignor Famagosta, who preached a sermon upon the importance of the Visitation. Having thus seen it fairly set on foot, St. Charles started himself on the appointed task of visiting the rest of his province, beginning with Cremona. His suite consisted of only six persons, and though in conformity with the decrees on the subject, at the charge of the clergy of each parish, he ordered that everything should be provided on the most frugal scale that he might not be burdensome to any one.

Nicolò Sfrondato, Bishop of Cremona, was absent at the time on important business, but the clergy of the city received him with great reverence, omitting nothing which could tend to show their obedience. As usual, his first care was to invite the people to unite in public prayer and solemn procession for the success of his work, during which time he gave Holy Communion to upwards of eight thousand persons, who flocked from all parts to receive the Bread of Angels at his hands.

Although this diocese was of great extent and thickly populated, St. Charles completed its visitation in the

was overrun by the Turks, when he took refuge in Rome, and was employed in the visitation of the dioceses of Ravenna and Urbino, and finally was made Bishop of Bergamo.

space of three months. In his zeal he cheerfully laboured by night as well as by day, abridging the little time he allowed himself for sleep. All these labours came upon him at the hottest season of the year, which aggravated his fatigues. He was, however, greatly encouraged by the success of his work, the clergy and people yielding everywhere to his gentle words, and still more to his saintly example. God was pleased to encourage His servant by a miraculous cure in the person of Signor Bartolomeo Scalvi, who was raised from his bed and a dangerous illness after receiving a visit from the saint, as we read in documents of the ecclesiastical tribunal of Cremona, in the process concerning the miracles of the saint. His authority and zeal were efficacious in bringing about a salutary reform among the clergy and in the convents of nuns who had not yielded due obedience to their Bishop, who was much consoled on hearing of the results obtained by the Cardinal, who may indeed be said to have been an apostle in his diocese, both by his holy example and the liberality he exercised towards the poor.

He concluded this visitation in time to return to Milan on the feast of the Nativity of Our Lady, the anniversary of the dedication of the Cathedral of Milan. He then prepared to visit the diocese of Bergamo, which in temporal government was under the Republic of Venice. When the Venetian senate was informed of his intention, they sent express orders to the magistracy of Bergamo to receive him with special honours, and to give him every assistance in the work he had undertaken, as a testimony of the devotion entertained towards him by their ancient Republic. These orders were scrupulously obeyed, and the Bishop and clergy emulated this example, for Federico Cornaro,[1] who then occupied the Episcopal chair, was a vigilant pastor of souls.

The saint observed the same order in this visitation as in the preceding, but his labours were rendered more fatiguing by the mountainous character of the country, and the rugged paths over which he had to travel. His efforts were, however, greatly blessed, as the devout Bergamese people flocked in crowds to listen to the exhortations and receive Communion from him. Everywhere men and women forsook their toils to fill the churches, so that in one day he gave Communion to as many as eleven thousand persons. These and other episcopal functions often kept him whole days in the church, but he never tired or was troubled by his exertions. The magistrates of the city, moreover, encouraged the people by their example in joyfully attending the religious offices. Among other tokens of esteem, a public oration was delivered by their direction, to thank him for having thus revived the ancient practice of metropolitans visiting the churches of their province.

During his stay in this place St. Charles made a solemn translation of the bodies of the holy martyrs, Firmus and Rusticus, which gave rise to some difficulty and confusion. These sacred bodies were preserved in the church of some nuns in a suburb of the city.

---

[1] Afterwards Bishop of Padua and Cardinal, died at Rome 1590.

Finding the convent ill-adapted for the purpose for which it was used, St. Charles wished to remove it to another site, intending, at the same time, to make the translation of the holy relics with solemnity. But the inhabitants of the vicinity rose up in a body on hearing that they were to be deprived of their treasure. With great violence they came to the church before the time appointed for the removal, forced the priest who had charge of the relics to point out their resting-place, before which they stationed themselves, defying any one to approach or touch them. When the Cardinal expressed displeasure at their violence, the rioters sought to make their peace with him, affirming that they had erred through ignorance. St. Charles was soon satisfied, and gave them absolution from censures they had incurred at the church-porch, pointing out, at the same time, the gravity of the offence that had been committed. He then carried out the ceremony of translation with all due honours, those who had at first opposed him assisting in the procession. The sacred relics were deposited in a larger church, and the devotion of the people for their holy martyrs was greatly increased. They likewise conceived great veneration for the saint, and were not slow to perceive that he was even more distinguished for holiness than report had spread abroad. When he left them to return to Milan, the whole city turned out to take leave of him, following him to the gates, and gazing after him with yearning hearts.

CHAPTER VIII.

THE JUBILEE OF THE HOLY YEAR KEPT AT MILAN.

1576.

ALTHOUGH St. Charles had obtained from the Holy
Father the Jubilee of the Holy Year for his diocese,
he did not publish it till the year 1576, so as not to
interfere with pilgrims going to Rome itself. He then
addressed to his flock a pastoral letter, breathing a
spirit of tenderness and fervour, and enlarging upon
the graces offered them. He called upon them to show
their gratitude for so great a benefit by doing their
best to gain it. With great severity he denounced the
prevailing vices of the age, reproving especially the
vanity of the female sex as unworthy of their Christian profession, and the root of many mortal sins.
The Jubilee was given them as an opportunity of
repairing the past and entering upon a new life, the
end proposed by the Church in granting indulgences.
He concluded by giving them some rules for gaining
the full benefit of the Jubilee. Four Stational churches
were appointed as follows : the cathedral, the great
church of St. Ambrose, and those of St. Laurence and
St. Simplicianus. Attached to the pastoral letter were

certain directions for the Jubilee, and the prayers to
be used in the churches.

For the greater benefit of strangers visiting the city
on this occasion, he directed Luigi Bascapè, one of
the Canons of the cathedral,[1] who was a member of
his household, to draw up an account of the churches
of Milan, and the holy relics deposited in them.   Father
Giovanni Battista Perusco, of the Society of Jesus,
Provost of San Fedele, also drew up a little handbook
for gaining the Jubilee.

The order of the processions, the days and churches
for the devotions and the special prayers, the confessors for the different churches, were all set down
and published.   The churches, by his direction, were
fittingly decorated during the whole time of the Jubilee,
the relics in each exposed, with great reverence, for
the devotion of the faithful.   In each church a tablet
was fixed in some conspicuous place, with an account
of the relics there deposited, and another with a list of
hymns to be sung, and prayers most appropriate for
each saint.   The Divine Offices were ordered to be
sung with more than usual solemnity in the cathedral
and in all the collegiate churches.   In all the churches
the Salve Regina and some other prayers were to be
sung every evening during the Jubilee, in the Stational
churches with especial solemnity.   The churches were
to be provided with divisions of wooden panelling to
separate men from women.   Curtains had previously
served the purpose, but as a greater concourse of persons might naturally be expected during the Jubilee,

---

[1] Afterwards Bishop of Novara.

St. Charles thought that a solid wooden barrier would act as a surer preventive of possible scandals.

In special cases he granted dispensations in accordance with individual circumstances, as regarded the visits, though he would not allow them to be made on horseback or in a carriage, but required all to go on foot ; but for the old and sick he made the conditions easy.

For the convenience of pilgrims from the country large crosses were set up by the rural deans and parish priests to point out the roads, and to remind them of the Passion of our Lord. Hostels also were made ready for the reception of pilgrims of both sexes. As these preparations had not been made without considerable expense to himself, he placed these houses under the supervision of some of the chief nobility, who were to take care that there should be no lack of what was needful.

The Jubilee was begun on the Feast of the Purification of Our Lady. After the procession of candles St. Charles celebrated mass pontifically in presence of the Governor, senate, and magistrates of the city. He preached on the singular grace conferred upon them by the Holy Father in granting them this Jubilee, and exhorted them all to avail themselves of it worthily in a spirit of true penitence, and in the practice of alms-deeds and good works. He then had the Brief of his Holiness read, as well as the regulations he had himself drawn up for the observance of the holy season, together with his decree concerning the reverence due to churches and holy places. On the three following

days he ordered processions, viz., on Wednesday, to
Great St. Ambrose ; on Friday, to St. Laurence ; and
on Saturday, to St. Simplicianus. The Forty Hours'
prayer was held before the Blessed Sacrament in the
cathedral to pray that God would infuse the spirit of
true devotion into the souls of His people. He also
sought to increase the fervour of the people by trans-
lating to the cathedral the body of St. Monas, Archbishop of Milan, from its resting-place in the church
of St. Vitalis, which, sometimes called La Faustiniana,
belonged to the Cistercian Fathers, to whom he had
granted leave to take it down, transferring the cure of
souls to another church in a better situation.

On the evening of Tuesday, the 5th February, the
saint went to St. Vitalis, together with his Canons, and
placed the relics of the saint in a shrine lined with
silk, deposited upon the altar, before which they
watched in turn during the night. On Wednesday
morning, the clergy, regular and secular, assembled for
the first procession to St. Ambrose, and were followed
by the nobility and magistrates, together with the
Apostolic Visitor, to the church of St. Vitalis, where
the two Prelates took the shrine upon their shoulders,
formed procession again back to the cathedral amid
lighted tapers, to the sound of trumpets and singing
of hymns. The people declared that heaven itself
had taken part in their joy by dispelling the clouds
which on the previous day had threatened a storm.

Upon their arrival at the cathedral the body of the
saint was laid upon the High Altar, while the Cardinal
in a few words recounted the praises of St. Monas, who

was the sixth Bishop of Milan, and one of its citizens, belonging to the ancient family of the Borri, endeared to the Milanese by his zeal during an episcopate of fifty-nine years. To him was due the division of the city into a hundred and fifteen parishes, and at his death he left the whole of his patrimony to the diocese. The ceremony of the translation was brought to a close in the evening by the deposition of the relics in the *Scurolo*, or crypt of the cathedral, the Apostolic Visitor preaching on the occasion.

The second procession to the church of St. Laurence took place on Friday; and on the following day that to St. Simplicianus, where another translation of relics was made, viz., that of the bodies of the holy martyrs Fidelis and Carpophorus, which after being laid in the abbey of Arona, and when all record of the exact spot where they rested had been lost, were discovered by the Jesuit fathers under the high altar of the church when it came into their possession. As St. Fidelis was the chief patron of their church in Milan, it was deemed but fitting that his body should be removed thither. St. Charles gave his consent, and directed the Fathers to place the relics in the church of St. Simplicianus, whence he would himself translate them to St. Fidelis.

The people of Arona, however, were loth to part with their treasure, and appealed to the Cardinal, praying him to support their claim. The saint was glad at heart to find the spirit of devotion in his flock, and consoled them with a promise that a portion at least should remain in their church. In the meantime he proceeded with the translation, which took place on the Saturday with the same ceremonies as before.

The next day, Sunday, closed the Forty Hours' prayer, which had been attended by numbers of devout worshippers, as a separate hour of watching had been fixed for each parish, chapter, convent and confraternity.

In making the visits to the Stational churches St. Charles himself was first and foremost. He frequently went in company with his Chapter, and also attended by his household, who walked along in order of two abreast while he followed. Often he would go barefooted, but so that none could observe it:[1] on the way they recited psalms and hymns and litanies. When they arrived and knelt down in prayer, the people following in after them, the saint would then turn round and urge them in a few fervent words to compunction and penance, finishing with giving them a blessing with the relics that were exposed. It was often late in the evening before he returned, though he was fasting all the while, as also were those whose devotion had prompted them to accompany him.

He earnestly exhorted all thus to visit the churches, and to facilitate this end he abbreviated the fifteen days of the Visits. The whole city seemed constantly alive with the various streams of devout worshippers, while their hymns of praise resounded on every side.

---

[1] At this time the saint had recourse to artifice to hide his austerity, wearing shoes without any soles in order to have the pain only of going barefoot without the praise of men.—O.

So judicious were the regulations of the Cardinal that
the most perfect order reigned throughout the throngs.
His calls to penance found their response in many
breasts, so that long processions of penitents might
often be seen clothed in sackcloth, scourging themselves
as they went. There were seen also many of the
nobility, and especially ladies, also in sackcloth, their
feet bare, with ropes round their necks, crucifix in
hand, wending their way to the churches. It was
as if the penance of Nineveh were renewed in Milan.
Most consoling indeed was the spectacle; and many
hands were lifted up to Heaven in thanksgiving for
the zeal of their holy Pastor.

Every part of the diocese furnished its procession
of pilgrims all moving to the common centre, all
desirous to gain the Jubilee, and though they came
from afar, both men and women often went barefooted.
For their bodies their Pastor provided sustenance, as
for their souls. As each company reached the cathedral
he either addressed them himself or deputed some one
to do so in his stead, and then administered to them
the Bread of Life. In the hostels, where everything
needful was in readiness for them, he used to visit
them and supply anything wanting from his own
bounty. There were often as many as six thousand
seated at the tables where their repast was spread.
He washed their feet and performed for them every
office of charity, while many looked on and wondered,
moved to tears at the sight. While the tables were
laid out with meats for the body, spiritual food was

not omitted, for certain religious were appointed to exhort them during their meal to holiness and piety of life.

Whilst thus unwearied in his labours for those of his people who were living in the world, the Cardinal did not forget the needs of those who were shut out from the public devotions in cloisters. As the choicest of his flock, he drew up special rules for their Jubilee, their prayers, and the adoration of the Forty Hours in their enclosures. He sent them also special directions that they might have every assistance and that the fruits of the holy season might be gathered in most abundantly by them.

While solicitous for the souls of others he did not neglect his own, increasing his prayers and alms as well as the works of penance he was wont to exercise; such as fasting and discipline, the use of the hair shirt and sleeping upon boards. It is reported by some members of his household that he adopted this last-named austerity in satisfaction for an act of negligence which he attributed to himself, though it was really no fault of his, owing to which some of the pilgrims found no beds ready for them.

In the midst of the Jubilee it was reported that the plague had broken out in Venice and Mantua; and the Governor of Milan in his regard for the public health felt bound to prohibit any from entering Milan who did not bring a certificate that the place whence they came was free from infection. This order putting a stop to the processions, the Cardinal contented himself therefore with repairing the loss in some degree by making use of the faculty he had received from the Holy See to extend the benefits of the Jubilee to other places. He abridged also the number of days and times of visiting the churches, so that none might be deprived of its privileges.

Note on p. 356.—"St. Monas."

This saint is reckoned the sixth Bishop of Milan, circ. A.D. 182-238, and flourished during the pontificates of Popes St. Eleutherius, St. Victor, and St. Pontianus.

CHAPTER IX.

1576.

DURING the Jubilee, the Cardinal held his Fourth
Provincial Council. It had been fixed for the 10th
May in this year, and though his time was so much
taken up with the devotion of the time, he would not
forego any of the usual ceremonies, or diminish his
labours; so that he seldom had more than two or
three hours' sleep. The Bishops of the province
attended its deliberations together with the Apostolic
Visitor, and decrees of further reform were confirmed
and published.

There was in Milan at this time a physician, Giovanni Angelo Cerro by name, by whose advice St.
Charles was guided in medical matters. He, in turn,
gained so much from his intercourse with the saint,
that he used to practise great charity towards the poor
of Christ, and to give them medicine without fee or
reward. Moreover, when he was called to a better
life he left his property to the Archbishop of Milan

and the Provost-General of the Oblates of St. Ambrose in charge for the poor, who have held his name in benediction.

This worthy physician took advantage of the assembly of Bishops in Milan to point out to them that the health of the Cardinal was endangered by his austerities, more particularly by his sleeping upon boards, which would, he affirmed, shorten the life of the saint.

The Bishops, in consequence, used their best endeavours to induce him to moderate this severity to himself. St. Charles replied, that he had not forgotten that the Apostle spoke of "*our reasonable service*,"[1] and that his penance was always guided by a prudent discretion. However, he listened to them with humility, thanking them for their advice, which he knew sprung from their affection towards him, but at the same time urged that what he did was not disproportioned to his strength. In order that he might not seem to set little store by their counsel, he consented to use a covering over the boards which served him for a bed, though it was only of sackcloth, and a little straw for a pillow.

The Apostolic Visitor had now finished his labours in carrying out the decrees of the Council of Trent, and after having fully secured the Archbishop's right of visitation of various hospitals and pious foundations, he left Milan.

This visitation had given great satisfaction to the Cardinal. In his sincere desire to see his diocese thoroughly reformed, he rejoiced that another should

---

[1] Romans xii. 1.

examine into his work and point out to him his defi-
ciencies. He would often say that experience had
taught him the great benefit of this supervision ; for
no man has sufficient natural light to see his own
faults, although he be sharp-sighted enough in discern-
ing those of others. In his visitation of other dioceses
he found many defects that threw light on his own
shortcomings, whilst the visitation made by others of
his own diocese enlightened him as to many failings
that had hitherto escaped notice.

His labours terminated, Monsignor Famagosta took
occasion to announce his departure to the people. He
added that he had found everything in such excellent
order that he had been much edified thereby, and that
there was nothing left for him but to confirm what
had already been done by their Pastor. The Cardinal
replied with humility, that the words of St. Peter
might be appropriately used by himself, " *We have
laboured all the night, and have taken nothing, but, at
Thy Word, I will let down the net :*"[1] he had hitherto
done nothing, but that, at the word spoken by the
Apostolic See through its appointed Visitor, he would
again let down the net, in the confidence that he
should not fail to obtain a blessing. In this way he
wished to testify his affection and reverence towards
the Holy See, and thank the Bishop for his labours in
the diocese.

The next undertaking of the saint was the translation of more relics. The Fathers of Mount Olivet
had lately rebuilt their church of St. Victor, anciently

[1] St. Luke v. 5.

called La Porziana. It became necessary, therefore, to transfer the relics of St. Victor and other saints from the old to the new building. St. Charles accordingly verified the relics with great care, and in so doing . discovered among them, to his surprise, the body of St. Satyrus, Confessor, brother of St. Ambrose, duly authenticated.

On the day before the feast of St. James, he arranged the relics in seven rich shrines, and held the accustomed vigil before them. Early the following morning, he returned home ; and, at the appointed hour, went with a procession of clergy and people from the cathedral to the church of St. Victor. Here they took up the sacred shrine, which was borne in turns by the Cardinal with his Canons and the Fathers of Mount Olivet. The procession was followed by great numbers of people, and the houses on the way were all decorated. Arrived at their destination, the holy relics were laid upon the High Altar during the day, to give opportunity to the people to satisfy their devotion. In the evening St. Charles returned, and the seven shrines were arranged in due order in presence of notaries. The relics of St. Victor and St. Satyrus were placed beneath the High Altar, and the others, being unknown, were deposited in a subterranean chapel or *scurolo*, constructed for the purpose by order of the Cardinal. He did not, on this occasion, invite the attendance of other Bishops, on account of the plague which had broken out in March near Arona, on the Lago Maggiore, which news naturally filled men with anxiety. For the same reason, St.

Charles put off his visitation of the diocese of Brescia, which he had announced, as he was loth to abandon his beloved city in a time of danger.

The fears of the people were not unfounded. It was not long before the dreaded pestilence made its way into Milan itself, where the Cardinal remained, busied in carrying out the recommendations of the Apostolic Visitor.

Note on p. 362.—"*Medical matters.*"

St. Charles did not entertain a very high opinion of physicians. To the Bishop of Cremona, afterwards Gregory XIV., on his return from Padua, whither he had gone to consult them for the stone, he wrote as follows : "I congratulate you on your return from Padua in a better state of health, and am glad that you have escaped safely out of the hands of the doctors, whom I recommend you to avoid as far as possible, a course which will go far towards keeping you in good health. Only go to them in the last resort."

Note on p. 364.—"*Fathers of Mount Olivet.*"

Or, Olivetans, a Benedictine congregation, so called from their principal monastery on Mount Olivet, near Arezzo. They were founded by St. Bernardo Tolomei, of Sienna, in 1319. In the beginning of the sixteenth century the church of St. Victor in Milan was given to them, and in 1560 they began to rebuild it, and opened it again in this year, 1576.

Book IV.

CHAPTER I.

MILAN VISITED BY THE PLAGUE.

1576.

Before the holy season of the Jubilee had drawn to a close, a certain prince of high degree [1] paid a visit to Milan. Some of the nobles, desirous to pay court to him, prepared to entertain him with tournaments and other public games and spectacles. All this was at the very moment when the Cardinal was earnestly engaged in endeavouring to unite all his people in exercises of devotion. He readily discerned the hand of the enemy in this work, leading his people away, and cooling their fervour by these excitements. What, indeed, could grieve him more than to see these snares spread for them, and the piety he had striven to enkindle smothered by vain attractions of the world?

Yet so it was. The last day of the holy season had hardly closed when a flourish of trumpets and drums

---

[1] This was Don John of Austria, who was sent at this time into Flanders by Philip II.—O.

announced the beginning of these diversions.   The
streets which had lately been paced by penitents in
sackcloth now reeled with crowds of maskers in the
gaudy liveries of the world.   These were evidences of
a lightness and instability of purpose which wounded
the heart of the saint.   Great indeed was the grief
with which he foretold the punishments which would
shortly come upon his infatuated flock.   I well remember the sorrow with which he used to speak of it.
One day he put into my hands a letter from the
archpriest of Monza, Jerome Maggiolini, a native of
Milan and friend of his own, telling how his people
were dying in numbers every day of a dire disease
which the doctors took to be fever.   When I had read
it, he observed that the doctors were mistaken—it was
the plague; and he added, speaking without reserve,
that the people of Milan had called down upon themselves the wrath of God by their ingratitude and for-
getfulness of His mercies; that the intelligence we
had just received was but the forerunner of afflictions
in the future, and we might rest assured that there
was no help but to throw ourselves on His mercy
with prayer and compunction of heart.   I spoke of
the excellent sanitary precautions which had been
taken to prevent the spread of the malady.   But he
answered with a sigh, that mere human precautions
could not prevail against the avenging hand of God..
No more was said on that occasion, but I well understood how certain he felt of the truth of his words.
And it was so.   In the midst of these diversions the
plague was discovered in the heart of the city.

Then mirth was changed into mourning. The prince, in whose honour this unseasonable merry-making was held was the first to take fright and fly to Genoa in hot haste, followed by the Governor and many of the nobles, leaving the city full of dismay.

Very different was the conduct of the Cardinal. In the midst of the revels news had been brought him of the serious illness of Antonio Scarampa, Bishop of Lodi, and he had immediately set out to visit him. On reaching Melegnano, about half-way, the tidings came that the Bishop had already passed to his rest. He therefore put on mourning, and reached Lodi in time to officiate at the funeral rites of the deceased with all his accustomed devotion, and was so engaged when three cases of plague were announced, two at Milan and the third at Melegnano.

Although he was not unprepared for the blow, it was with sorrow that he saw the hand of God stretched out in punishment upon his beloved flock. Neither did he hesitate for a moment to return, and passing through the city had an opportunity of witnessing with his own eyes the trouble of the citizens at being suddenly deserted by the nobles, their alarm and confusion, not knowing what to do for the best.

The presence of their Pastor restored confidence, and the whole city gathered round him, now their only hope. Falling on their knees around him, they bathed his feet with their tears, and besought him to take pity on them. Passing through their midst, he made for the cathedral, as was his wont, and there offered up his prayers. Mounting his horse again, he went to the house of a lady of the Rabia family, near the church of La Scala, where the plague had broken out, and found some Ursuline[1] nuns there, ignorant of the nature of the malady. He immediately took steps to isolate them, placing them in a vacant convent in the ward of the Porta Comasina, and keeping them apart in different cells for a time, thus preserving them both from harm to themselves and from spreading the contagion among others.

On reaching his own house he was met by a deputation of officers of the crown and members of the municipal council, begging him by the love he bore his people to aid them in their necessity; acknowledging that God was chastising them, and feeling utterly at a loss what to do. In their perplexity they came to him as their father to learn how to mitigate the evils by which the city was stricken.

In reply he assured them of his earnest desire to devote himself to their aid in this time of need, and begged them to take courage, and on no account to abandon the city, as others had done; promising that God would amply reward them for any public services it might be in their power to render in alleviation of the distress. Thus he dismissed them consoled and strengthened in mind.

Being fully persuaded that this visitation had been sent as a chastisement for sin, he gave himself up to prayer with greater frequency and fervour than usual to avert the anger of God, and to ask for light to know and grace to do His holy will. These

---

[1] Belonging to a community founded by the saint himself.—O.

prayers he accompanied by increased fasts and austerity of life, depriving himself of his straw pallet,[1] sleeping upon bare boards, with only a sheet for coverlet, and spending great part of his nights in prayers and tears, chastising in himself the sins of others in order to appease the indignation of God against his flock.

Besides this he ordered three solemn processions of all the clergy and people, which were attended by great numbers of the religious orders and of the magistrates. When they came to the churches he preached to the people, exhorting them to do penance, and reproving boldly the shortcomings of the rulers of the city in delaying so long to turn to God and to repentance, the true means of propitiating Him; adding that one offence among others which called down this scourge upon them was the edict which had not been repealed, forbidding the meetings of confraternities of penitents and others, thus preventing many spiritual exercises[2] and means of invoking the mercy of God. Among other evil consequences of this, he mentioned that the people, debarred from these ways of devotion on festival-days, had been tempted to give themselves up entirely to vain pastimes and amusements. Finally, he exhorted all to amendment of life, and to good works of almsgiving and visiting the poor and sick.

[1] On his return from the hospital one day he sent thither the straw pallet which he used in deference to the wishes of the Suffragan Bishops, expressed at the last Provincial Council. Another that was substituted he also despatched to the same place, forbidding any more to be given him, as he intended to sleep on bare boards.—O.

[2] The saint referred here to the processions which had been forbidden.

Notwithstanding the saint's exertions in moving the people to appease the Divine anger, the plague continued to extend its ravages day by day, God so permitting it in His unsearchable judgments. It was no longer the district of the Porta Comasina that suffered, but from every part of the city came rumours of the plague, so that the hospital of St. Gregory without the walls was restored to its original purpose as a pest-house, and the infected were sent thither to be separated from the rest of the community.

Page 367.—" A certain prince of high degree."

Sir W. Stirling-Maxwell, in his "Don John of Austria," 2 vols., 1883, does not seem to beware of a visit of this prince to Milan at this time. According to him we find Don John in May 1576 at Naples, by August 22 he is at Barcelona, by September 22 in Madrid, on October 31 at Paris on his way to Flanders, vol. ii. p. 116, 122. Don John visited Milan from Vigevano in May, June, and July of 1574, p. 54, and invited Henry III. of France, then at Venice, on his way home from Poland, to visit him in the Lombard capital, but the invitation was declined.

Page 372.—" The house of a lady of the Ralia family."

This occurred on August 12, 1576. On the day before, August 11, there had been a case of plague in the Porta Comasina district.

CHAPTER II.

1576.

THE friends of the Cardinal were well acquainted with his self-devotion and intention of risking his life in the service of his people. Fearing the hazards to which he would be exposed, they begged him not to run into danger, urging that he could make ample provisions for the relief of the sufferers by means of others, while he himself withdrew to a place of security. But they could not shake his resolution; nothing would induce him to abandon his flock—rather would he die with them. His confidence in God was so great that he felt no doubt whatever that He would take care of him in the midst of dangers. In order not to follow his own will, he consulted certain persons in authority who were not likely to be biassed by human respect, begging them to speak their minds freely, considering his duty as Pastor and the distress of his flock. He made this appeal more willingly because he had received instructions from Rome, urging that he was under no obligation, and ought not to imperil his life by remaining in the midst of the contagion.

The opinion he asked for coincided with this view, but he was not satisfied with it, though reasons were given. He cited the examples of many of the saints who had not counted their life dear to them, and quoted the homilies and epistles of Bishops, showing that pastors of souls are bound to stand by their flocks in such dangers. They made answer, that these were counsels of perfection, not of obligation. His reply was characteristic: That in this case he was bound to follow such counsels, for the episcopal office is a state of perfection. This they could not gainsay, but praised his good intentions, and begged him to use all possible caution, and at least to keep from contact with infected persons. He made them this promise, whenever he could do so without detriment to his pastoral office, though it seemed well nigh impossible, for every time that he was seen in the city the terrified people flocked round him throwing themselves at his feet as their common father and imploring his assistance. Not satisfied with obtaining his blessing, they strove one with another to kiss or touch his garments, as if they had no hope of safety but through him. How could he find in his heart to thrust from him his beloved children in the very hour of their distress? This was a matter in which, with all his self-control, he could not check the tenderness of his heart.

Thus confirmed in his purpose of ministering to the plague-stricken, with true prudence he, in the first place, made the offering of himself entirely to God, not knowing when He might think fit to call him away. While ordering his spiritual affairs, he did not overlook temporal matters, but made his will,[1] by which he bequeathed to his relations only what the law required, leaving all the rest to the Great Hospital of Milan for the poor, reserving only a few legacies to other pious foundations and to members of his household. Nor did he neglect to provide for masses and prayers for his soul; and chose at the same time the most lowly position in the cathedral for his tomb.

Having made every preparation for his end, though only eight-and-thirty years of age, he gave himself up entirely to his people. By going in person from house to house he became acquainted with all infected as well as suspected cases. Wherever he turned his steps he saw sights of misery — wretched victims abandoned to death, without help either for body or soul, a spectacle that pierced his heart with grief.

The worst cases he found in the hospital or pesthouse of St. Gregory outside the walls, a quadrangular building, divided into a number of cells like a monastery of regulars, enclosing a large open space, with a chapel open on all sides for the greater convenience of the inmates; the whole surrounded by a moat full of water like a fortress, so that it could only be approached by the gate. In this place was an immense gathering of the plague-stricken, as well as of those suspected of infection, all in distress and misery. When the officers of the municipality heard of a case of suspected plague, they immediately shut the sus-

[1] Signed by him on the 9th September, 1576, in Latin and the vernacular. In it he indicated the day of his death.—O.

pected persons up in their houses, or else removed them to this hospital, where they were destitute of all succour, their bare unfurnished cells being little better than prisons.   Their misery increased every hour by fresh arrivals of fellow-sufferers, among them perhaps a father, a mother, or children, whom they saw perish before their eyes, without assistance, without the sacraments, without being able themselves to render them aid of any kind.

When our saint reached this abode of misery, there pierced his ears the cries of sufferers, who rushed to the windows, stretching out their hands to him, with tears and groans begging his compassion.   Some mourned the loss of relatives ; others shrieked with pain, imploring aid for body and soul with a lamentable chorus : " O most pitiful father, forsake us not; O holy Archbishop, great Cardinal, have pity upon us; dear Pastor of our souls, help your poor abandoned children ; O leave us not without giving us your blessing."

Far less was needed to move the heart of Charles with the deepest commiseration.   Tears poured from his eyes, and all the more abundantly because he was not able to relieve their necessities on the spot. He gave them, however, all he could—words of comfort and promises to spare nothing in order to minister to their wants.   The sight of his tears and sympathy was balm to the hearts of these poor creatures, who relied confidently on his promise of assistance.

CHAPTER III.

WHEN Charles had returned home and entered his own apartments, the remembrance of what he had seen seemed to weigh heavily upon him. Leaning back against the wall for support, and looking at those who had accompanied him, "Have you fully realised," he said, "the depth of wretchedness of these poor people, not plague-stricken alone, but forsaken of men, and what is far more deplorable, destitute of spiritual succour, not a single priest being found to take compassion upon them? It is I who am the cause in not having been the first to set the example of aiding them. Still, if God does not send them help in other ways, I know my duty." In these words he plainly showed his intention of serving the sick and administering the sacraments with his own hands.

He had already begun to distribute alms, but his charity took a still wider range. Not satisfied with sending to the hospital a supply of provisions and necessaries, he despatched thither a quantity of his furniture, including even his bed. He sent, too, all the silver plate [1] he possessed to the mint, to be coined into money for their relief; while to provide for the ever-increasing calls upon his charity, he directed collections to be made both in his own diocese, and sent into other parts to beg alms.

To supply their spiritual necessities, as he saw that the clergy of the town shrunk from the dangers of the plague, he procured a priest and lay assistants from the Swiss valleys, men whom custom had rendered indifferent to infection, and assigned the hospital of St. Gregory to their care. Still, this was far from being sufficient for the daily increasing numbers of those who were struck down. In this strait he turned to the regular clergy, hoping to find them more ready for the work of charity, as being more detached from the world, and leading a life of greater perfection. Nor was he disappointed. He found many willing to devote themselves to the work, with the consent of their superiors. He urged also upon those living in the world the blessedness of giving help, and many of both sexes were led to risk their lives for their brethren. For their use he wrote a little book, encouraging them to perseverance, and reminding them of the eternal rewards promised by God for their charity.

All the while his own visits and labours were unwearied. In the course of them he found it necessary to have with him only those who were

---

[1] All the silver plate he possessed consisted of a water-jug and basin and four plates, with spoons and forks to match. He had two pastoral staves of silver, one of which was certainly sold at this time, probably both, for we afterwards find mention in his letters of wooden ones.

most trustworthy, as they had to converse and sometimes remain a considerable time among infected
persons. He gave orders to the rest of his household,
as well as all others, to keep at a distance, as the
contagion was spreading more widely every day, owing
to the neglect of these ordinary precautions. He
found that his whole household united to put difficulties in the way; some, out of care for their own
health, quitted his service altogether; others, to prevent him from exposing himself to danger, were
chary of lending a hand to the work. Seeing the
trail of the serpent in this, he called all the disaffected
to him in private, and succeeded in infusing into
them his own spirit of sacrifice, so that they offered
themselves cheerfully to the work. He made special
rules also for the rest of his household, appointing
certain prayers and penances, to turn aside the anger
of God, with stringent precautions against infection.
For himself, he acted as if he were actually an infected
person, allowing no one to come near him or wait upon
him, and having a rod carried before him when he
went abroad, in order to keep off every one from
himself and his assistants, who were eight in number.

In the same way, that all might have access to him
without risk, he threw open his hall of audience with
a barrier or grill of lattice-work across it. He also
took the same precautions in the choir of the cathedral,
for the security of the canons and clergy during the
celebration of the divine offices which he never
missed attending at this time.[1]

[1] He had usually been present in choir on feast-days only.—O.

It was remarkable that during the whole time the plague lasted, neither he nor any who accompanied him had so much as a headache, though they were continually in attendance on the plague-stricken and those in their last agony. It was considered as a miraculous evidence of the blessing of God upon their labours. Three persons of the Cardinal's household were carried away by the pestilence, and they were not of his companions, but caught it owing to want of care and neglect of the rules he had laid down.

The ravages of the disease still continuing, as the clergy of the town still shrunk from contact with it, Charles sent to ask the Sovereign Pontiff if he could not oblige them to administer the sacraments to the dying. He asked Bernardo Carniglia, through whom the petition was sent, to procure the opinions of certain learned persons in Rome also, and to obtain for him the following faculties from his Holiness: viz., to dispense regular priests, who were willing to give themselves up to this work, from the obligation of obtaining the permission of their superiors; to appropriate to the service of the poor certain legacies and endowments intended for other pious uses; the faculty of absolving in cases reserved to the Holy Apostolic See; various indulgences for the service of the sick; plenary indulgences for the dying; the Papal blessing for rosaries and medals; and several particular indulgences for the exercises of devotion with special reference to the prevailing calamity when so many were daily called to their last account. He also asked for the privileges of St. Gregory's altar in Rome, for St.

Gregory's chapel in the hospital, that the souls of the faithful departed might be released from purgatory by the holy sacrifice of the Mass. Lastly, begging for these indulgences both for himself and his successor in case he should die during the pestilence, he besought his Holiness graciously to remember in his prayers the miseries of his flock, that God would be pleased to take away the plague—the just punishment of their sins, and that he would write as a father to his people exhorting the sick to patience in their sufferings and all cheerfully to help and to profit by this visitation sent by God to further their eternal salvation. As the ravages of the pestilence were not confined to Milan but threatened other parts, he prayed his Holiness to call upon the Bishops of those places as good shepherds not to forsake their flocks but to offer their lives for their people.

Gregory XIII., while loth to see the life of a Prelate whom he so highly valued exposed to risk, praised his charity and self-devotion and granted all his requests, promising him his prayers and support in all his undertakings, begging him to have some regard for himself and not to run into unnecessary danger, reminding him that the welfare of his people depended in a great measure upon his life, and that his death would be a loss not only to his diocese but to the whole Church. Soon after the despatch of this letter Bernardo Carniglia was called to his reward, and the saint's inquiry as to his power of obliging his clergy to attend to the plague-stricken remained unanswered.

The Holy See graciously granted all the above requests and sent a pastoral letter addressed to the whole province of Milan, calling upon all to fulfil the duty of Christian charity at this time of trial, and urging the sick to patience and trust in God. The Cardinal printed this letter of the Sovereign Pontiff together with an epistle of St. Dionysius of Alexandria, in which is described the charity of the Christians of his time towards each other under a similar calamity; also two sermons of St. Cyprian, one in time of pestilence, and another on almsgiving; a discourse of St. Gregory Nazianzen on the love we owe to the sick and to the poor; two homilies of St. Gregory of Nyssa on the care of the poor, and a letter of St. Augustine to Honoratus on the duty of not deserting our neighbour in distress. All these he had translated into the vernacular, as also the Pope's letter, adding at the end an account of the devotion of St. Bernardine of Sienna to the victims of the plague.

His next care was to call together all the secular clergy of the city, exhorting them earnestly to a self-sacrificing love of their neighbour, and not to set too high a value upon their own lives in these times of danger. He acknowledged that he desired nothing of them which he was not ready himself to do, and promised that he would himself administer the last sacraments to them if any should fall victims to their intrepidity. He gave it as his own opinion and that of many learned doctors, that they were bound to administer the sacraments of Penance and Holy Eucharist at whatever risk. His words did not fail of their effect. His

hearers one and all offered themselves joyfully to follow
in his footsteps, and were filled with so fervent a spirit
that they not only confessed and communicated but
also gave extreme unction to the dying during the
plague.

Yet after this it seemed that fear of the contagion
and the terrible appearance of the dying robbed many
of their self-possession when the time came for approaching the bed of death. Once more the saint
sent for those who had so failed, one by one, and
urged their duty upon them with so much force and,
where needful, with so wholesome a severity that they
were not known to be again wanting.

A noble action which occurred at this time is
worthy of record. The dead bodies carried out from
the hospital of St. Gregory during the night were
thrown into a public burying-ground adjoining, called
the Foppone, in order to be ready for interment the
following morning. On one occasion a poor wretch,
not quite dead, had been cast out with the rest amidst
a heap of putrefying bodies. Early in the morning
the priest of St. Gregory's was passing that way to
take the Holy Viaticum to some dying persons. At
the sound of the bell, the poor creature raised himself
upon his knees amidst the heaps of corpses, and turning towards the priest, exclaimed, " O my father, for
the love of God suffer me to receive the Holy Sacrament once more!" The priest did not hesitate for a
moment but hastened to give the poor man the consolation he so ardently desired. After receiving his
Saviour he laid himself down again, and a few minutes

later he was called away with every reason to hope for a favourable judgment from Him with Whom he had united himself on earth.   This action edifying in the dying man for his longing for the Bread of Angels, and in the priest for his charity amid so many plague-stricken corpses, was told from mouth to mouth and thought worthy of record by St. Charles himself in his little book called " A Remembrance for his Beloved People."

Having moved the clergy to do their duty, the Cardinal, for his own part, made every provision for preserving them from fatal consequences as far as it was possible, laying down precautions to be used also by lay-attendants on the sick, in which the office of each and every one was prescribed with minuteness and forethought.   They are to be found in the con-stitutions of the fifth Provincial Council of Milan, and are valuable for future emergencies.

While the saint was energetically attending to all these matters, the notables and chief men seemed to be thinking only of making good their retreat to their estates in the country, so that all those who were most needed to carry on the government were found to be absent. The evils produced by this state of things were increased by the Governor of the city being among the number.   Having ascertained the names of those who had not yet taken their departure, he sent for them and succeeded in banishing their fears and inducing them to remain and help in alleviating the general distress.   In order to carry on the adminis-tration of the city, having obtained the promise of assistance, he parcelled out the city into districts, assigning one to each person who undertook to visit and provide for necessitous cases in these parts. That everything might be done in order, he recommended meetings at regular intervals for consultation on the best way of relieving distress, and that one of the clergy should be present to give the benefit of his experience and advice in spiritual matters. This arrangement was found successful, and the improved condition of the poor greatly comforted the saint.

New troubles, however, awaited him. There arose a dispute between the municipal authorities and the officers of the crown as to which of them was bound to provide funds for carrying out these recommendations. In the meantime, all these good works were brought to a stand-still, and the poor plunged again into suffering. St. Charles witnessed their affliction with heartfelt compassion, having already exhausted his own means and done his utmost in begging alms. There was nothing left he could do but pray fervently that God, of His infinite mercy, would vouchsafe to send succour to His people in their need that they might not perish. At this time the Governor, who had taken refuge from the pestilence at Vigevano, was obliged to return to Milan on business with the Senate. The Cardinal seized the opportunity to expostulate with him in a spirit of paternal authority on his forsaking his post at such a time, and warned him of the chastisements he might expect from the hand of God if by his example he continued to encourage the nobility in their abandonment of the city and neglect of the poor and needy.

Mgr. Antonio Seneca, one of the deputies to whom the Cardinal had given the charge of the city, was the bearer of this letter to the Governor, who very promptly turned his attention to the needs of the people, and in conjunction with the Senate made such provision for them as amply to satisfy the anxiety of the saint on their behalf.

Page 385.—The Governor.

A new Governor, Antonio de Guzman, Marquess of Ayamonte, had been sent to Milan, after Luis de Requesens had gone to Flanders in 1573, and is the same who is referred to in page 369.

CHAPTER IV.

IN the meantime, the contagion was rapidly spreading,
and every hour brought to light new cases of plague
in the different parts of the city. No care or precaution seemed of any effect to stay its ravages, and
every one thought that it would be his turn next.
Men forsook their ordinary occupations to shut themselves up and avoid all intercourse with their neighbours. Hence arose a complete stagnation of trade,
and great distress among those whose subsistence
depended upon their daily labour. Large numbers
of servants and domestics were dismissed, and artisans and labourers were thrown out of employment.
Neither abroad nor at home could they obtain work,
because Milan was strictly cut off from all intercourse
with the outside world. In this pass they all betook
themselves to the Cardinal, as to a common father,
in full confidence that he could relieve them in their
destitution. It was a sight to melt a heart of stone
to behold the troops of these poor creatures marching
along like an army to throw themselves at the feet of
their Pastor in their last extremity. He received them

cheerfully, like a father distressed at their misery,
bidding them be of good heart, and promising them
aid.   Any one unacquainted with his strength of mind
and fertility of resource might indeed have thought
that this time he had undertaken more than he could
perform.   His own means had long been exhausted;
overwhelmed with debts, what could he do for the
crowds now gathered round him?

Seeing that some were strong and capable, he set
them as guards in various places where needed, others
he appointed to attend upon the sick, to disinfect their
clothes and the like.   The rest, three or four hundred
in number, he lodged for several days in the porch
of St. Stephen in Brolio, afterwards removing them
to more commodious quarters at Vittoria on the road
to Melegnano, eight miles from Milan, in a large
building raised by Francis I. King of France in
memory of his victory over the Swiss.   In order to
be of real benefit to them he was not satisfied with
supplying all their bodily wants, but gave them rules
for keeping order.   For the practice of their religion
he appointed some Capuchin fathers to administer the
sacraments and preach to them, and a judge, with the
consent of the authorities, for the correction of offenders,
and visited them himself, when he was able to do so.
Though the assemblage was large, and of some of the
roughest characters of the city, the discipline they
observed was remarkable, and they might indeed have
been taken for a religious community.   As their
maintenance required a considerable outlay, and we
know that he had already gone beyond his own

resources, it is evident that God blessed his means by multiplying them in his hands. At the same time he never neglected any ordinary means in his power, and when all funds were exhausted, he sent his poor round to the neighbouring towns marching in bands with a crucifix carried before them, singing litanies to move the faithful to give alms. Thus in one way or another they were sufficiently supplied. But as winter came on they began to feel severely their want of clothing, and as he could not bear to see them suffer, he set himself to devise some way of providing suitable garments for them.

He accordingly put in requisition all the hangings and draperies of his palace, and cut them up for this purpose, turning out all his stores, and stripping them of every article which could possibly be turned to account. He went round into every room to see that his orders were carried out, and allowed nothing to be kept back but a single change of linen for himself, and a coarse cloth which he used as a table-cover till his death, instead of a rich tapestry, of which it had once formed the lining. All these stuffs were made up into articles of clothing and cloaks with hoods, to be worn in chapel. Altogether it was reckoned that he gave for this purpose eight hundred yards of red and seven hundred of purple cloth, besides other stuffs and garments of his own which he freely added, keeping only what was barely necessary for his own use. Before this time he had sent to the hospital all clothes that he had left off wearing, besides his furs, which were of considerable value. Thus he had put the crown to his works of mercy by giving away all that he possessed.

Still even this stock was not sufficient to clothe all the poor of the city and neighbouring hamlets and of the hospital, so that he had to beg for more. The saint took particular pleasure in distributing these gifts with his own hands, in order that he might witness and share the joy of those who received them. In the midst of sadness men smiled when they beheld the array of motley colours we have described, like regiments of soldiers in different uniforms. But better than this, it led many rich men of the city to imitate his example, and to bestow the furniture of their palaces in the same way, while their wives cheerfully deprived themselves of their jewels and ornaments, and put them in the hands of the Cardinal, whom they acknowledged as the best administrator of their wealth.

Though every resource had been made use of to mitigate the evils of the pestilence, yet as its ravages seemed rather to increase than diminish, the saint renewed his oft-repeated warning that it was nothing less than a scourge from Heaven, and that their hopes must rest entirely on the divine assistance rather than on any human exertions. He reminded them of what many holy bishops, and particularly St. Gregory the Great, had done in like circumstances; how they had collected the people together, and with solemn processions and prayers besought Almighty God to have mercy upon them when they seemed to be given up to destruction.

In imitation of this example he directed three general processions to be made together with fasting, almsgiving, and prayers, during three days in the week, on the Wednesday, Friday, and Saturday, begging all to confess and communicate on the following Sunday, which happened to be the 7th of October, the anniversary of the victory of Lepanto over the Turks five years before, and holding out a hope of obtaining again the mercy of God. He also granted a particular indulgence, repeating his exhortations to the people to avail themselves of the time of penance offered to them, and by a true repentance to call upon God to take pity and remove the scourge of His anger. As a necessary precaution for avoiding contagion, he directed that the people of each . parish should walk separately in the procession—each parish under its own banner.

When the city authorities heard of the intended processions they did not approve of them, afraid lest the concourse of people should add fuel to the fire. But St. Charles, acting under the guidance of the Spirit of God, would not yield to mere human expediency, arguing that the real remedy for their evils lay in the very means proposed, quoting the example of St. Gregory, who had in a similar peril held a solemn procession, and God had been pleased to send His angel to announce that His anger had been appeased. In this way he entirely overcame their opposition, and these very magistrates themselves took part in the procession. On the 3d of October, when all the clergy and people were.

assembled in the cathedral, the Cardinal blessed ashes
with the usual rites, and put them on the heads of
all, though it was not the season of Lent. But he
did so in order to move the people to greater penance
and self-abasement, and to make a solemn recognition
of the submission due to God in their affliction. The
blessing of God manifestly attended his labours, for
the whole congregation was with one accord melted to
tears of penitence, as if a dew from heaven had softened their hearts. The procession then formed and
went to the church of St. Ambrose the Great, the
Cardinal himself closing it with a devotion and mien
so touching that no one could look upon him without
emotion. He wore a purple vestment in token of
penitence, drawing the hood down to his eyes, his
train sweeping along the ground instead of being carried in state. Round his neck he bore a rope like the
halter of a condemned criminal; in his hand he carried
a crucifix (preserved to this day in the sacristy of the
cathedral) on which he kept his eyes fixed throughout
the whole of the way, like a malefactor led forth for
execution. He considered himself to bear upon his
shoulders the burden of the sins of his people, and
offered himself in sacrifice to God for them, well
content to receive the chastisement due to them if
only they might be spared what yet remained to fill
up the measure of their retribution. This was in
imitation of holy King David, who, when the pestilence was carrying off his people at the thrashing-
floor of Areuna the Jebusite, seeing the destroying
angel at work, called upon God to wreak His anger

upon him and to pardon the people. The sorrow of
their beloved Pastor and father excited the same feeling in the breasts of his people, who, as he passed
along, made the streets re-echo with cries of "Mercy!
mercy!" As the canons and clergy wore a garb of
penance like his own, the appearance of the city
was that of a people whose hearts were full of
contrition.

At the church of St. Ambrose the Cardinal preached
on the words of the Prophet Jeremy, *Quo modo sedet
sola civitas,* "How doth the city sit solitary that was
full of people?"[1] and spoke of the sudden calamity
which had overtaken the prosperous and smiling city,
the Divine justice awakening their hearts to self-
knowledge, a spirit of penance and newness of life,
not sparing their sins, but denouncing them publicly
as the cause of this scourge from heaven. Not to
leave them without consolation, he bid them remember that the hand of God was upon them also for
blessing if they bowed themselves under it in patience.
His earnestness brought tears to the eyes of all his
hearers, and moved the coldness of their hearts.
Those who had come wrapt up in the instinct of self-
preservation, shunning contact with their neighbours,
now forgot themselves in their eagerness, clustering
round the pulpit to catch the words which dropped
from the lips of their inspired pastor.

This was the first time that he had preached from
this pulpit in Milan, having previously been used
to address the people from a seat placed in front of

[1] Jer., Lam. i. 1.

the high altar; but on this occasion, seeing the
assemblage which crowded the church, he thought
he should be better heard, and it was found to be
more advantageous for the people, so that he always
continued using it in future.

It pleased God, during this procession, to accept
the oblation of His servant, and to lay upon him
some part of the suffering for which he had offered
himself. As he walked along with bare feet, carrying a large crucifix in his hand, rapt in contemplation
of the passion of Jesus Christ, his foot caught in an
iron grating, so that one of his nails was torn off
to the quick. He would not, however, stop to apply
any remedy, but bore the pain without flinching, and
the roughness of the road. Every one was moved
to compassion, but he showed no emotion save that
of joy, that he was called to suffer for his flock.

On the other days of the procession he appeared,
still walking barefoot. Though he submitted to have
the wound bound up on returning home after the
procession, he removed the bandage afterwards, nor
would he have it replaced till after the procession was
over. When the surgeon came to dress it, and shud-
dered at the incision he had to make, the saint himself never showed that he felt any pain.

On the Friday the procession went to the church
of St. Laurence, where the Cardinal preached again,
taking for his text the dream or vision of Nabuchodonosor in the Book of Daniel [1] concerning the tree
which was shown to him green and flourishing, with

· [1] Dan. iv. 7.

the birds of the air sheltering in its branches, but which was suddenly cut down and destroyed, leaving nothing but a stump behind. He applied this parable to Milan and the sudden destruction that had overtaken it, striking terror into his hearers at the judgments of God, and filling them with compunction for their sins.

The third procession took place on the next day, Saturday, to our Lady's Church by St. Celsus, where there is always a great crowd by reason of the many graces bestowed here through her intercession. This, being the last, was the most solemn day, for St. Charles had desired that all the convents of regular orders, the collegiate chapters, and the heads of the parochial clergy should bear the relics preserved in their several churches, with lights in their hands, to move the people to greater devotion, and to ask the suffrages of the saints. On this occasion also he himself carried the whole time of the procession the relic of the Holy Nail of the Passion of our Lord,[1] taken from its shrine in the cathedral and borne on a great wooden cross, enclosed in a crystal case. He preached on this occasion on the instruments of our Lord's Passion, kindling the hearts of the people to love and confidence in God's mercy, and the intercession of His Holy Mother, the Patroness of the Church, for whom the Milanese people cherished a peculiar devotion from of old. On their return to the cathedral he laid the Holy Nail on the high altar, and began the devotion of the forty hours, with a meditation every hour on some mystery of the Passion, attended

---

[1] Placed by the Empress St. Helena on the trappings of her palfrey.

throughout the whole time by a multitude of the
clergy and people taking the watching in turn.   The
contemplation of the sufferings of the Son of God, and
the exhortations of the preachers to compunction and
amendment of life, moved the people not only to tears
of penitence and cries for mercy, but to a goodwill to
appease the anger of God.   At the close of these forty
hours, the holy Cardinal conducted another procession
longer and more fatiguing than the others—making
the round of the city, and carrying as before the Holy
Nail aloft, his feet bare and the rope round his neck.
In his desire that every part of the city should enjoy
the blessing of having this most precious relic carried
among them, he spared himself no fatigue, but visited
the six districts in turn fasting, bearing the weight of
the heavy cross all the day with the wound in his foot
still open.

Though the concourse of people was great, it was
observed that the plague made no progress during
these days, as might have been expected, and as
happened in the time of Pope St. Gregory at Rome,
when eighty persons died of the pestilence during the
processions.   This exemption was recognised as a
special privilege conferred upon our saint, and thus
was literally fulfilled his promise to the authorities
when they interfered with his arrangements about
the processions.

Still his zeal was not yet satisfied, and during the
continuance of the plague he kept both clergy and
people in supplication before Almighty God, not only
in Milan itself but throughout the diocese.   To this

end, beside the ordinary divine offices in the collegiate churches, which he required to be celebrated in spite of the risk of contagion, he made a point of keeping the great feasts in the cathedral with the canons, observing all necessary precautions, and directing the clergy of the cathedral to go in procession singing litanies and psalms on the Monday of each week to the church of St. Ambrose, and the rest of the collegiate chapters to go in turn to the cathedral on the other days, often joining them himself, going barefoot even in time of ice and snow.

On feast-days he appointed the litanies to be sung in all the churches before the High Mass, and a certain time to be devoted to mental prayer by all the people, the points being given out aloud by a priest appointed for this duty in each church. The same practice was observed throughout the diocese, so that the prayers of all his people might have been said to ascend to God " without ceasing," as in apostolic times.

Further, to encourage the people in these exercises and in the corporal and spiritual works of mercy, he opened the Church's treasure of indulgences according to the faculties given by the Holy See for certain prayers and works of charity, granting them to physicians, surgeons, and nurses, to those who buried the dead, to those who took charge of orphans, and for every kind of service rendered in love of our Lord.

He was careful to guard against the assaults of the enemy of mankind, and prepared to crush each new form of temptation as it arose. One of the most dangerous at this time was a superstition which spread among the simple and uninstructed people recommending certain charms written and printed on cards and engraved also on rings and medals, which they thought protected them against infection. These were no sooner brought to the notice of the saint than he issued an edict prohibiting their distribution, and denouncing them as impostures condemned by holy Church, offensive to the majesty of God, and suggested by the spirit of falsehood. By this means he saved a number of simple souls from falling a prey to the snares of Satan.

CHAPTER V.

THE PEOPLE, BY THE SAINT'S ADVICE, OFFER THEMSELVES
BY VOW TO ST. SEBASTIAN——FURTHER PROVISIONS
AGAINST THE PLAGUE.

1576.

THE anger of God was not yet appeased, and His scourge still hung over the city, notwithstanding the prayers and penances of the people and their Pastor. From day to day the plague-spot appeared in some fresh place, till the whole city might be said to be steeped in the disease, and it became necessary to devise some new means against its progress.

It was in this crisis that the unflinching faith of St. Charles was seen. Though the wrath of God seemed unappeased, and His judgments to fall heavier the more earnestly the people prayed, his trust never faltered for an instant. When the pestilence was devouring his flock he continued steadfast in his faith that God would ere long deliver them. Full of this assurance, just at the time when the outlook seemed most hopeless, he one day in a sermon in the cathedral promised them that if they only continued their practice of penance and purpose of amendment, the plague would disappear from among them before Christmas-tide. This prophecy was much discussed at the time, and when it was fulfilled by the event it was freely acknowledged that only the Spirit of God could have revealed it to him, as all probability, so far from bearing him out, told directly against him, as new cases of contagion were published daily.

As his confidence was invincible, so also was it altogether free from presumption, and he was not deterred from continuing his prayers by his foreknowledge of returning health, or discouraged at the moment by their seeming fruitlessness. He was always urging the people to increase the fervour of their prayers, and was ever giving them fresh opportunities of enkindling their devotion. Though all that men receive through the intercessions of the saints is from the hand of God, yet he knew well it is His good pleasure to work by means of instruments, and that the genius and intellect of man is given to serve Him in difficulties and trials.

When every effort seemed to have failed, he recommended them to make a particular application to the glorious martyr St. Sebastian, who was held in special honour by the Milanese as a native of their city. His intercession had before this time put an end to the ravages of pestilence in the pontificate of St. Adeotatus, A.D. 672, when Rome was desolated by this terrible scourge, and the dead lay in heaps in the public ways, and nothing stayed its virulence till an altar was erected to St. Sebastian in the church of St. Peter *ad vincula*. Following this example, St. Charles

encouraged the Milanese to make a solemn promise to
restore the ruined church of the saint, to provide for
the celebration of a daily mass there in perpetuity, to
keep his feast with due honour, and the vigil as a
fast, to make a solemn procession on the anniversary of this day, viz., October 15, for ten successive
years, and every year on his feast day. In making
this vow we see that St. Charles had two objects
chiefly in view : to increase the veneration paid to the
saint, and to keep up in the minds of the people the
remembrance of their deliverance, as an incentive to
watchfulness against those sins which had provoked
the infliction.

The worst was not yet, however, over. The hospital of St. Gregory was filled to overflowing, and
numbers daily applied for admission. In union with
the municipality, St. Charles decided upon adopting
two important sanitary measures. The first was to
construct temporary hospitals for the sick in the
country, at some distance from the city, six in number, corresponding to the six districts, defended by
ditches and walls, so as to prevent communication
between the sick and the sound ; the other was the
establishment of quarantine within the city, in order
to restrict all intercourse leading to the spread of
contagion.

The condition of the city at this time was so
wretched that it recalled the Lamentations of Jeremias
over Jerusalem. St. Charles himself thus describes it :
" The city might at this time be likened to that great
tree which was shown to Nabuchodonosor in a dream,

reaching to heaven, and spreading out its branches to
the ends of the earth.   O city of Milan, so wast thou
in the days of thy greatness exalted to heaven, and
thy riches penetrated unto the utmost parts of the
world.   Men and beasts and fowls of the air were
nourished by thine abundance.   Peasants came from
afar to labour under thy shade, and nobles delighted
to take up their abode in thy palaces.   But now how
is thy wantonness and pride suddenly cast down, so
that thou art become a by-word in the mouths of men!
Thou art shut up within thy walls; thy wares and
thy merchandise are cut off.   None come any more to
dwell with thee, to enjoy thy fruits, and to traffic in
thy markets, nor even to adorn themselves with thy
inventions, nor to learn of thee new fashions of vanity,
but thou art shunned alike by gentle and simple, and
canst tempt no one by thy pleasures or riches to meet
the poison of thy breath.   How great is the misery of
those who must perforce dwell with thee!   If they
escape the ravages of the pestilence, few there are who
are not numbered among the suspected and banished
to the discomforts of the hospital, or, what is worse,
obliged to crave a shelter in the huts without the
walls, where they are lucky if they find straw to lie
upon, the greater number having to sleep under the
dew of heaven, in the haunts of beasts, where soldiers
hem them in, lest they should carry the plague-spot
elsewhere.   What more need be said?   Thy streets
and public places are deserted, thy churches are
empty, thy markets closed, thy houses left desolate.
O Milan! famished and hard-pressed, begging aid

from villages and hamlets around that once depended upon thee, how art thou humbled and brought low by the sudden shaft from the hand of God!"

From these words of the saint we may gather how great was the distress in which this once-thriving city found itself; we have it on his authority that there were as many as sixty or seventy thousand poor, who, being thrown out of employment by the stagnation of trade, and failure of the ordinary channels of labour, were dependent upon the alms of the charitable for their daily bread. This was of course a heavy drain on the public purse, and the controllers of the city found themselves obliged to borrow money on the security of the tolls and customs.

Throughout this extremity the saint continued his almsgiving without reserve, though forced to embarrass his income for many years in advance, and was constantly reduced to such straits that his steward had often to go, now to one, now to another, to beg means for the day's expenses, as if he had himself been one of the poorest.

And though often hard beset, he was never abandoned by the Providence of God in whom he implicitly trusted, and who often aided him miraculously in times of greatest need. This was manifested particularly on one occasion. He had been busy the whole day providing for the necessities of the destitute. On returning home in the evening he found there was nothing in the larder for his own household, and no means of obtaining any provisions, everything having been distributed among the poor. The saint withdrew without a word to his own apartment, in all probability to pray, while his chamberlains and assistants in the labours of this trying period stood around with arms crossed, supperless, yet never doubting that God would provide for them. Just at this moment a person of consideration knocked at the door, accompanied by a porter carrying a bag of a thousand crowns, and requested an audience of the Cardinal, at whose feet he laid the money as an offering. This gave great consolation to the household, as being a wonderful instance of the care of God for them. These favours from heaven caused the saint to exercise greater charity still towards those in distress, and to urge those who had means at command to do the same. In many instances his exhortations had the best results, the wealthy often despoiling themselves of their most valuable effects that they might have more to give away. Among the most benevolent was Pomponio Cusano and his brother Agostino.[1]

The number of the needy continued, however, to increase in the long season of distress, and Milan, no longer able to provide for their necessities, was forced to have recourse to the neighbouring cities and towns for aid. Many of them responded with alacrity to this appeal: the store of provisions contributed by the people of Casal Maggiore gave most seasonable succour, and was particularly worthy of remembrance as a mark both of generosity and loyalty.

While the Cardinal busied himself in behalf of the suffering members of his flock, his charity was seen most especially in his solicitude for the poor little ones

---

[1] Afterwards made Cardinal by Sixtus V.

who lost their mothers in the plague. When it was impossible to find foster-mothers for them all, he had them supplied with goats' milk. These little nurslings were his especial charge, and he took particular pleasure in rescuing them wherever he came across them, for sometimes when going round the city by night he descried them on door-steps, sometimes lying by the side of the dead bodies of their parents; but wherever they might be, they always received at his hands the care and tenderness of a father.

Page 401.—"*The city might at this time be likened.*"

This is an extract from the *Memoriale al suo diletto popolo,* Part I. chap. 1, printed in the Acts of the Church of Milan, Part VII.

CHAPTER VI.

SPIRITUAL CARE OF HIS FLOCK DURING THE PLAGUE.

1576.

THE spiritual care of his flock in this time of pestilence weighed particularly on the mind of the saint; for while he did not neglect their bodies, his principal solicitude was for the salvation of their souls. In his daily visits to the sick in the hospital or in the huts beyond the walls, his first inquiry was as to their spiritual welfare, in order to provide them with every assistance and consolation. The first priest whom he had placed at the hospital had fallen a victim to his own want of caution, so he procured another in his place from Switzerland. He then appointed a Capuchin father, Paul Belintano, over the establishment, to keep order and correct offenders. This father did good service in keeping all the officials in the regular performance of their duties. When the huts beyond the walls were erected he had to find priests to attend to the administration of the sacraments there, as the parochial clergy were now confined to the city by the rules of quarantine. In this emergency he had recourse to the Regular orders,

having received a faculty from Rome to dispense with
the consent of their superiors in case of refusal. He
sent accordingly for certain fathers who were noted as
good confessors, and begged them to undertake the
care of the sick in the following address, taken in
substance from the life of St. Charles by Monsignor
Bascapè, Bishop of Novara.

" Reverend Fathers,

" I have no need to describe to you the miserable
state of this city, since it is open to the eyes of all,
nor to rouse you to compassion, for no one can be so
hard-hearted as not to feel for the afflicted. Yet this
I will say, that it is no ordinary calamity which we
have now to endure. We see men in the hour of their
need deprived of the presence and support of those
nearest and dearest to them. We see them torn from
their abodes and dragged to a place of suffering, which
is more like a stable than a hospital, and this with
little or no hope of again beholding their relatives or
homes. This would be grievous indeed even if it only
concerned the frail bodies which must one day perish,
though there would then be this consolation, that they
would soon be rewarded for their pains by an eternity
of joy. But here it is worse than this: it is not their
bodies alone which are in danger of perishing, it is
their souls, for which I plead. Though reduced to a
condition so desperate, they have none to minister to
their needs in spiritual things. Shall we not be
heartless indeed if we stand by and stretch out no
hands to help ? Shall we see our brethren and fellow-

citizens, our friends and relatives, not only deprived
of comforts in their sufferings, not only tortured with
pain and the apprehension of a terrible death: but
shall we stand idly by and see them without any of
the consolations of religion, while they call on us with
tears to take pity on them, while their very looks tell
us, when they have lost their voices, that their days
are without help and their end almost without hope?
Shall these things take place before our eyes, and we
give no relief? O reverend fathers, here is your
opportunity to prove your title to the name of religious,
to effect all your good desires and resolutions, to serve
God by acts of heroic perfection. This is the time to
show forth the excellence of your institute, that you
are striving to be saints and to lead perfect lives, for
it is chiefly by works of piety and mercy that perfection is to be shown. O turn not your backs upon
an occasion of serving God in a way so charitable and
so necessary, reject not the prayers of these wretched
suppliants. It is a work that falls more clearly to
your share, for the city clergy have their hands full in
a season of such distress. We know that they are faithful in performing their ordinary duties, and that they
could not suffice for more than this even if they were
in greater numbers than they are. But besides this,
if they were to mingle with the plague-stricken, they
would be shunned as bearers of contagion among their
own people, so that we should have to provide other
clergy for parochial duties. We have exerted ourselves
to procure the services of priests from the country,
and some have offered themselves, but they do not

suffice for all that is required of them, and there are numbers of patients in the huts beyond the walls who are altogether without the ministrations of the Church, because we have no priests to send to them.

"It is to you then we look in this emergency, to you who, living in a state of perfection, are obliged by your profession to make no account of temporal considerations, but to despise them, whenever you may thereby serve God more perfectly. To you we look, who ought to be ready to lay down your lives for the love of God and your neighbour, especially when it is a question of saving souls. For it was thus that the Son of God died for us, and thus many saints have done, whose example you as good religious are bound to follow.

"But you will say, perhaps, that in the case of the sick, whose cause we are pleading, your good offices are not so essential, seeing they may be saved without you. We do not now dispute the point, nor will we consider the matter on a ground so low. The holy law of the Gospel, and the example of the saints, teach us to exercise generosity. The saints knew no law but that of charity, and never shrunk from devoting themselves to such works as this which we now propose to you. Jesus Christ our Lord in His own person bears out the lesson. Though the Son of God, He gave Himself of His own will to a death of shame upon the cross, for friends and for enemies.

"It is He who invites you to take part in the work. Though we have spoken of the duty of not counting our lives dear to us in His cause, we do not wish you

to understand that there is of necessity danger to
health or life.   By God's grace it is far otherwise,
and with ordinary caution and attention to rules, risk
may be avoided, as is done by those priests who have
hitherto laboured here.   But this we say, that if it
should please Almighty God that any of us should
catch the infection and die, that it would be a glorious
end, rather deserving the name of life, for dying thus
in the service of God and of our neighbours, it is most
certain that we should attain to life eternal—that life
which the saints and martyrs have made the end and
aim of their labours upon earth.

" Moreover, it is an opportunity of showing our
gratitude to God, and laying up a treasure of merit
for ourselves, making a generous return for the love
which the Son of God has lavished upon us, offering
up our lives in His service and in that of His plague-
stricken brethren, even as He laid down His life for
us on the cross, nay, even as He gives it to us His
priests every day in the Holy Sacrifice of the Mass.

" Who is there among you whose heart is so cold as
not to respond to the call of our dear Lord, to whom
we are so bound ?   Who can refrain from offering
himself, his health and life, and all that he has, in
sacrifice to Him ?   Shall we suffer ourselves to be
overcome by the fear of death ?   In any case we must
die ere long.   What security have we, again, that if we
abandon our duty in keeping out of the reach of pestilence, that the just judgment of God will not over-
take us, and thus punish our inordinate affection for
our perishing bodies ?   Believe me, reverend fathers,

it is an easy thing to fall a victim to this common visitation. We have innumerable examples before us of those who have hedged themselves round with every possible precaution, but have nevertheless perished. For it is a scourge sent by God for the chastisement of our sins, and who shall deliver us from the hand of His power when it is His will to search us out ?

" Far better for us, therefore, would it be to abandon ourselves to God by entering upon this holy work for love of Him, and in satisfaction for our sins—thus, so to speak, restraining His arm, and calling upon His mercy.

" Dear fathers, what shall I say more ? Shall I reproach you with the example of laymen, who, for a little temporal gain, expose themselves to far greater danger in their attendance than is required of us— touching them, handling them, and waiting upon them in every way ? But I will go further, and say there are many of them who do this, not for fee or reward, but from pure love of God. This we know of ourselves, for many have placed their services freely at our disposal. And shall *we* do less, His priests, who are the recipients of His special favours, who make profession of lead- ing a spiritual and perfect life ? Shall we suffer our- selves to be outstript by people in the world ? shall not the love of God have greater weight with us than mere interest and gain has with them ? Have we not indeed our own true interest at heart ? Is not the reward of glory which God will render us in His eternal kingdom more to us than perishing gain is to them ? Think of these things, beloved brethren and

fathers, and show not yourselves to be so weak and
faint-hearted that laymen shall rise up in judgment
against you and condemn you.

"If any of you are withheld from offering yourselves by reason of not having the permission of your
superiors, though we will not believe that the charity
of any superior is so weak that he would not wish to
second your good desires, know that the Sovereign
Pontiff hereby releases you from all obligation of
obedience on this occasion: and we have received
ample faculties from His Holiness to authorise you to
come even against the express will of your superiors.
Let not this therefore distress you. Far from incurring any guilt of disobedience, you will be doing what
is most pleasing to His Holiness, to which he himself
exhorts and invites you.

"I call upon you one and all therefore to devote
yourselves generously to this work worthy of your
high calling, and to make your service a special oblation to Almighty God, who has vouchsafed to charge
Himself with the reward of all you do for Him.
Moreover, I ask it of you as a favour personal to
myself, of which I shall never be unmindful. For I
assure you, you will hereby relieve me of a burden
which oppresses me beyond measure, and I shall be
greatly rejoiced when I see you occupied in saving
these souls committed to my charge, and so dear to
me, that I may say I bear them graven on my heart.
You may imagine the grief and anguish I feel to see
them in danger of perishing eternally for want of
spiritual assistance. I do not doubt, however, that

you will readily offer yourselves that I may send you out to them, or that the example of the first-comers will inspire many others to do likewise. When the work is once begun, God, I know, will move many hearts to carry it on. But as the risk of those who are first to offer themselves is greater, let them rest assured that their reward shall be higher. Fear not, my brethren, ever to be forsaken under any circumstances that may arise; I myself will keep my eye upon you, and will never forsake you. If it should please God that any of you fall a prey to the disease, and there should be none to serve you, I will attend you myself and have every care for your souls. For my own part, you are my witnesses, that from this hour I devote myself to minister to you in holy things. I am firmly resolved that no weariness, no fatigue, no peril, shall make me quail from fulfilling my pastoral office, or from doing everything in my power for the souls which God has committed to my keeping."

Such was the substance of the address delivered by our blessed Pastor on this occasion, but it was spoken with so great unction and earnestness that every one of the fathers who heard it was moved with a great desire to do his bidding. Twenty-eight offered themselves on the spot, to the great joy of the saint, who accepted their services with gratitude, and immediately appointed their work to each. From day to day their numbers increased, the Capuchin fathers being among the foremost to come forward, and from that time there was never any lack of priests during the continuance of the plague. St. Charles provided them all with lodging and maintenance in his palace, where they all dined together in the common refectory, though not without observing the usual precautions. The proportion of those who were carried off by the plague was not large, viz., two Jesuits, two Barnabites, and two Capuchins, God being pleased to accept the offering of themselves they had so generously made. They may be compared to those priests who ministered to the plague-stricken of Rome in the time of the Emperor Valerian, of whom the Roman Martyrology thus speaks under the date Feb. 28: "At Rome the commemoration of many holy priests, deacons, and others, who in the time of the Emperor Valerian, during the ravages of the plague, willingly went to their death in ministering to the sick, and have always been venerated as martyrs by the faithful."

We may gather in this way some idea of the work which God was pleased to accomplish by means of His servant. We see him with a few words not only moving so many to expose themselves to the peril of their lives, without hope or thought of reward in this world, but inspiring them with a strength and a confidence, in which they were ready to undertake whatever labours the saint appointed them. This was the source of untold blessings, for St. Charles was now enabled to provide the sick with aid and consolation, and the departed with solemn rites and the offering of the Holy Sacrifice for their repose. Thus, the last hours of the agonising were soothed, and greater numbers were able to enjoy the last blessing of the saint and the plenary indulgence at the hour of death. A stricter watch was kept over clothes and things which might carry infection, as well as over persons appointed to disinfect them, so as to prevent thefts and the purloinment of valuables which the deceased might have about them. These priests likewise gave good example and encouragement to the parochial clergy by fearlessly living among the sick of whom they had the charge, in order to be on the spot to render them assistance at any hour of the day or night.

Still kindled by his compassion for the suffering people, the saint continued to turn to account his powers of persuasion in procuring the help of the laity. When spiritual needs were so far provided for, he renewed his efforts for the relief of their bodies, by inducing both men and women to serve without payment for the love of God. For this purpose, as he went his rounds of the city, he would stop when he came to any elevated place, where he could be well heard, and addressing the people who were sure to run in crowds to hear him, exhort them to come generously to his aid for the love of our Lord Jesus Christ. When he had finished, there would come a number of persons, like so many soldiers of the cross, to have their names enrolled in a book which he kept for the purpose. After this he gave them his blessing, and showed them what they would have to do, investing them with his own hand with a habit of sackcloth, as a badge of the work they had undertaken. He then dismissed them with words of encouragement, which filled them with so much fervour, that they never shrunk from the lowest offices of attendance upon the sick, or from exposing themselves to every risk. God was pleased in many instances to accept the sacrifice they made of themselves, and to give them eternal life in exchange for this temporal existence. To the sick their services were of the greatest benefit, for as they were undertaken from motives of pure charity, so they were performed in a spirit of cheerfulness and generosity very different from that of a hireling.

This brings to my mind a touching episode of the times, in which the spirit of self-devotion was brought out in a striking way. The pestilence had seized upon a house opposite the Archbishop's palace, from the windows of which was seen a melancholy sight. Three children lay in one bed stricken with the plague. Two boys were already dead, but the third, a girl about ten years of age, was still alive, but likely soon to follow them. The poor mother was there alone, for every one else had fled from the house, but so great was her fear of the malady that she dared not approach to give any help, even though she saw two die before her eyes and the third almost at her last gasp. Their sad condition was brought to the knowledge of the Cardinal, who, when he had satisfied himself of the fact, felt great compassion for the poor child, and sent for an Ursuline nun who had previously put herself at his disposal, and gave her the charge of the little sufferer. The sister, having removed the two dead bodies, applied such remedies to the survivor as the case required, so that the child shortly revived. The next day, however, she had a relapse, and while the nun was disposing her for death she expressed an earnest wish to receive the Cardinal's blessing. She was accordingly carried to the window, and a messenger was sent with the child's request. The Cardinal was at the moment in the refectory, but immediately rose to give her his blessing from the window. After this the disorder took a fresh turn, and after being taken to the hospital the child was within a few days restored to health, but the nun in her stead was seized by the contagion, and rendered up her soul to God.

CHAPTER VII.

MINISTRATIONS TO THOSE IN QUARANTINE WHO WERE OFTEN VISITED BY THE SAINT.

1576.

GREAT was the satisfaction the saint derived from the results of his labours, for he now saw the sick provided with every consolation they could have had in their own homes. Both he himself and all his priests, by a special privilege from the Apostolic See, were enabled also to grant the plenary indulgence at the hour of death.

There was another part of his flock which now began to claim his care. It did not escape him that the forty days of quarantine, if given up to idleness, afforded many temptations to sin; he therefore was heedful to provide that this time should be spent so as to promote the glory of God and the salvation of their souls. In the first place, he required the clergy to make it a time of penance and fasting, as they were just now entering on the season of Advent; and urged on the laity the duty of confession and communion before beginning it. Next, in order to sanctify the time, he directed that every one should hear Mass devoutly every day ; and to give effect to this order, he erected altars at the crossways and conspicuous places, where Mass was said daily, so that all could assist from their windows. In the same way he arranged for confessions to be heard, sending priests round at stated times from house to house, the confessor sitting on the doorstep outside, and the penitent kneeling within, the door serving as a barrier. The parish priest went round with the Blessed Sacrament on Sundays, and gave holy communion on the doorsteps to all, as if they had been cloistered religious. He also made arrangements that each district should keep seven times of prayer throughout the day and night, singing psalms and hymns in two choirs, after the manner of a chapter of canons, and saying suitable prayers, each hour being announced by ringing the great bell of the cathedral. When it sounded, all the inhabitants attended at their windows, a priest or other person appointed began the prayers, and all the people on their knees made the responses, each having the book of prayers which the Cardinal had printed for the purpose. It was a sight to see, when all the inhabitants of this populous city, numbering little short of three hundred thousand souls, united to praise God at one and the same time, sending up together an harmonious voice of supplication for deliverance from their distress.

Milan might at this time have been not unfitly compared to a cloister of religious of both sexes serving God in the inclosure of their cells, an image

of the heavenly Jerusalem filled with the praises of
the angelic hosts.

To provide still further against the evils of idleness, St. Charles sent round a pastoral letter, suggesting how the rest of their time might be profitably
spent in mental prayer and spiritual reading, and
granted special indulgences to those who practised
these exercises and prayed for the sick.

While he was thus intent in keeping all well employed, he was always the first to set an example of
punctuality in fulfilling his own obligations, as the
head and guide of all. Every day, and we may say
every night, he visited the hospital, the huts, or some
part of the city, according to a plan he had laid down,
allotting a separate district to each day of the week.
He never returned home till he had accomplished this
duty, though it was often ten or eleven o'clock at
night. By these constant visits every one was kept
up to his work, and his continual presence encouraged
all to persevere. At the same time, it was a consolation to him in the midst of his toils to see his people
in tranquillity of mind, praising God and labouring to
save their souls in a time of perplexity and distress.
By this means, too, he obtained an immediate knowledge of the needs of his flock; for as he passed along
the streets, those who were confined to their houses
by the quarantine were sure to run to the windows
and beg his blessing on their knees. Thus every one
had an opportunity of making known to him, as to
their common father, all their needs; for their confidence in him was so great, that many laid open to

him their sorrows, which they had no mind to publish to the committee appointed to provide for temporal distress. And this was the case with the respectable classes also. In order that he might not forget any of these numerous' appeals, he carried a book with him, in which he noted down their tale, and always left them encouraged and consoled. Beside the regular rations which he distributed to the necessitous, he was always accompanied on his rounds by two priests[1] on horseback, carrying a store of articles for the sick, which he would distribute among the poor with his own hands, as well as alms where he saw there was need; and he would take the opportunity of inquiring whether his orders had been carried out, so that his little book was no bare collection of facts, but was the means of the removal or alleviation of distress. Nor did his charity stop here. He was always ready to enter the infected houses to go to the bedsides of those in their last agony, in order to dispose them to die in the love of God. We have seen him groping his way in through a window, or climbing a ladder, to enter when the door was closed; for he would rather have suffered any inconvenience than that one soul should be left without aid, and its salvation imperilled.

Time would fail us to tell of his many charities, or of the cures following upon his blessing, which may be read in the processes of his canonisation. It may be sufficient here to speak of the general estima-

[1] Among these were Ottavio Abbiato Forrero and Griffith Roberts, canons of the Cathedral, and Ludovico Moneta, one of the chaplains of the household.

tion in which he was held by all the people, who
looked upon him as an angel of God, rejoicing whenever they saw him, as if he came to open heaven to
them. His zeal, moreover, seemed to overflow upon
all the priests who served under him, and made them
emulate his fervour and self-devotion in administering
the last sacraments to the sick, who at that time were
passing to a better life. But while his solicitude for
all his flock was great, he spent himself with all his
heart upon those priests and others who at his wish
had given themselves up to the service of the plague-
stricken; always holding it to be his especial charge
to see that they wanted for nothing, and himself to
administer to them the last consolations.

Page 421.—Griffith Roberts, note.

Griffidio Roberti, a native of Wales, was Canon Theolgian of the Chapter,
and one of the confessors in ordinary of St. Charles. Book VIII. chap.
xxiii. Oltrocchi's note here describes him as one of the saint's almoners
at this time of the plague. In a memorandum drawn up in 1588, probably by Count de Olivares and Cardinal Allen, he is recommended for
one of the Welsh bishoprics. See *Records of English Catholics* (London :
Nutt), vol. ii. p. cvii., Introduction.

CHAPTER VIII.

1576.

IN pursuance of his resolution to fulfil all the offices
of a good shepherd to his flock, St. Charles thought
himself bound to give the sacrament of confirmation
to those who were as yet unconfirmed and in danger
of death. For though not a sacrament absolutely
necessary to salvation, he could not let any die without having this grace. He gave notice, therefore, to
all those who were unconfirmed, to prepare themselves
for receiving it devoutly. He then went through the
streets in his pontificals and anointed the candidates
with the holy chrism from door to door, with all
solemnity possible under the circumstances. Out of
reverence to the sacrament, it had not been customary
to admit children under nine years of age to it, but
although the Cardinal had made it his practice to
confirm every Pentecost in different churches, still
several thousand persons presented themselves to
receive it on this occasion. Among them it is thought
must have been many who were already sick of the
plague.

When he went on the visitation of his diocese, of which we give an account in the next chapter, he continued in his purpose of not suffering the plague-stricken to die without confirmation, and administered it first in the town of Sesto on the road to Monza, where the pestilence had made great havoc.   While he was so engaged, a great number of the infected testified their desire for the sacrament.   The saint turned to Father Ludovico Moneta, and asked his opinion of what he ought to do in the case.   The good priest would not give any counsel but, that if the Cardinal thought fit to grant their request, he would gladly assist.   While the saint stood in doubt, a number of the poor creatures, moved by an extraordinary desire for the holy chrism, fell together at his feet.   The attendants frightened at the risk, cried out to them not to come too near.   But when St. Charles perceived the strength of their desire, he would not send them away, saying, " It is the will of God ; let them come for their consolation." After confirming all who presented themselves, he perceived a number of people lingering at some distance, who durst not approach.   Inquiring why they did not come, he was told that they considered their cases too bad and the danger too great.   " Shall we then," said he, " let them die without the sacrament ?   Nay, let them come also."   After this he never hesitated any more, but confirmed all who desired it, how great soever the danger might be, and he was often called upon to confer the sacrament even in the houses of the dead, not unfrequently upon the dying, and on one occasion, at Trezzo, a man fell dead at his feet the moment after he had received the chrism.

In his visits to the sick he found himself called upon at times to administer the sacrament of baptism also. For there were many cases of children born in the temporary huts, whither the mothers had been removed on the plague-spot appearing, and as they were in danger of death, he baptised them and then sent them out to nurse. One case of a little negro girl, whom he met with in this way, was very remarkable on account of a miracle which he afterwards worked upon her.

He frequently had the consolation of fulfilling the promise he had made of giving the last sacraments to the parochial clergy and some of the other priests who had devoted themselves to the care of the sick. This was the case with the parish priest of San Raffaele, in Milan. It was reported to the Cardinal that he had caught the infection, and he immediately presented himself at his bedside, and perceiving his case to be desperate, bade him prepare himself for receiving the last rites, which he would administer himself, assuring him that he would not lose sight of him as long as he was alive. The following day he returned to give him Holy Communion and Extreme Unction, and with this intention said Mass that morning in the church of San Raffaele, and gave Communion to the priest's acolyte, who died of the plague. He then changed his vestments in order to administer the sacraments to the sick priest in his own room. His attendants, among them Monsignor Seneca and Bernardino Tarugi, were

panic-struck at his purpose, but did not venture
either to interpose between the saint and his zeal,
or to follow him in his heroism, but hung back
in fear and hesitation.   St. Charles nevertheless
turned towards the chamber of death in his pontifical
vestments, with the Blessed Sacrament in his hand.
He was met on his way by John Baptist Capra,
Deputy Governor, and Alfonso Gallarato, his Lieu-
tenant, and other members of the City Council,
who had come together to beg him on their knees
in the name of the state not to expose his precious
life to risk.   They urged that he was endangering
himself without any necessity, since any priest might
act for him ; and were accompanied by several priests,
who were ready to go in his place, rather than
that he should be exposed again to danger.   They
bid him reflect what would be their condition if the
venture should prove fatal to him ; that his beloved
city and diocese would then indeed be left desolate,
and the poor and the sick be in despair.   Thus all
the religious exercises he had instituted would fall
into disuse, and his priests, whom his example had
encouraged to attend the plague-stricken with so
much charity, would lose heart when they had their
Pastor no longer with them.   They prayed him, therefore, for the love of Jesus Christ and his flock, to
listen to them, and if he had no regard for his
own safety, at least to consider the entreaties of his
spiritual children.   St. Charles stood firm, however,
still bearing the Blessed Sacrament, and listened to
all they had to say, while the tears rolled down his

cheeks, as he perceived the sincerity and earnestness of their affection which had brought them to his feet. Yet he would not suffer himself to be carried away by these human feelings from the duties of his episcopal office; but answered them briefly, that while he fully appreciated their attachment, he prayed them not to take it ill that he could not abandon his purpose. " Was he not," he said, " especially the pastor of his priests, and how could he exhort them to risk their lives for their people, if he, their head and Archbishop, feared to put himself in the same danger for them, and, moreover, broke his word so often pledged to them, that he would administer the last sacraments to them ? The lives of all were in the hand of God, and if it should please Him to call him to Himself at this time, they were not to distress themselves, but have confidence in His mercy, on which alone the safety of the city depended, and He would provide them with a better pastor."

As it was clear that he had already counted the cost, and that his resolution was not to be shaken, they had perforce to let him go on his way without further hindrance, only testifying by their sorrow the reluctance with which they saw him prefer the duties of a simple priest to his own so highly valued by them all. He went to the sick-room, and closing the door upon himself and the plague-stricken patient, gave him Holy Communion. Then perceiving him to be near his end, he gave him the last anointing and disposed him for death. Thus fortified with the sacraments, the blessing of his Archbishop, and the plenary indulgence for the hour of death, the sick man passed to his rest.

Here we must mention a memorable example of fraternal charity in a priest who is still living, Aloysius Chignolo, of the Church of 'St. Paul at the meeting of the ways, who carried his devotion to the sick so far that he not only, like the Cardinal, attended upon them in their last moments, but washed and prepared their bodies for burial after death.

Shortly after this event we have narrated, the saint was informed that the parish priest of St. Peter in Caminadella had been seized by the malady and was in a precarious state. He at once set out to visit him, but the sick man hearing of his intention and unwilling that his Pastor's life should be endangered, went down into the church just at the moment of the Cardinal's arrival, who was much surprised, knowing him to be in a dying state. He gave him Holy Communion, and then made him return to his bed, and would have anointed him there, but the priest rather than let him stay longer in such a place assured him it was not yet time. The saint persevered, however, and returning the next morning to give him Extreme Unction, found that he had prevailed upon some pious persons in attendance to bring him down again into the church. But St. Charles, knowing him to be at the point of death, had him carried up again to his bed, while he followed in his pontificals, and regardless of the fetid atmosphere gave him Extreme Unction, staying with him through his agony, and recommending his soul to God till he breathed his last.

The Saint after this, discharged the same offices for the parish priests of St. Victor near the theatre, and of St. Babylas; and, indeed, in every case that occurred, his example encouraging all to look to the safety of their brethren rather than their own. Yet, he invariably adopted every precaution of prudence, and never ran any risk where there was no need. Still more cautious was he where others were concerned, and when he had been engaged where there was danger of giving infection to others, he would isolate himself for several days, doing everything for himself during that time, and he required all priests who attended the sick to observe the same rule.

Page 427.—" He would provide them with a better pastor."

On another occasion, when Ottavio Abbiato Forrero, one of his canons, begged the saint not to wear himself out with so many anxieties, he replied, "God grant I may wear out indeed! then He would give you a better pastor."

CHAPTER IX.

ST. CHARLES VISITS ALL THE PLACES IN HIS DIOCESE INFECTED WITH THE PLAGUE.

1576.

THE plague had not confined its ravages to the city, for more than a hundred towns and villages of the diocese had suffered from it. Everywhere St. Charles was at pains to provide the same means of relief, the same prayers and processions, as he had used in the metropolis. For this purpose he sent round those on whose judgment he could rely, with instructions to carry out his wishes. Difficulties were thrown in his way by the civil officers, who misunderstood his intentions; but he overcame all obstacles by prudent management. When he had brought both spiritual and secular matters into good train at Milan, he thought he could then visit the rest of his diocese without in any way neglecting the capital.

Wherever he appeared, his presence seemed to infuse fresh life and hope into the panic-stricken people; fear and despair vanished at his approach. No wonder; for by kind words and sympathy he everywhere

assuaged the sorrows of the suffering, and silenced
repinings, filling them with courage to endure all for
the love of God, in satisfaction for their sins, to win
an eternal crown. Those whom he found at the point
of death he cheered with the bestowal of the plenary
indulgence and with fatherly consolations. He mul-
tiplied these blessings by stirring up the clergy to
emulate his exertions, and to devote themselves with
their whole soul and strength to the service and salvation of their flocks.

To those who were spared by the pestilence, he
likewise made it a time of edification by showing
them how God's judgments were abroad, and that
they too might expect to perish unless they did
penance for the sins which had provoked them. He
denounced openly the vices of the age, rebuking those
who profaned holy days and seasons by unseemly
diversions or by servile work. Still more severe were
his strictures on vain display in female attire, which
he declared to be destructive to devotion, and the occasion of a number of sins and scandals, calling down the
vengeance of heaven.

His warnings were on one occasion signally enforced
at Inzago, a place which had been terribly devastated
by the plague. While he was preaching to the people
there of the judgments of God, and calling upon them
to do penance, he noticed among his hearers a lady
decked out in a style of ostentation little suited to
the occasion. The ill-timed display called forth a
severe reprimand from the saint, who addressed her
personally, pointing out her levity, and ending with

the solemn denunciation, "Wretched woman! thus to trifle with your eternal salvation, when you know not that this day may not be your last in the world!" The next morning she was suddenly called to her account, a calamity which brought a salutary fear on all who had heard his words.

In many places huts had been constructed at a distance, in imitation of those at Milan, for the reception of the plague-stricken, and wherever this was the case he had little wooden chapels erected where Mass might be said every day for the sick. Wherever it had been found necessary to carry the dead outside the towns for burial, he consecrated graveyards; and this rule was to him another occasion of great fatigue, for he would never omit any part of the customary ceremonies, and was consequently obliged to remain for a long time exposed to the burning rays of the sun and the exhalations of decaying corpses. The fortitude with which he endured these inconveniences was particularly remarked at Inzago, where they were more than usually intolerable.

In his journeys he was entirely taken up with the care of the sick, and made all his arrangements with a single view to this end, viz.: travelling with haste, taking his scanty meals by the way, allowing himself the least possible time for sleep, and taking that little rest on a chair or a table in order not to run any unnecessary risk of infection. It required no ordinary degree of temper and judgment to keep all things in order in the midst of these difficulties.

There was an impression abroad in spite of his being

continually brought into contact with desperate cases of plague, that by a special grace he could not be a means of conveying infection, and therefore no one feared to approach him. Many noblemen took pleasure in attending on his progress. Others insisted that he should go and lodge with them. Among these was a gentleman named Pozzo, who forced him, together with all his suite, to pass the night at his house in the town of Perego. Though the Cardinal was very unwilling, lest there should be risk of infection, his host would take no refusal, saying he feared no danger while the Cardinal was with him. His hospitality was greatly appreciated by the saint's household, who had for many nights been strangers to any better beds than boards or tables.

There were occasions when the saint had to put up with very different treatment. Thus, one day at Gallarato, he had taken up his quarters at the house of the rector, when the mayor (podestà) of the place sent a guard of soldiers to surround it, with orders to forbid all entrance and egress, alleging that the Cardinal was a " suspect," and that he was determined to preserve the town from the infection. This exercise of authority over ecclesiastical persons was, of course, displeasing to the Cardinal, who hinted that the functionary would be incurring the censures contained in the sacred canons. The next morning, therefore, when all the chief persons came to visit him before his Mass, the mayor himself being among the number, he felt it his duty to take some notice of the matter, in order that it might not be made a precedent. Accordingly, the Cardinal made a remonstrance in forcible terms, tempered with his characteristic mildness, forbidding him to be present at the celebration of Mass or to enter the Church, as having laid himself open to the censures of the Church. Upon this the mayor humbly acknowledged his error, and craved pardon of the Cardinal; and his friends interposing their good offices, the saint, who desired only confession of the fault and amendment, readily released him from censure. This example served as a warning to others, so that during the whole time the plague raged, the ministers of the Church were never again interfered with, and went wherever they would, provided only with the Cardinal's licence, without let or hindrance from any one. .

The prolonged absence of the saint from Milan, at a time when communications between the different parts of the diocese were sedulously avoided, occasioned a rumour that he had fallen a victim to his zeal. It was bruited abroad not only in Milan, but in the remote towns of the province; many bishops publicly lamenting his loss, and at Verona, the Bishop even celebrated Mass for the repose of his soul. In Milan the mourning was loud and general; the mere thought of his death seeming to render every one beside himself for grief. When the saint himself heard of the report, his tender heart would not suffer him to leave his people one moment longer than necessary in suspense on his account. He hastened to change their sorrow into joy by returning back to

Milan with all speed. As usual he went in the first instance to return thanks in the Cathedral, and his arrival was immediately made known by the glad peals of the bells. This was the signal for universal rejoicing, which was greatly increased on his going to visit those who were confined to their dwellings by the quarantine—all rushing to their doors and windows to assure themselves of his presence.

While all his flock thus enjoyed the benefit of his care, none received a larger share than the different communities of cloistered nuns. He kept them constantly occupied in religious exercises, praying that it might please God to preserve them from the disease, and to moderate His indignation against the city. Further he protected them by wise precautions from every risk of contagion. As many of them were very poor, he took care that they should not suffer want; providing them out of his own means and begging alms for them especially at Rome, where some of the Cardinals gave generous contributions to their necessities. Thus by the grace of God they were wonderfully preserved. To his great consolation, out of the whole number of convents in his diocese only two were infected, and those slightly, showing that the anger of God had been turned aside by the prayers of so many of His handmaidens.

The malady reached the Great Seminary of Milan, and there was great alarm, but owing to the precautions taken its ravages were speedily stayed, two students and one Jesuit Father alone being carried off.

CHAPTER X.

CORRECTION OF DIVERS FAULTS IN THE CLERGY AND PEOPLE—PROCLAMATION OF A JUBILEE.

1576.

THE immunity enjoyed by the saint in the midst of the dangers by which he was beset was universally ascribed to the special favour of God. Neither he nor any of the persons who accompanied him on his errands of mercy ever caught any infection during the whole time the pestilence lasted. Yet he never made use of any antidote but a sponge dipped in vinegar which he carried in his hand in a little perforated case. It was always his maxim that in all matters pertaining to the exercise of his office, a Bishop ought not to encumber himself with precautions, that he ought to fulfil all that is required of him, and leave the rest entirely to God's good providence. In all those things which are not of obligation, he thought he ought not to tempt God by incurring unnecessary risk, but to adopt every precaution prudence might dictate. He used also to lay down this rule for the guidance of his chaplains and others, often going so far as to dissuade them from exposing themselves without necessity.

The virulence of the plague and its protracted duration had produced a great fear of death among the Milanese. The Cardinal, who had all along recognised the prime cause of the visitation and the only true means of removing it, was not slow to improve this salutary fear and make it a means of drawing his people to do penance and abandon all evil courses. Like a good shepherd, he was most anxious to cure the infirmities of his flock by providing them with every remedy for their various needs, with sermons, with the Sacraments, exhortations, and warnings, both in public and in private, and in this way brought back a number of sinners into the way of peace, especially among the upper classes and hardened sinners, two sets of persons most inaccessible to grace in ordinary times. He used to say that he reckoned this visitation of pestilence among his great consolations, as it had enabled him to work many conversions among his people. For when men find themselves face to face with death, their hearts are softened through their fear and expectation of the Divine judgments, and are thus prepared to listen to counsels of amendment.

It is an old saying that while the scourge of God brings the just to penance, it often tends to harden the reprobate, and it was verified at this time. There were some among the people who made it a time of more deliberate indulgence in sin than usual, taking advantage of the difficulties the quarantine placed in the way of bringing offenders to justice, to carry on their vicious practices. But though the rod of human justice might fail to reach them, the scourge of God overtook many, as happened in a well-known case.

Some Milanese nobles had gone for safety to a town at some distance. Having taken up the notion that there was no better preservative from contagion than leading a merry and self-indulgent life, they formed themselves into a Society to which they gave the name of the "Academy of Love," and abandoned themselves to all manner of profane and sensual pleasures, as if quite forgetful of their eternal salvation and the counsels of their pastor. But the hand of God found them out, and while they thought they had made themselves quite safe from every approach of the dreaded foe, the plague-spot suddenly appeared in their midst. No effort sufficed to stay its ravages, and there was not a house which escaped its visitation. It was remarked that nowhere else had its havoc been so frightful, and it was readily acknowledged that God had thereby designed to punish in a signal manner the dissolute life of these blinded sinners. The more so that it was equally noticeable that in those places where the warnings of the saint had been heeded, the pestilence passed them over or touched them but slightly.

In preaching penance and amendment of life, the Cardinal was careful, as usual, to set the example of practising what he recommended. Accordingly we find him at this time increasing his mortifications and setting himself with fresh fervour to gain greater holiness of life. Thus, among other things, he deprived himself of fires, also of flesh meat, and of the collation usually taken on the evening of fast-days, thus only taking food once in the day; and he resumed his habit of sleeping upon boards. These hardships were not slight to one so delicately brought up, while the toils of his laborious career made them all the more severe. He began also to make it his practice to preach to the people on all festivals and twice in the week during Lent, also to attend the funerals of the canons both on account of good example as well as for his own interior perfection. During all this time he was carrying out his measures of reform, appointing visitors and others to see their proper execution in the different parts of the province. He put into force his regulations to secure the proper reverence for holy places, such as requiring the closing of the side doors of many churches, which people were prone to make use of as an easy way of passing from one street to another, as well as other important rules for the maintenance of order and discipline among the clergy, striving by exactness and paternal admonitions to raise them to a more perfect standard, in order that they might be as much respected for the sanctity of their lives as for their holy vocation. In carrying out these measures he observed that the ancient and once universal practice of shaving the beard had in many cases fallen into disuse, and it had become very general among the clergy to trim it according to the fashion of the age among men of the world. He judged that this salutary season, as he was wont to term it, was favourable for obtaining the abolition of this abuse, and he accordingly addressed his pastoral letter of the 30th December, 1576, to his clergy upon this subject, calling upon them to conform to the ancient usage, which was still observed by some priests

of Milan, although in other places it had altogether
disappeared with other good customs. He showed
how high their state was above that of the laity, and
that it behoved them to walk worthily of their calling
as consecrated to the service of God, letting their outward demeanour bear witness to the recollection of
their hearts, and that above all they should eschew
all ostentation and display. In concluding he touched
upon some of the mystical lessons which the practice
might be thought to symbolise, and exhorted them to
adopt it willingly and promptly. At the same time
he himself appeared in public, conforming to the
custom he recommended, and thus by exhortation and
example shortly obtained general observance of the
rule, notwithstanding some little reluctance on the
part of certain dignitaries. Having established the
custom, he further enforced it by a decree of his next
synod; and took care that it should not again fall into
abeyance during his life. Thus, an example was set
which produced fruit in other parts also, and the
Milanese clergy were seen shaven and shorn, disciples
of their great Cardinal.

Gregory XIII. had granted a general jubilee as a
means of inviting all the faithful to penance and
prayer, that God would vouchsafe to remove the
scourge of pestilence which was desolating other
parts of Italy as well as Milan. St. Charles was
desirous of publishing this jubilee in his diocese as
soon as the quarantine should be ended; but when
he came to confer upon the subject with the magistrates, he found them averse to closing the quaran-

tine, or to affording any facilities for renewed intercourse among the people for fear of opening up new
fields for the spread of the plague. It was their
mind on the contrary to prolong the quarantine until
the city should be declared free from all trace of the
disorder. The Cardinal would not dispute the point
with them, though he was sorry that his people
should be deprived both of the application of the
treasures of the Church and of the benefit and consolation of visiting the churches and hearing the
Word of God at the holy season of Christmas. He
wrote to represent this to the Governor, who kept
himself at a safe distance at Vigevano, and to warn
him against putting his trust too exclusively in
human remedies, pointing out that God had already
shown His mercy by greatly mitigating the infliction,
so that what remained was rather to be looked upon
as the consequence of the pestilence than the pestilence itself. Neither did he omit to remind him that
by the merciful providence of God it was manifest no
evil had resulted from the earlier processions, though
they took place at a time when the disease was raging
most fiercely, and there was therefore the less reason
to expect any harm now when the malady had almost
exhausted itself. His reasoning failed to remove the
prejudices of the Governor, and the Cardinal yielded
the point, deriving satisfaction from the fervour with
which the people followed the exercises of piety he
had prescribed for them.

He deferred the publication of the jubilee, therefore,
till the spring of the following year, 1577, when he

held processions like those before described, and attended by a great concourse of persons. The saint also appeared in the same penitential garb, his feet bare notwithstanding ice and snow, and, together with his canons, threw himself prostrate on the ground, while the litanies were sung, beseeching God that He would be propitious to His people and graciously grant their supplications. This sight touched all hearts and moved them to contrition, in preparation for receiving the sacraments of penance and Holy Communion, and the benefits of the jubilee. He preached on each of the three days with an unction and fervour that moved the congregation to tears.

Not only in Milan, but throughout the whole diocese, numbers of people were led to follow the example of their holy pastor, walking in the processions barefoot, and showing every sign of penitence and sorrow for sin.

Page 441.—The Governor.

This Governor is Antonio de Guzman, Marquess of Ayamonte, who came on the departure of Luis de Requesens to Flanders, p. 319.

CHAPTER XI.

THE OBSERVANCE OF THE FIRST SUNDAY OF LENT—
BLESSING OF THE CITY.

1577.

THE fast of Lent, as it was originally observed in the
Church, consisted of six entire weeks, or forty-two
days, leaving, when the Sundays were omitted, only
thirty-six, or a tithe of the whole year. To make it
correspond with the number forty consecrated by the
fast of our Divine Lord, St. Gregory the Great made
it commence four days earlier in the Roman calendar.
The Church of Milan, which has always kept to the
Ambrosian rite, had never changed the original practice. But in process of time the people yielded to
the temptation of beginning the fast one day later,
thus reckoning the first Sunday in the carnival time,
not only eating meat, but giving themselves up to
profane amusements. This abuse had even entered
the sanctuary, and it had become customary to make
the divine offices conform to this perverted usage by
inserting therein alleluias, versicles, and antiphons
of rejoicing. Thus the practice in a vicious circle
reacted upon the habits of the people and seemed to

sanction their misappropriation of the day to sports and pleasures.

From the beginning of his episcopate St. Charles had condemned this abuse, and had brought a great many of the people to the general Communion and the sermons and other religious exercises, but there was still a large number of worldly persons who preferred to spend the day in their own fashion. He, therefore, found it necessary to adopt more vigorous measures, and resolved to make the religious observance of the day a matter of ecclesiastical precept.

However, before doing this, he consulted with several prudent theologians at Rome and Milan, and addressed a pastoral letter to his flock on the subject, dated March 1, 1576. In this letter he ordered that the observance of the day should be proclaimed simultaneously with the jubilee of the Holy Year, knowing that men's minds would thus be better inclined to the ordinance. He proved, by reference to St. Ambrose, St. Augustin, and St. Gregory, and other doctors, that this Sunday was commanded by Holy Church to be observed as the commencement of the Lenten abstinence, and that it was so observed not only in the time of St. Ambrose, but also of later Archbishops of the city, citing in confirmation of this a constitution of Ottone Visconti, who was elected in the pontificate of Urban IV. He exhorted laymen affectionately to accept the ordinance in a Christian spirit, as dutiful children of the Church, and the clergy also, that their example might rouse and encourage the laity to do the same; and lastly, forbade the celebration of marriage on that day under any circumstances.

The injunctions of this letter were obeyed by most persons, and when the people were humbled by the scourge of the pestilence, and ready to acknowledge their dependence on the mercy of God, a favourable time seemed to have arrived for fully carrying out its observance. This he did by publishing a general edict to the effect, and afterwards still more stringently by a synodal decree, so that at last this day was kept according to pristine observance. There still remained some who rebelled at the restriction of their pleasures, but their opposition was before long overborne by the cheerful acquiescence of the better-disposed on the one hand, and by the signal chastisement which befell some of the profane worldlings on the other.

To mention but one such event, a member of a noble family having engaged in a perverse spirit to set at nought the ordinance of his pastor, sat down on that day to eat meat in defiance of the prohibition; but it so happened that without any cause to which he could ascribe his inability, he found himself unable to swallow a single morsel. Recognising his error, and having done penance, he was remarked afterwards for his careful conformity to the precepts of the Church.

The fear of contagion having now passed away, with the return of mutual intercourse in the city there came new labours for the saint. Instead of allowing himself some relaxation, he girded himself up to undertake fresh toils. It seemed to him to be a season for working good among his people, and he would not let the opportunity slip away unimproved. While the remembrance of their deliverance was fresh in their minds, he resolved to make a general visitation of the city and diocese. He accordingly wrote a pastoral letter, dated February 2, 1577, to the people, announcing this intention, and calling upon them to prepare themselves for it, so that it might bring forth fruit. The following is an extract :—

" Out of the pastoral solicitude of our office, we have at this time resolved to renew the bonds which unite us together, as if those ties and obligations were to begin this day, and as if those words of God, spoken in a like case by Jeremy the prophet, had been uttered to-day : 'Lo I have set thee this day over the nations, and over kingdoms to root up and to pull down, and to waste and to destroy, and to build and to plant.' When Judas Machabeus, the pious captain of the Hebrew people, had mourned in sackcloth and ashes the desolation of Jerusalem and the Temple, and the affliction of the priests and people, God gave him strength and courage to repair that terrible overthrow. Thus his first care was to visit the Temple and to set priests of blameless lives, zealous for the law of God, to purify, restore, and adorn it, while he deputed others to fight their enemies, who, from the hills round about, strove to impede the work. So now our first care shall be to visit the whole of this city and diocese, sharing our labour and solicitude with the priests our fellow-workers ; sending some to look to the reparation and decoration of the material temples, the discipline of the ministry, and all things pertaining to the worship of Almighty God, commissioning others to watch over the spiritual care of the people, strengthening them with blessings and sacraments and the arms of spiritual warfare against the temptations of the enemy, as well as to correct errors and abuses, to punish the perverse and those who set stumbling-blocks in the way of amendment of life,—all, in various ways, labouring to build up and perfect in Christian discipline the souls committed to our care. For it is not only necessary to take away things that soil and stain, we have to adorn the spiritual edifice with the beauty of holiness. It will be our earnest endeavour, with the help of God, to cut off all occasions of sin both public and private, to overthrow the dominions of the devil, to implant the love of God, of devotion, brotherly love, and works of piety, to purge all the people, their houses, their families, and every soul from foul offences—from the indwelling of evil and the profanation which the inordinate love of earthly things works in the soul. This purgation is the real work we have to do in order to be entirely delivered by God's mercy from the plague and to be preserved in the future from its contagion."

These words suffice to show us the spirit in which the saint undertook his visitation. During its course he solemnly blessed the houses of the people, a ceremony of ancient use, to resist the invasion of the spirit of evil, to drive away pestilence and sickness, and to make them more worthy to be the dwelling-places of our angel guardians. He explained the value of this blessing in his pastoral, pointing out the way in which they were to prepare for it, as he had before directed heads of families to arrange for the blessing of their houses with holy water on the vigil of Christmas, according to the Ambrosian rite followed at Milan. He particularly impressed upon them the duty of removing everything which did not accord with Christian morals and might offend the most pure eyes of Almighty God, such as profane and lascivious pictures, light and sinful books, cards, dice, masks, and all things which might be occasions of sin,—furnishing their dwellings instead with holy images, with spiritual books, and all things likely to kindle devotion and the fear of God. He begged them to prepare themselves by Confession and Communion to receive grace from God and heavenly benediction. He printed a little book containing the psalms and prayers for this holy function and the ceremonies to be observed ; giving directions to the clergy not to bless houses where there were excommunicated persons, women of bad character, usurers, and other public and notorious sinners, where public gambling or anything else was carried on contrary to Christian piety. In this way he hoped to purge the city and diocese of profanity, and to introduce a true and perfect standard of practice.

The visitation was then begun with the usual state and ceremonial. The Milanese hailed it as the signal and earnest of returning health and peace to see their Archbishop once more passing through their streets in the splendour of his office, where they had a short time before beheld him toiling painfully along in the garb of penance, borne down by the weight of their sins. They all ran to the cathedral to rejoice their eyes with the sight. Leaving the cathedral, he went on to bless every part of the Archbishop's palace, and the house of the Canons annexed. As he proceeded to bless the houses of the laity, who had them all adorned duly to honour the ceremony, the evil one, full of malice at this manifestation of piety, moved the envy of the officers of the crown, who pronounced it an infringement of the royal jurisdiction. Finding upon consultation that the Governor was inclined to support them in this view, they pressed their objections so urgently upon the Cardinal, that he thought it well to yield, though he could not but grieve to see a good work so soon cut short.

CHAPTER XII.

WITH Lent came fresh anxieties for our saint in the shape of new impediments in the way of the spiritual progress of his flock.

It had been discovered that some of the persons employed to disinfect the clothes and other things belonging to those who had died of the plague had purloined certain of them for their own use, and in their haste to hide their booty had not taken care to cleanse them properly. This, it was thought, might occasion a new outbreak of the pestilence, and as one or two cases had really occurred to cause alarm, the Governor by the advice of the Council renewed the quarantine. This time, however, it was not acquiesced in so readily by the people, many of whom would not absent themselves from the Lenten services and sermons. But when the festival of the Annunciation came, which is always kept in Milan with solemnity, drawing great multitudes of strangers on account of the perpetual plenary indulgence, granted by the Sovereign Pontiff in form of jubilee to the cathedral and the great hospital alternately, nothing could keep the people from availing themselves of the opportunity of grace thus thrown open to them. It was manifest that God had been pleased to enkindle great devotion in the hearts of the people, for not content with visiting the churches appointed for gaining the jubilee, they crowded to every shrine and place of worship, as if they could never be weary of praising God and rendering thanks to His saints, by whom their lives had been preserved in the midst of the plague; and they rejoiced with each other in visits of congratulation, as if they had returned from exile or imprisonment.

It was a more serious matter, however, that the decrees of the magistrates against the thefts were disregarded and the penalties set at nought. No progress was made till the Cardinal took the matter in hand, and at Easter-time published an edict on the serious nature of the offence, giving all concerned to know that it was a mortal sin, not only as a theft, but also on account of the injury to their neighbour, by endangering their lives and multiplying sources of infection. He laid the penalty of excommunication upon all who should thereafter be guilty of this offence, reserving absolution to himself. At the same time he gave directions to Confessors respecting the cases of those persons who had thus been blinded by avarice.

After this he obtained permission from the Governor for every one to leave their houses for the Paschal Confession and Communion, according to the precepts of the Church. All were greatly consoled by this favour, and it was so pleasing to God, that no case of infection occurred, although the churches were daily thronged : nor was there any further need to make quarantine regulations.

In his zeal to do honour to his Divine Master, the saint bethought himself that the Holy Nail of the Passion, which is one of the chief relics of the Church of Milan, had not in times past received that veneration to which it was entitled, having been but seldom shown for the devotion of the people. He determined to institute a solemn procession and to carry the relic himself through the city in state every year on the Feast of the Invention of the Cross, May 3, starting from the Church of the Holy Sepulcre,[1] as having a particular reference to the Passion of our Lord.

From this church the saint led the first procession in honour of the precious relic of the Passion, followed by the Governor, and magistracy, and the people of the city, the women and children excepted, who were not yet allowed to leave their homes. On the morning of the feast he had the relic taken from its shrine in the church and placed on a monstrance of elaborate workmanship. It was then set on a cross in a crystal and silver case and carried by the Cardinal himself in full pontificals during the whole procession under a canopy borne in turn by the Governor, the senators,

---

[1] This church was built in the year 1100 by Benedict Roccio Cortesella, upon the model of that at Jerusalem, in memory of a signal victory of the Crusaders in Palestine the year 1099, when they delivered the Holy City from the Infidels, and made Godfrey, Duke of Lorraine, their King. Cortesella on that occasion headed a band of seven thousand Milanese, who much distinguished themselves.

and principal nobles of the city. Through the whole way he kept his eyes intently fixed on the precious relic of Redemption, while his thoughts dwelt on the sufferings of the Saviour of the world, till the tears ran down his cheeks. The people were not slow in responding to the invitation their pastor had given them to show it honour, hanging draperies from their windows and following themselves in numbers, each parish with its proper banner, and each one with a light in his hand, like an army of Christian soldiers. The weather lent another charm, for the morning had opened cloudy, but at the time the Holy Nail was taken from its shrine the rain ceased, and the sun shone till the close of the ceremony, when the rain again fell in torrents. On arriving at the Church of the Holy Sepulcre, the Cardinal took several gold pieces from his almoner, and dropped them into a box at the door to set an example to the people of offering their alms in honour of the Passion of our Lord. On the return of the procession to the cathedral, the Cardinal sang a solemn Mass, and preached to the people, beginning with the story of the Emperor Heraclius, who when vested in the insignia of his imperial dignity—the mantle and the diadem—was not found worthy to carry the holy cross on which the Son of God was lifted on Calvary, but was forced to lay aside his trappings before he could raise that tree of scorn. This he applied to himself, and said that when that morning he saw the violence of the storm, he had felt a misgiving that God had sent it on account of his unworthiness. He then spoke of their spiritual needs,

bewailing the insensibility of those who had not made
good use of the season of God's visitation, through which
they had just passed, but continued to live at ease ;
and exhorted them to show their gratitude to God, and
their perpetual remembrance of the bitter Passion of
His Son, which they were especially bound to have
graven on their hearts, as they had in their midst this
precious token of His sufferings. After the Mass, the
relic was left exposed on the High Altar for forty hours'
adoration, at the close of which the saint again preached
from the words of the prophet Isaias : " Behold the
hand of the Lord is not shortened that it cannot save,
but your iniquities have divided between you and your
God ; "[1] in which he lamented the ravages of sin in
the soul of man, comparing it to a wall of separation
preventing our prayers from reaching the ear of God,
and standing in the way of His grace which He would
pour into our hearts according to our needs, and which
but for that obstruction would have softened them,
even though they had been hard as stone. In another
discourse he spoke of the brazen serpent which Moses
set up in the wilderness, by gazing on which the people
were healed of their wounds, as a figure of our Divine
Lord, who, being raised upon the wood of the cross,
gave salvation to us miserable sinners, and freed us
from the penalty of eternal death, drawing thence
motives of love to God, who had by such means delivered us from our sins. Moreover, He had been
pleased to leave the people of Milan one of the sacred
instruments of His Passion, stained with His very

[1] Isaias lix. 1.

blood. He spoke so movingly that there was not a person present whose heart was not pierced and filled with the love of God. And it was manifest that the Spirit of God both spoke and worked by him. He remained in the church all the forty hours, from the early morning till late at night, without taking any food or rest. When the devotion was over, he carried the Holy Nail once more in procession round the cathedral, and then while it was placed again in its shrine, he remained on his knees in the pulpit, discoursing to the people ; and so fervent was he in his veneration, that he moved the people to cry aloud to Heaven for mercy in tones that would have moved the hardest heart. To help their devotion, he had facsimiles made of the nail[1] for distribution among the people, so that they might keep them in their houses. This procession and devotion is repeated every year at Milan, and attracts multitudes of people from all parts.

---

[1] One of these he had made with great care, and after touching the original with it, sent it to his Catholic Majesty King Philip II.

CHAPTER XIII.

CELEBRATION OF THE JUBILEE AND PROCESSIONS IN FUL-
FILMENT OF THE VOW TO ST. SEBASTIAN—PRAYERS
FOR THE REPOSE OF THE SOULS OF THOSE WHO
DIED OF THE PLAGUE.

1577.

THE city did not yet obtain complete freedom from
the pestilence. Ever and anon alarming rumours
would be heard that the plague-spot had again been
seen. The Cardinal himself was afraid that there
might be yet remaining among the people traces of
the old leaven to stir up the anger of God, and to
cause the scourge to be again raised in His hand.
To provide against another visitation, he obtained
from Rome the faculties to publish a jubilee to perfect the purification of the souls under his charge,
and to make them fit to appear before the face of
God. This jubilee was published in the July of this
year, 1577. He called upon the people to co-operate
earnestly with him, and really to begin a new course
of life, and prepare themselves with their whole soul
and strength, to receive their share of the treasures
now put within their reach. He then held the three

customary processions, preaching every day, and urging his flock to avail themselves of these spiritual aids.

About this time there was offered him another occasion for showing his love and solicitude for his people. The plague had broken out at Brescia. The intelligence grieved him, for the love he bore the inhabitants of that city. Still more was he grieved when he heard that its Bishop had taken flight, alarmed because some of his household had caught the infection, abandoning his flock to their fate. It needed no more to induce the saint to visit this afflicted people and offer them all the assistance in his power. While he was preparing to start for the place, the Bishop himself found means to prevent his undertaking the journey. St. Charles did not, however, give up the cause of the people of Brescia, but wrote to their pastor to remonstrate with him, and to beg him to return forthwith, at the same time giving him rules for his guidance—the results of his own experience. The Bishop complied, and on his return, the Cardinal sent to him Father Paul, the capuchin, who had done so much good at the hospital.

In pursuance of the dedication to St. Sebastian before mentioned, the Council general of Milan had collected a large part of the funds necessary for re-building the church of that saint, and the foundations had been prepared. After Mass on the vigil of our Lady's Nativity, St. Charles laid the first stone of the church in memory of the deliverance of the city from pestilence, through the intercession of this glorious martyr.

From this constant desire of making every religious ceremonial productive of lasting fruit among the people, St. Charles addressed another pastoral letter to his flock in October of this year to prepare them for the worthy celebration of the procession in honour of St. Sebastian, which was fixed for the 15th of that month. This preparation he made to consist in three days of fasting and prayer, to obtain the entire removal of the scourge of pestilence which still lurked in this city, as well as the deliverance of the other towns and provinces which had been visited by it; and more especially as a mark of contrition for past sins and of amendment of life. He exhorted them also to give abundantly of their substance in alms on the first day for the church of the Holy Sepulcre; on the second, for the ruined church of Great St. Laurence, which he wished to rebuild; and to encourage the people to greater liberality, he foretold that the Queen of heaven would show great favour to this church, which indeed came to pass. For God vouchsafed to work many miracles by her pictures which the saint had painted on the walls of this church, bringing a great concourse of people, by whose alms the building was greatly advanced. Their alms on the third day were to be devoted to the hospital for mendicants, which he was preparing to found in Milan. He then recommended all to go to Confession and Communion on the following Sunday, in order to gain the indulgence he had obtained for them from Rome. This indulgence was likewise granted to all other places in the diocese which had followed the same course of fasting, almsgiving, and prayer as in

Milan. The procession to St. Sebastian's was then solemnly celebrated, and alms offered for the completion of the edifice.

The victims of the plague who had experienced the care of the saint were no less objects of his solicitude now that they were buried out of sight of men. Many of them indeed had left no one behind to remember them. After Martinmas he set himself to gain for them the suffrages of the faithful throughout the diocese, and ordered the solemn office for the dead to be offered three times in their behalf in the cathedral, requiring the city clergy to be present; and at two other collegiate churches, with the attendance of the clergy of their respective districts. In the convents of Regulars, and in all the parochial and collegiate churches of the diocese, he required that each priest should say a Mass for the repose of their souls. Nor did he forget to admonish the laity to offer up their prayers for their deceased brethren, writing a pastoral letter exhorting them to assist at the said offices by their suffrages, alms, and visits, particularly to the seven stational churches of Milan. To move them more powerfully to lend their assistance, he dwelt in this letter with great force on the intensity of the pains suffered by the souls detained in purgatory.

While he was engaged in forwarding these works of charity, at the return of spring, news was brought him of disorders of no small moment which had occurred in the Swiss parts of his diocese, such that, if they were not speedily repressed, worse might follow. Upon these representations, he set out without loss of time, and travelled so rapidly that he accomplished in a day and a night what was usually reckoned as two days' journey. Leaving Milan late one night, he reached Biasca, in the valley of Bregno, two hours before daybreak of the second day, passing over Monte Cenere at midnight. As the mountain paths were all frozen or covered with snow, it was necessary, where they were very steep towards Bellinzona, for him not only to dismount, but to climb on his hands and knees, which were cut, and bled profusely. He paid little or no attention to them, however, and after a couple of hours' rest set himself to repair the mischief that had arisen. He visited some of the towns in these parts where the plague had penetrated, doing all he could for the relief of the sufferers, and giving Communion to great numbers of the infected. This new instance of his self-devotion increased the fame of his sanctity throughout these parts, as well as the sorrow of the people when he left them to keep the Christmas festival in Milan.

CHAPTER XIV.

PUBLIC THANKSGIVING TO GOD FOR THE DELIVERANCE OF
THE CITY AND DIOCESE FROM THE PLAGUE.

1578.

IT was now manifest throughout the city and diocese of Milan that God had been pleased at length to remove the scourge of pestilence, notwithstanding the apprehensions entertained by some timid people that a fresh outbreak might occur in the spring. The Cardinal, who was confident that the prayers of the people had been heard, urged his convictions so forcibly upon the municipal authorities, that he succeeded in driving away their fears, and obtaining their consent to put an end to the regulations of quarantine.

Here was a fresh opportunity to lead the minds of his flock heavenwards, and St. Charles did not fail to make use of it. We cannot but be struck with his watchfulness in seizing such occasions, and his energy in improving them to the glory of God and salvation of souls. In the first place he published a little book, entitled " Instructions to the people of the city and diocese of Milan for the Christian life

in every class of persons," intended to be a rule to
all for their spiritual guidance to help them in living
holily in the world, teaching them to consider that
the reign of sin ought to have passed away from
among them with the pestilence, which had been
sent as its scourge, and that it behoved them from
henceforth to lead a new life of spirituality and perfection.   This was accompanied by a pastoral letter,
dwelling on the obligation which rested upon every
one to show his thankfulness to God for extinguish-
ing the plague, by trying to lead a life pleasing to
Him.

He further required all the clergy and people to
join in public acts of thanksgiving, including three
processions and sermons ; in the last of which he
carried a sacred relic, followed by all the clergy, the
magistrates, and the people, passing through every
quarter and principal street, stopping at several
places where altars had been erected, so that,
although beginning at an early hour, they did not
return to the cathedral till late in the day.   On each
of the three days of the processions, he desired that
every priest should say a Mass of thanksgiving, and
that in the evening on its return, the Te Deum
should be sung at the Ave in every collegiate, parochial, and regular church.

On the return of the third procession to the
cathedral, he commenced the devotion of the Forty
Hours, after carrying the Blessed Sacrament round
the church.   During the whole time of these forty
hours the Saint remained in the church, addressing

the people from the pulpit every hour. These processions were likewise observed in all parts of the diocese, as he had directed the rural deans to procure the attendance of clergy and people, that none might be wanting to this duty of rendering thanks to God for His mercies. He also printed a little book of devotions and prayers proper to the occasion. Finally, he brought the whole action to a close by another procession round the cathedral, in the same order as before, with clergy and people and each parish with its banner.

In his sermon on one of these days he spoke confidently of the deliverance of the city as being miraculous; and in a book which he published about this time, entitled " Memoriale," he used the following words :—" There is one thing, my children, of which we must make mention, which will make us appreciate more fully the magnitude of the mercies we have received at the hand of God. And it is this, that it was not to this city alone that this favour was granted of quenching the plague, but to the whole diocese, and that in so marked a manner, that it was at one and the same time that health was restored to both. Nearly one hundred places of this diocese were infected, and at this moment there is not one spot which is not perfectly freed from it. Praised be the name of the Lord always, and by all, but chiefly by us who have tasted of His loving-kindness." Again, in the seventh chapter of the second part of the same work he says :—" Have always before you this great benefit which God has so miraculously worked for you, and never be at any time unmindful of His mercy."

In another place, still speaking of their deliverance, he says:—"This is no effect of our prudence, which indeed failed us at the very outset, and left us bewildered and lost; nor is it due to the skill of physicians, who have not yet discovered so much as the origin of this malady, much less the means of counteracting it; nor does it come of tender care for the sick, for they were at the first outbreak deserted by their nearest and dearest. No, my children, no; let us never fail to acknowledge this—it was the effect of God's mercy alone. It is He who has stricken us, and He who has healed our wounds—He who has scourged us, and He who has comforted us. He has taken the rod of discipline into His hand, and by His touch has changed it into a staff of support."

In the same way, in another place he brings forward reasons why this deliverance was delayed, and why God did not at once grant the prayer of His people. "It was thus that, by deferring the time of restoration to health, God taught us day by day more and more plainly the vanity of the hopes which many placed in human efforts—taught us also that it was the work of His hand—and by this means pointed out to us the true way of restoration. He did not heal us all at once, that we might know that He required of us perfect conversion and amendment."

The faith and confidence with which he made these assertions at a time when the rest of the population was hovering between fear and hope, doubtful whether the disease did not yet lurk among them—was taken as a proof that he could only have known the truth by revelation from God, and that this immunity had been granted by Him out of regard to the merits of the saint in answer to his tears, his prayers, and penances.

St. Charles himself seemed never to think that he had returned praise and thanks enough to the Divine Majesty. Over and above the public acts we have mentioned, he wrote letters to all the bishops of the province exhorting them not to suffer God's mercy to be forgotten, but to stir up the people to show their gratitude in earnest. To this appeal they readily responded, and at the same time testified their thankfulness to him for having obtained this mercy for them. Among others, Nicolo Sfrondato, Bishop of Cremona, afterwards Cardinal and Pope, under the title of Gregory XIV., not content with congratulating him by letter came to Milan on purpose to repeat them by word of mouth. While there he preached in the cathedral before the Governor, senate, and magistrates, upon the greatness of the mercy shown to them; edifying them by the lessons he taught, and gratifying them by so public a recognition of the merits of their beloved pastor.

To render their gratitude still more lasting the saint undertook another work, entailing upon him considerable labour, the publication of a book entitled, " A Remembrance for his Beloved People of the City and Diocese of Milan." It was intended to keep up their remembrance of the calamities and miseries of the time of pestilence, and of the mercy of God in delivering them from its horrors. I have called this book a work of great labour, because to write it he would not interrupt any of his other duties, but subtracted from his already scanty modicum of rest all the time that he required for its composition. This was not done without great violence to nature, and his secretary observed that need of sleep would overcome him from time to time, yet that he would soon rouse himself and take up the thread where he had dropped it, without requiring the repetition of what had gone before ; as if he had kept his attention alive to the matter he was dictating, in a way which seemed quite miraculous. But other persons of sound judgment have thought that what the secretary took to be slumber, was rather an abstraction of his mind in God, and a species of rapture, being guided to this conclusion by the loftiness of conception, lucidity of expression, and tone of spirituality which pervades the' work, from which it seemed to them that he had been in those moments lost in contemplation, and that he afterwards dictated the ideas he then received from God.

The moment the city of Milan was released from the restrictions of the quarantine, her former extensive relations of commerce were resumed on all sides, and a concourse of strangers as great as ever filled her streets. Much wonder was felt when, on taking a census of the victims, it was found that during the whole period of the plague not more than seventeen thousand persons had died in the city, and eight thousand in the rest of the diocese, of which number a

hundred and twenty were ecclesiastics ; whereas, at the
last visitation in the year 1524, fifty thousand had
died in four months in Milan alone, and an incalculable number in the other towns and districts. In this
the Milanese discovered another proof of the blessings
they had derived from the labours and merits of their
Pastor.[1]

[1] St. Charles, at this time, urged upon the Pope, Gregory XIII., the
foundation of an English College at Rome.

Note on page 38, vol. I.

*The episode of Dom Bartholomew of the Martyrs, O.P., p. 38–47, is not
found in Giussano's Life, but is taken by permission from the Life of St.
Charles by E. Healy Thompson, Esq., and from that of the Venerable
Dom Bartholomew, translated by Lady Herbert, see Chapters xx., xxiii.,
and xxv.*—EDITOR.

END OF VOL. I.

www.ingramcontent.com/pod-product-compliance
Lightning Source LLC
Chambersburg PA
CBHW020448270326
41926CB00008B/529